Last R

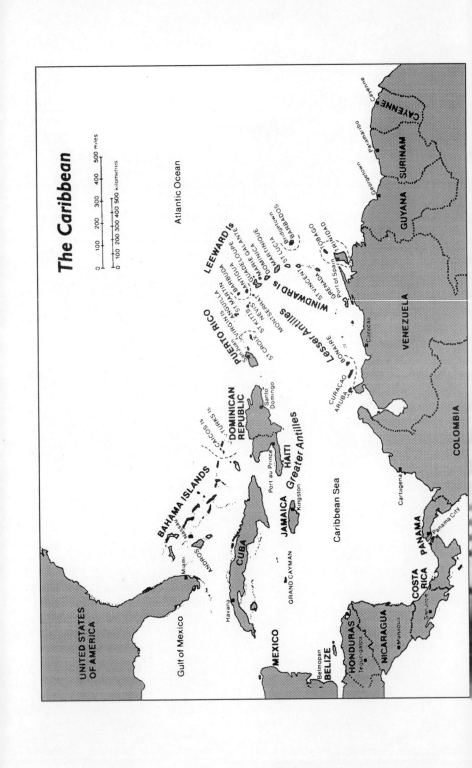

The Caribbean

Last Resorts

The Cost of Tourism in the Caribbean

Polly Pattullo

CASSELL

Cassell
Wellington House
125 Strand
London WC2R 0BB

First published 1996

Published in association with
Latin America Bureau (Research and Action) Ltd
1 Amwell Street
London EC1R 1UL

Distributed in North America by
Monthly Review Press
122 West 27 Street
New York, NY 10001, USA

British Library Cataloguing-in-Publication Data
A catalogue record for this book is available from the British Library.

ISBN 0–304–33693-9 (hardback)
       0–304–33692-0 (paperback)

Cover photograph by Philip Wolmuth

Typeset by Ben Cracknell

Printed and bound in Great Britain by Biddles Ltd, Guildford and King's Lynn

Contents

Foreword

The governments and leaders of the Caribbean have finally and almost unanimously come to the view that tourism is anything from 'an important', to 'the most important', to 'the only' means of economic survival for their states. Indeed, the first economic summit of the newly formed Association of Caribbean States (ACS), held in August 1995 in Port of Spain, Trinidad, focused on tourism, trade and transport. Those present included Presidents Fidel Castro of Cuba, Ernesto Zedillo of Mexico, Rafael Caldera of Venezuela, Violeta Chamorro of Nicaragua, Cheddi Jagan of Guyana and almost every prime minister from the Anglophone nations of the Caribbean Community.

Yet, as acceptance of this view of tourism as an indispensable economic tool spreads, it is essential that we avoid the twin dangers of unthinking triumphalism on the part of the industry's advocates or uncritical acceptance by governments and the general public.

Last Resorts: The Cost of Tourism in the Caribbean by Polly Pattullo is a timely and penetrating study of this subject. At the beginning of the book, Ms Pattullo juxtaposes diametric views in St Lucia concerning the beautiful and deeply symbolic pair of volcanic cones, the Pitons. The pragmatists proposed a site between the Pitons for a new hotel complex, the Jalousie Plantation Resort and Spa, as an exclusive enclave for the diversion of the wealthy. The idealists opposed the plan on grounds that ranged from concern for the delicately balanced ecosystem to resistance to the desecration of history. Poet and Nobel Laureate Derek Walcott, holder of the Order of the Caribbean Community, spoke with cutting passion of those who 'make a fast buck off a shrine'.

Last Resorts explores the question, who won when Jalousie was opened in 1992? The contest which preceded the hotel's opening becomes a metaphor for the problems which lie at the heart of Caribbean development; and in describing the intense controversy surrounding the issue, the book lays bare the contradictions at the heart of tourism itself.

The vacation industry is clearly here to stay. But the question which we dare not ignore is whether we, the Caribbean people, are going to have the wit and the will to make it the servant of our needs. If we do not, it will become our master, dispensing pleasure on a curve of diminishing returns while it exacerbates social divisions and widens that legacy of colonialism: the gap between small, comfortable minorities and large majorities barely surviving at the social margin.

In succeeding chapters, Polly Pattullo examines the effects of tourism on Caribbean culture and the region's environment and social cohesion. Of particular importance is her analysis of the threat posed by the booming cruise ship industry.

The Caribbean, from Cuba to the Cayman Islands, from Haiti to Tobago, needs tourism. Indeed, this industry is now commonly described as 'the engine of growth' for the region. Yet if its underlying dynamics are not understood, it can be an engine of short-term cash enhancement and long-term disaster. The danger lies in an industry increasingly based on the all-inclusive resort, walled off from the surrounding countryside and importing its food and furniture, its designs and designers, its fabrics and fashions from the US mainland.

On the other hand, with proper planning and popular participation, the tourism sector can become the best market for a great variety of products and activities, involving whole industries, professional groups and individuals. It can be the primary target for our architects and builders, for our artists and crafts people, as well as our farmers. In short, tourism can provide a vital stimulus to regional production, the reason for enhanced regional trade with the transport to carry it, and a vital catalyst for a process of regional integration which can spread beyond the immediate scope of the hotels and their guests. In addition, hotel workers, for example, can be encouraged to become part of the shareholding structure while the industry itself sponsors local theatre groups and provides sports facilities for the youth. If all such goals are pursued, tourism could become an engine of self-sustaining growth for the whole region and a means towards the greater empowerment of all its people. This was, in fact, the hope behind the first ACS summit and the rationale for its agenda.

Last Resorts leaves no doubt that there is no room for triumphalism, yet no need for despair. Anyone who reads it will know why we must proceed with care and, equally, how action that is both bold and wise can place the tourism industry at the service of all. Polly Pattullo has brought a keen mind and lucid style to one of the most important issues of our times.

MICHAEL MANLEY
September 1995

List of Illustrations

Acknowledgements

My thanks to my helpful editor, James Ferguson, for asking me to write *Last Resorts*; to those who read all or parts of the manuscript, in particular, Edward Cumberbatch, Lennox Honychurch, Anne Walmsley, Martin Mowforth, Peter Prince and Ros O'Brien; and, above all, to the people of the Caribbean – whether ministers or tourism officials, hotel workers or beach vendors – who so generously offered information and advice. And to my friends in Dominica, especially those living or working in the Roseau valley, who first inspired me to think more closely about the future shape of the Caribbean tourist industry.

CHAPTER 1

The Lock and The Key:

History and Power

Jalousie Plantation Resort and Spa lies in a sweeping valley sloping down to the sea between the Pitons, the two great volcanic cones on the west coast of St Lucia. The site is one of the great landscapes of the Caribbean; from land, sea or air the Pitons rise up green, steep and pristine. A handful of miles away is Soufrière, the oldest town on the island, of faded charm and high unemployment. Tourists arriving at Soufrière on picturesque two-masted schooners and catamarans are told not to throw coins into the sea for the teenage divers hanging around the jetty. They are then whisked through the town to visit the nearby 'drive-in volcano'. Those bound for the luxuries of Jalousie – 'the closest thing to paradise on earth', the brochure claims – pass through swathes of cocoa, banana, citrus and avocado before turning off on to a new and better road, the approach to Jalousie. If they cared to look to their right they would see Malgretout ('In spite of everything'), a home for the poor and old, where figures move slowly along a wooden verandah.

Jalousie opened in 1992 – but only after a bitter battle. Those who supported the development included the government, Soufrière's opposition MP and some local people; they believed that Jalousie's investors would bring jobs to a depressed part of St Lucia and foreign exchange to the island as a whole. At a meeting held in the town to discuss the issue, young men from Soufrière blew conch shells and shouted 'We want Jalousie'.[1]

The anti-Jalousie protesters argued that not only were the Pitons the national symbol of St Lucia and a sacred site for the island's first inhabitants, the Arawaks, but their rich and fragile ecosystem was too precious to disturb. They wanted the area to be held in common for the benefit of all St Lucians and not sold off to foreigners to turn into a ritzy ghetto for white tourists.

In a passionate article in a local newspaper, St Lucia's Nobel Prize winner Derek Walcott, wrote: 'To sell any part of the Pitons is to sell the whole idea and body of the Pitons, to sell a metaphor, to make a fast buck off a shrine…'. He said that the debate was being conducted at a level which would argue that 'a casino in the Vatican' or 'a take-away concession inside Stonehenge' would provide extra income and jobs.[2] Selling the Pitons, he concluded, was like selling your mother into prostitution. At that time, the government was also considering the offer of an American investor who wanted to run a cable car up the Petit Piton and flatten the summit of Gros Piton to build an 'Amerindian village' and restaurant.

An alternative plan, put forward in a report by the Organization of American States in 1989, recommended that the whole area of the Pitons, including the Jalousie estate, be turned into a locally controlled and managed national park. It was argued that this option would not only protect the environment, but it would be the sort of tourist attraction which would generate employment through locally owned businesses such as guesthouses, restaurants and guiding services. The report estimated that the park would create 400 new jobs in the area, as well as offer opportunities for small entrepreneurs.[3]

In the end, and despite the influential voices of the protesters, the government went ahead and gave permission for Jalousie to be built.

Jalousie is owned by the Swiss-based M Group Corporation, headed by A. Pascal Mahvi, an Iranian-born business man who bought the land, once a copra estate, from Colin Tennant, an English aristocrat and former owner of the nearby island of Mustique. (Tennant, otherwise known as Lord Glenconner, now runs a self-consciously down-at-heel bar nearby called 'Bang Between the Pitons'.) Managed by Resort Services, an Ohio-based subsidiary of the M Group, the US$60-million, 320-acre resort has 115 cottages and suites (with plunge pools), four restaurants, a ballroom, the Lord's Great Room furnished with Tennant's antiques, tennis courts, a helicopter pad, a hydroponic farm for growing non-traditional crops and tight, high-tech security. For US$350 to US$475 per day in the 1994 high season, guests enjoyed all meals, unlimited drinks, water sports, saunas and beauty treatment and cable television in an 'ambiance of tranquility and serenity'.

On hand to deliver this service were nearly 400 workers, all, according to the management, St Lucians except for 14 expatriates (in 1994) in the most senior posts. Besides providing jobs for local people, the Jalousie management said it also helped the town of Soufrière by supporting a school, a sports organization and the queens' pageant, a kind of beauty competition.

Yet the links between guests and St Lucians appeared strictly controlled. In the manner of the 'all-inclusive' concept, in which guests pay for all their holiday needs in advance, non-guests cannot enter the premises without buying an expensive pass. Local fishermen are no longer allowed to work the bay where guests now lie on imported sand. The management maintains that the resort respects the environment: the low-storeyed buildings, it says, blend in with the landscape and, except for the Great House, are invisible from the sea, while special mooring facilities for yachts protect the coral reef from damage. The environmentalists said that this was too little, too late; the reef, they claimed, had already been damaged by silting, the after-effects of construction work, and Amerindian relics had been destroyed when the tennis court was built, probably over a burial site.

By then, however, Jalousie was featuring in international tour brochures. It had become one of hundreds of beach resorts in the Caribbean which seek to capture bookings from holidaymakers and honeymooners seeking their 'away-from-it-all', fleeting moment of tropical luxury.

What is important about the story of Jalousie is that it is so typical. There are countless Jalousies in the Caribbean. As such, it raises questions about sovereignty (when beaches and valleys become foreign fields). It also presents dilemmas about the environment, and about social and cultural relations between visitors and hosts. The decision of the St Lucian government, worried about its balance of payments, to welcome a foreign company willing and able to build a glittering pleasure dome and so provide instant foreign exchange and jobs has been repeated time and time again by other regional governments. Indeed, in the economic and political climate of the 1980s and 1990s, governments, with few exceptions, fell over themselves to make such an equation. Like St Lucia, they have thrown out alternative proposals which offered longer-term solutions based on sustainable development.

Those decisions have been crucial. For the circumstances and conditions under which projects such as Jalousie have come into being reflect the shape of Caribbean tourism. In a wider sense, they also go some way towards explaining the dynamics of Caribbean societies over the last quarter century.

Changing Landscapes

Some 32 million people live on the islands of the two archipelagos which straddle the Caribbean Sea between the main continental landmarks of Florida in the north to Venezuela in the south, and the 'mainland' territories of Belize in Central America and the Guianas in South America. There are great disparities of size and population. Tiny Saba has 1,100 people on 11 square kilometres, while Cuba has a population of 11 million. Of the chain of small islands in the Eastern Caribbean, Trinidad is by far the largest (with a population of 1.1 million), and the rest are what are known as microstates, with populations mostly below 300,000. The distance from Belize in the west to Barbados in the east is some 2,000 miles; flying time (if you could fly it non-stop, which you can't) would take nearly as long as from Los Angeles to New York.

Despite such geographic and demographic distinctions, the Caribbean has a common heritage, moulded by slavery, colonialism (English, French, Spanish and Dutch) and the plantation. Its people are a reflection of that historical background: the indigenous (and now almost extinct) Amerindian, European colonizer, settler and adventurer, African slave, indentured East Indian, labouring Chinese and Portuguese, small-town merchant Arab and Jew. All such peoples have fashioned the Caribbean of today, forging Creole societies in which old loyalties and traditions, dominated by Africa and Europe, compete now with the great power and hegemony of North America.

In the second half of the twentieth century, the Caribbean has been preoccupied with fundamental change. Many former colonies became nation states, like the already independent countries of Haiti, the Dominican Republic and Cuba, and began to etch out their own political, economic and cultural paths. Yet, like other regions of the Third World, the old economic patterns – dependency on foreign investment and the export of raw agricultural products – persisted.

During this process the tourist industry became part of the landscape. By the 1990s, all Caribbean territories were in the tourism business, as the politicians proclaimed it 'the engine of growth'. An image of movement and acceleration, of power and prosperity had been touted to launch Caribbean peoples into 'development' and 'modernism' out of their poverty on the periphery of the world.

It was not just politicians (of all persuasions) who favoured this process. Invoking similar mantras and, more importantly, helping to make it all happen were the facilitators, the ranks of consultants, diplomats, international lending agencies and development banks. The third protocol (1986–90) of the Lomé Convention, which enshrines Europe's special relationship with states in Africa, the Caribbean and the Pacific, also recognized the 'real importance of the tourism industry' and provided a broad range of financial provision (in contrast to earlier versions of Lomé dating from 1975 in which tourism was barely noted). All these bodies agreed that tourism made economic sense for both tiny, underproductive islands as well as for larger, more diversified but still struggling, debt-laden, Third-World economies, such as Jamaica or the Dominican Republic.

Such ideas also found favour with the important West Indian Commission which recognized 'the strategic position that tourism has come to occupy in the region'.[4] The Commission was set up in the early 1990s by the Caribbean Community (Caricom), the 13-strong, English-speaking regional grouping, to seek an economic and political way forward for the region in the footsteps of the British West India Royal Commission of 1897 and the Moyne Commission report, published in 1945. The Commission's 1992 report, *Time for Action*, welcomed the fact that all Caricom countries were now 'openly committed to nurturing in their economies a tourism sector geared to their particular endowments'.[5]

The Caribbean's share of world tourist arrivals is less than 2 per cent, but this is triple that of South Asia's, more than double that of Oceania and larger than that of South America or West Asia. The insular Caribbean ranked ninth in the world on the basis of its tourism receipts in 1990, according to the International Monetary Fund; and by 1994 the Caribbean Tourism Organization (CTO) estimated that its 34 member states grossed US$12 billion from tourism. The following year, the CTO announced that the region's tourism industry would grow by 6.3 per cent annually over the next 16 years, at 'almost twice the projected 3.6 per cent world tourism growth rate'.

Armed with the statistics, it was hardly surprising that *Time for Action* viewed tourism as a key instrument of development and modernization. 'Out of the tourist industry radiates stimuli for a wide range of industries producing goods and services; this is the concept of tourism as an axial product. Viewed in this light, the tourism sector can play an important role in the diversification and transformation of the region,' it declared.[6] The challenge for the Caribbean, according to the report, was to retain, and possibly increase, its share of the world tourism market.

These arguments, however, were not new. They had been around in the 1950s, and then in the 1960s with the advent of long-haul air travel and the rise of the consumerist West. Those decades, conveniently so for the rich foreigner looking for new holiday spots, also coincided with the decline of the Caribbean's traditional plantation economies and the search for an economic replacement. For the Caribbean, one solution was migration; there is a certain irony in the fact that tourists began to arrive in the Caribbean in greater numbers just as the poor of the Caribbean began their own more onerous journey in the opposite direction to work. For those who stayed, the chosen alternative was to turn primarily agricultural economies into pastures for pleasuring the leisured. International bodies such as the World Bank and the United Nations endorsed tourism for the Third World; an Organisation for Economic Cooperation and Development (OECD) publication had reported in 1967 that tourism was a 'promising new resource for economic development'.[7]

By the 1990s such views were being voiced more vigorously – some would say more frantically – than ever. Despite all the debate about the disadvantages of tourism to fragile, Third-World economies and cultures, the region had become even more dependent on tourism. By then, too, the choices had narrowed, with the Caribbean saddled by debt, prices for its goods and raw materials in decline and traditional protected markets under pressure as old colonial loyalties faded.

More fundamentally, a fragmented Caribbean found itself increasingly marginalized as the world rearranged itself into free-market trading blocs, such as the North American Free Trade Agreement (NAFTA) and the European Union (EU), while the Anglophone Caribbean's own regional bloc, Caricom, and the wider Association of Caribbean States made, in comparison, painfully slow progress. The effect, as the CTO put it in 1995, was clear: 'Trading blocks such as the NAFTA and the European Community have made it increasingly difficult for traditional Caribbean manufacturing and agricultural industries to remain competitive, giving tourism an even higher priority throughout the region.'[8] Stringent structural adjustment programmes imposed on many territories on the advice of the International Monetary Fund also promoted tourism.

Politically, too, by the end of the Cold War, the region appeared marginalized. It no longer generated much political interest except when refugees from Haiti or Cuba threatened the Florida coast or when there was an outcry over drugs. In any case, the Caribbean was by then largely controlled by governments sympathetic to the USA and had become locked into a North American agenda. If there were alternatives to tourism, no governments appeared poised to investigate them. Such conditions lent themselves as never before to tourist expansion.

By the 1990s, those countries which had previously eschewed tourism or had only developed it at the margins began to embrace it. The collapse of oil prices, for example, led to a new interest in tourism for both Trinidad and its sister island Tobago. Similarly, in Aruba tourism replaced an earlier dependence on oil: nearly 6,000 hotel rooms opened in the decade after the closure of the Exxon refinery in 1984. In agriculture-led economies, there were similar shifts; the crisis in the banana industry in the early 1990s forced Windward Island governments to put tourism at the top of the agenda. St Lucia and Grenada redoubled their efforts, while St Vincent and Dominica entered the tourist business seriously for the first time. Poor performances in sugar and bauxite exports and the debt burden pushed Jamaica towards greater tourist activity. In Cuba, economic isolation after the collapse of Soviet communism provoked rapid tourist development. Even Guyana began to include tourism in its new mixed-economy strategy.

While tourism has made footprints in nearly every territory, these have differed in shape and size, form and style. Patterns of growth have reflected a range of factors, some dependent on natural features and geography, others on economics and politics, both within the region and globally. Furthermore, growth has taken place at different speeds. Some countries joined in early and enthusiastically, others latterly and reluctantly as their options diminished. Some, whether pioneers or late-comers, are now in the big time, and others just have bit parts. Some boast marinas grand enough for Greek shipping magnates and cultivate exclusive hide-aways for retired rock stars. A few have mountain wildernesses and rainforests; more have casinos, karaoke competitions and Jolly Roger pirate cruises.

Such disparate stages in tourist 'development' could be plotted on the graph of what has become known as the Butler model of tourism's life cycle. According to Butler, the first phase is the 'exploration' of a remote and unspoiled spot. Then come the stages of involvement, development and consolidation as more hotels are built and mass tourism arrives. In time, the high spenders move on and the 'product' stagnates; attempts to stop the decline with down-market tourism fail; and social and environmental deterioration begins. The Butler model then suggests that only the choice between stagnation and rejuvenation remains. In the worst scenario, tourists leave, discarding the people and the environment. What was once poor and unspoiled is again poor but now spoiled.[9]

Examples of these stages have been identified in the Caribbean although nowhere yet has quite reached the terminal phase. The model, whether accurate or not, has cast its shadow over the Caribbean's tourist industry and has helped to concentrate the mind over the potentially damaging effects of tourism, not just in the Caribbean but worldwide. It also illustrates the complex relationship between what guests want and what hosts supply.

The History

In the Caribbean, what most guests want is the beach with its creamy sands and clear seas. That has, almost everywhere, been the point of seduction. Yet the beach was not where the industry first began.

At the end of the nineteenth century, the first tourists to the Caribbean were attracted not by its sea and sand but by its invigorating climate and balmy air (islands such as Jamaica no longer evoked associations with disease). 'The island possesses great natural beauty, and its warm, healthy climate is recommended by the medical faculty,' boasted Elder, Dempster & Co.'s promotional literature for its 1905 winter tours for 'health and pleasure' sailing regularly between Bristol and Jamaica.

At that time, the tropical seascape was more likely to be admired from a verandah than from the water's edge. The particular sea-view would depend on the traveller's nationality; the English, for example, went to their colonies of Barbados or Jamaica, the French to Martinique, the Dutch to Curaçao. The Americans, for reasons of geography, went to the Bahamas and Cuba, both close to the Florida coast. At that time, too, it was exclusively the wealthy who had the time and money to travel. Early advertising blurbs for shipping lines advised 'Winter in the West Indies'; it was all too fashionable.

While wealthy east-coast Americans made winter trips in their large yachts, land-based visitors stayed in the first hotels. The Royal Victorian Hotel in the Bahamas opened in 1861 at the cost of more than US$130,000. In the Eastern Caribbean, Crane Beach, on the wild east coast of Barbados, opened in 1887, while in Jamaica, Titchfield Hotel, a look-alike Victorian stately home, opened in Port Antonio in the next decade. By 1915, Cuba had 72 hotels, over one-third of them in Havana, where everything from polo to fishing was laid on for the holiday-maker.

Then the sun, which had once been seen as a coarsening threat to white skins, became the new icon. The age of sun, sea and sand tourism had begun although it was still only the rich who were able to enjoy it.

Between the wars, visitors rented or bought houses in the manner of the old plantocracy. Ian Fleming and Noel Coward spent time near Port Antonio in Jamaica. Not far away lived Errol Flynn on his very own Navy Island. There, Flynn gave parties for film stars and popularized rafting down the beautiful Rio Grande, using the rafts which had once carried bananas down river to take his friends on all-day picnics. Cuba also gained its own reputation for macho carousing and gambling in the manner of Ernest Hemingway, one of its expatriate American residents. By the 1950s, tourism had become Cuba's second largest earner of foreign currency after sugar and the island welcomed more than 300,000 tourists a year, most of them American.

When tourism overtook sugar as the major foreign-exchange earner it pitched the Caribbean into a new historical phase. It happened, for the most mature tourism economies such as Jamaica and Barbados, with the introduction of regular non-stop international jet services in the 1960s. With that, a less exclusive form of tourism, alongside the luxury market, also became possible.

It was then that the scramble for tourist dollars broadened and deepened. With the potential for a mass market, the multinational organizations such as hotel chains and tour operators began to show serious interest in the region. This was particularly true for the nearby

American and Canadian markets, which had long provided the majority of visitors to the region. By then revolutionary Cuba had been boycotted by Washington, and Puerto Rico and the Bahamas had taken over as the choice destinations of the USA. Countries, other than old hands like Jamaica and Barbados, were also beginning to be 'discovered'. Some of the rich even bought their own islands: the Rockefellers bought part of St John's in the US Virgin Islands; St Vincent and the Grenadines sold Mustique for £45,000 (including the rights of the local population) and also leased away Palm Island on a 99-year-lease for a total rent of US$99.

This growth, however, took place against the first stirrings of concern that it was not all 'fun, fun, fun' in the sun. From the investors' point of view, the Caribbean seemed expensive and inefficient. At the same time, two worldwide recessions in the 1970s kept the tourists at home and the costs up. In the Caribbean itself, intellectuals began to question the co-option of the region by foreign interests, viewing it as demeaning and as recolonization by other means. 'Tourism is Whorism' was a phrase coined at the time. The Black Power movement gained its own impetus in the Caribbean as island states struggled from colonial to independent status. The way tourism appeared to be underpinned by racism became an important issue.

William Demas, then president of the Caribbean Development Bank, lamented the tourist industry's effect on Caribbean peoples: 'We welcome foreigners, we ape foreigners, we give away our national patrimony for a pittance to foreigners and, what is worse, we vie among ourselves in doing all of these things.'[10] It was not, however, just the opinion-formers who were dissatisfied with tourism. In 1966, Jamaica's director of tourism complained that the 'biggest problem we are facing isn't "selling" Jamaica to the tourist, but "selling" tourists to the Jamaicans'.[11]

Such views were not uncommon during those years. However, island administrations (with the exception of Cuba and the other territories which avoided tourism for whatever reasons) continued to promote beaches and sunshine. Their increasing dependency on tourism was pointed up by the contemptuous views of foreign hoteliers and tourism 'experts' who credited themselves with the islands' survival. For example, the American travel industry spokesman who wrote in the trade magazine *Travel Weekly* in 1972: 'Without the large hotels, most of the islands would dry up and blow away .... Hilton is probably doing more to further local island cultures than anyone else, including the islanders themselves'; or the official overseeing a multi-million dollar aid project in the Eastern Caribbean who commented, 'only tourism and drug traffic keep these islands from going down the tubes'.[12]

At that time, however, a different voice was attempting to gain a hearing. In the 1970s, Jamaica and Grenada (see Chapter 9) both deliberately attempted to use tourism as a tool of social and economic development for their people. Neither island wished to curtail its tourist industry, but both governments believed that there were serious flaws in the way it functioned. They were convinced that they could excise the negative aspects of tourism and make it work for their people rather than for foreigners.

In the event, the invasive hand of US politics and capital intervened and, for both Jamaica and Grenada, what they called 'new' tourism never had much of a chance to develop. Instead, mass tourism became entrenched by the 1980s. Even hurricanes and a series of recessions in the Western world appeared only to cause temporary, if worrying, blips on Caribbean tourism's ever-rising growth rate.

The Numbers Game

In 1994, 13.7 million stayover tourists (visitors staying at least 24 hours) and some 2.3 million cruise-ship passengers visited the region. For stayover tourists, this was more than an overall six-fold increase on the figures for 1970, while cruise-ship arrivals had increased at an even faster rate. Some territories had seen a far greater growth rate. Anguilla's stayover arrivals increased from 1,000 in 1970 to 43,705 in 1994; visitors to the Turks and Caicos increased from 2,000 to 70,946 in the same period, while the Dominican Republic's arrivals grew from 63,000 in 1970 to approaching 2 million in 1994. These three countries also recorded the greatest increases in visitor expenditure, with Antigua, St Lucia, Belize and Dominica making the next greatest gains.[13]

The number of hotel rooms per country likewise increased, in some cases dramatically. The 'newer' destinations showed enormous growth, with the Dominican Republic, for example, increasing its room count from 3,800 in 1980 to 26,801 in 1993. Many others doubled (Antigua, the British Virgin Islands, St Lucia) or tripled (Anguilla, Aruba, Belize, St Kitts) their room numbers. The most stagnant were the 'mature' destinations such as Bahamas and the US Virgin Islands, while Barbados lost one-sixth of its rooms between 1980 and 1993 (from 6,680 down to 5,580), and poor Haiti's room capacity dropped by 50 per cent.

In 1994, the most popular destination in the Caribbean was the Dominican Republic with some 1.9 million stayover visitors. The Bahamas came second with 1,516,031, followed by Jamaica (976,635), Puerto Rico (790,263), the US Virgin Islands (683,044), Cuba (617,284) and St Maarten (585,000): together these accounted for more than half of stayover tourists and for around three-quarters of the Caribbean's total receipts from tourism. Those territories with the smallest number of stayover tourists included Guyana and Surinam, whose numbers of genuine tourists were difficult to assess, followed by the tiny British dependencies of Montserrat (21,285) and Anguilla (43,705), and the Dutch dependencies of Saba (28,844) and St Eustatius (10,000 to 15,000).[14]

Overall, the 1994 figures for stayover tourists represented an estimated 4 per cent increase over 1993,[15] less impressive than the 9.9 per cent increase in 1993 over 1992 which had prompted fulsome praise from regional tourism pundits.

Tourist officials and government ministers pore over the regular reams of statistics (arrivals, countries of origin, number of rooms, occupancy rates, visitor expenditure numbers and percentage changes) as classical diviners once peered into animal entrails for inspiration. In what has become a numbers game, orchestrated by politicians and administered by officials, more has become better.

This attention to arrival figures is understandable given the importance attached to tourism. It has become a last resort. For as statistics show, for two decades tourism has distinguished itself as the *only* steady growth sector for the region. As Jean Holder, Secretary-General of the CTO, explains: 'What is unique about the Caribbean is that it is more dependent on tourism than any other region in the world. Tourism receipts are 25 per cent of our total exports. There is a great deal riding on it.'

In 1993, the Economist Intelligence Unit's report on the industry said: 'Tourism is the only sector of regional GDP that has consistently increased its share of total income during the 1980s. In some places, tourism accounts for up to 70 per cent of national income directly and indirectly.'[16] The report also noted that without tourism the region's current account deficit during the 1980s would have been nearly four times higher than its reported US$11 billion. In Barbados, for example, a net deficit in 1986 of some US$315 million on the balance of trade was transformed into a small balance of payments surplus, largely as a result of some US$324 million earned from tourism.

Six Caribbean countries earned more from tourism in 1992 as a share of exports (if tourism is defined as an export rather than 'invisible earnings') than they did from all other sectors. These were Antigua (65.1 per cent), the Bahamas (72 per cent), Barbados (59.3 per cent), Grenada (54.3 per cent), St Kitts-Nevis (58.4 per cent) and the Dominican Republic (50.9 per cent).[17] In other, somewhat more diversified, economies such as Jamaica, tourism also made a very significant contribution to export earnings. Belize, Grenada and St Lucia, for example, earned more from tourism than from banana exports. This classic reversal of fortunes, from agriculturally dependent to tourist dependent, is now also true for the old sugar-based economies such as Barbados, the Dominican Republic, Jamaica and Trinidad and Tobago, where tourists have become more 'valuable' than sugar.

Similarly, tourism revenues offset more than 41 per cent of the Caribbean's total import bill in 1990. Not surprisingly, tourism contributes most to the import bill of islands such as Antigua and Barbuda (73 per cent) and the Bahamas (72 per cent), and least to islands such as Trinidad and Tobago (7 per cent) and Dominica (16 per cent) with a smaller tourist industry.[18]

If tourist numbers alone were the key measurement of development, then giant steps indeed would have been taken in the Caribbean over the last couple of decades. However, an increase in numbers is not necessarily a guarantee of increased expenditure.

One way of looking at the statistics is to work out the amount each tourist spends against the number of tourist arrivals. In Barbados, for instance, the total number of tourists (cruise and stayover) increased between 1989 and 1993, yet visitor expenditure per person fell from US$660 to US$640. St Maarten managed to increase its spend per tourist arrival over the same period, but from a lower base (from US$267 to US$318). At the other end of the scale, upmarket Anguilla (with no cruise ship arrivals) increased its arrivals from 28,400 to 36,700 between 1989 and 1993 *and* its visitor expenditure per person from US$989 to US$1,180.

These sort of variations indicate that visitor 'spend' must depend not just on heads on beds but on other factors: room occupancy rates, length of stay, the wealth, interests and social class of the tourists and the available range of attractions and shopping.

Room occupancy rate, which is calculated by expressing the number of occupied rooms as a percentage of all available rooms over a specified period, is one useful measurement of economic return. In the first major study of the structure and organization of tourist accommodation in the Caribbean, the average year-round room occupancy rate for the region in 1987 was estimated at 65 per cent, compared to 81 per cent for Hawaii and 58 per cent for Mexico.[19] However, this figure obscured wide country variations. By 1993, four countries returned under 60 per cent occupancy rates: the Bahamas (56.8 per cent), Barbados (53.7 per cent), Martinique (55 per cent) and Trinidad and Tobago (54.5 per cent). In contrast, the highest occupancy rates were Aruba (79.5 per cent), the Cayman Islands (71.1 per cent) and the Dominican Republic (75 per cent). While rates have fluctuated over the years for most countries,

Aruba and the Dominican Republic have returned consistently high occupancy scores.[20]

In some cases rapid hotel development has created a lopsided industry where too many rooms chase too few tourists, especially in the slow summer season. Both the Bahamas and Barbados were described by the Economist Intelligence Unit in 1993 as 'having clearly overdeveloped and are failing to attract sufficient visitors to fill their available accommodation'.[21] In St Maarten, an explosion of hotel building in the 1970s, when the number of rooms escalated from 400 to 3,200, brought the room occupancy rates tumbling from 70 per cent to 45 per cent. The occupancy rate was still poor by the 1990s. 'We want to put a freeze on hotel rooms, otherwise things will go from bad to worse,' says Cornelius de Weever, director of the division of tourism in St Maarten.

Occupancy rates also depend on the relationship between the number of incoming flights and the number of hotel rooms. Tobago, for example, a small and somewhat underpromoted destination, experienced low occupancy rates in the early 1990s when not enough flights arrived at the upgraded Crown Point airport to fill its new hotels. 'We are now concentrating on the room occupancy. Once we've got that we can bargain with the tour operators,' comments Claud Benoit, a member of the Tobago Assembly. Grenada's low occupancy rate at the end of the 1980s was probably a result of similar difficulties but by 1993 showed an improved rate of 68.8 per cent.

Low occupancy rates (and seasonality) have a particularly painful impact in the Caribbean where high hotel construction and running costs, high food import bills and relatively high pay rolls all contribute to low profit margins. Total revenues per room in the Caribbean in 1986 were more than US$46,500, compared to the average worldwide of US$29,510. Yet the profit margin per room was estimated at only US$5,000 in the Caribbean compared with US$7,705 worldwide and US$11,500 in the Pacific.[22] The result is that room rates in the region are some of the highest in the world, rising to US$1,000 per night for a suite in chic St Barthélémy. So even high visitor expenditure does not necessarily solve problems or bring greater economic benefit if there are high internal costs and high import bills (see Chapter 2).

A Question of Control

Such figures illustrate part of the complex economic nature of the Caribbean tourist industry. Yet they do not reveal another crucial dimension of the region's ever widening and deepening dependence on tourism. This is the question of control.

Historically, Caribbean economies have been driven by external forces. In many ways, tourism has not changed this, although in recent years there have been certain shifts towards local control in some states.

From the beginning, however, US interests and capital dominated. This was particularly true, for instance, in Jamaica. In the last decades of the nineteenth century, bananas from Port Antonio began to be shipped to the east coast of the USA. The business was run by the United Fruit Company, owned by a Massachusetts sea captain called Lorenzo Baker. Bananas went one way and tourists, who went the other way, spent five luxurious days on board the banana boat before arriving in delightful Port Antonio. There, Captain Baker put up his passengers at his newly built Titchfield Hotel where American staff served them imported American food. In contemporary economic parlance, Captain Baker had achieved 'vertical integration', controlling the two essential planks of the tourist industry – travel and accommodation.

The captain's enterprise did not go unnoticed. There were, as there would be later, two schools of thought. Some Jamaicans welcomed his business as a model for US investors to develop the island's resources. Others deplored the situation whereby foreigners came to Jamaica 'to take out of it fortunes'.[23]

The steamships of the nineteenth century have now become jumbo jets and those first guesthouses have turned into luxury hotels. But for the Caribbean the economic issue remains the same. Who profits from tourism and controls its parts: land and hotels, labour and management, transport, marketing, distribution, entertainment? Is it the descendants of the United Fruit Company, the transnational companies in New York, London and Paris who run the airlines and tour operators and many of the hotels? Is it the local governments who reap the taxes and duties generated by tourism or the local elites who accrue commission fees as wholesalers and importers and who now own and manage hotels? Or do the Caribbean workers in the industry – the guesthouse owners, waiters, taxi drivers, farmers, tour guides – also benefit? Or, indeed, have those with nothing to do with the industry indirectly benefited from tourism?

Airlines, tour operators and travel agents and hoteliers are the key players in the tourist industry jigsaw. These three institutions, in particular the airlines and tour operators, are largely owned, controlled and run from outside the region. Sometimes, through vertical integration, they are corporately linked, controlling every stage of the tourist's holiday.

For example, the British company Airtours plc is not only a tour operator, but is also an airline, a travel agent and a cruise line. Now the world's third largest holiday company with profits of £75.8 million in 1994, it started as a tour operator in 1978 offering holidays at the cheaper end of the market. First selling Caribbean holidays in 1987, it bought an up-market tour operator, Tradewinds, in 1993 to complement its Airtours programmes. By then it had also bought two travel agents, which were renamed Going Places, now with 625 high-street outlets. In 1991 it launched its own airline, Airtours International, with a fleet of 20 leased aircraft, including two 767s for long-haul flights. In 1995, it also started up its first 'Caribbean Calypso' cruise, 27 nights for £1,599. Airtours, then, can provide every sort of Caribbean holiday and can look after the tourist from start to finish.

Another example of such vertical integration is KLM, the Dutch airline. Besides owning 40 per cent of the regional airline ALM, it has a financial interest in Golden Tulips, the Dutch hotel group operating in Curaçao, Trinidad, Bonaire and Aruba. It also has agreements with another major hotel group and a tour operator which buy seats from KLM. Thomson Travel Group, one of the largest of the UK's tour operators, also owns the charter airline Britannia Airways. The link works the other way for British Airways, one of only two scheduled airlines flying to the Caribbean from the UK; it also owns a tour operator, British Airways Holidays.

The Airlines

It was the introduction of the long-haul jet aeroplane in the early 1960s which transformed the Caribbean, bringing it within reach, both technologically and financially, of the ordinary holiday-maker. Every day of the year, airport departure boards in Miami, New York, London, Paris, Toronto and Amsterdam flash up Caribbean destinations – Montego Bay, Nassau, Antigua, Fort de France and so on.

Yet for the most part it is not Caribbean-owned airlines which shuttle to the sun. In 1992, foreign airlines controlled nearly three-quarters of the seats to the region, with American Airlines alone picking up more than half of those seats. American Airlines, KLM, British Airways, Air France (the last three reflecting old colonial links) and foreign-owned charter companies dominate the Caribbean skies. In contrast, regional airlines get a tiny slice of the schedules. In 1991, nine regional airways (Air Aruba, ALM, Air Jamaica, Bahamasair, BWIA, Cayman Airways, Guyana Airways, LIAT and Surinam Airways) scrambled around for just 29 per cent of seats from the USA, 19 per cent of seats from Canada and 15 per cent from Europe. These small, under-equipped, state-owned regional airlines are not only outclassed by the international carriers but, in their struggle to survive, they lose phenomenal amounts of money. In 1992, for example, Air Jamaica's operating deficit totalled US$5 million.

The effect was, as the Economist Intelligence Unit report pointed out in 1993, that the regional airlines were 'at the mercy of the major airline blocks of North America and Europe'. In addition, said the Unit, the collapse of PanAm, TWA and Eastern Airlines meant that the Caribbean was dangerously dependent on American Airlines, a situation which was causing 'great concern'.[24]

This vulnerability means that the big suppliers can not only elbow out smaller airlines but, through their market power, can also decide route strategies (developing 'hubs' such as Puerto Rico was a favourite device in the 1980s), schedules and fares and control reservation systems. For example, it was a blow to Trinidad when British Airways announced its withdrawal of direct flights to Port of Spain in 1994; and in 1995 St Lucia suffered when American Airlines decided to drop two of its weekend flights out of New York.

British Airways has traditionally played tough in its routing strategy. In 1985, in a secret deal with the Antiguan government, it paid US$280,000 for exclusive rights to the London–Antigua route, thereby denying landing rights to BWIA, the region's only locally owned airline flying to Europe. This arrangement ended in 1992, and by then BWIA had managed to expand into continental Europe, gaining a foothold in Zurich and Frankfurt. Yet those routes remained vulnerable, never more so than in late 1994, when rumours spread that BWIA's new private-sector American owners were plannning to axe the European routes. In the event, reassurances were given that the routes were safe, to the relief of St Lucia and Grenada especially, both heavily dependent on a growing European trade.

Plans for the Caribbean region to pool resources and amalgamate their own airlines 'to make use of economies of scale instead of being burdened by them'[25] and to counter the giant international carriers have not been successful. In 1993, a modest proposal by the CTO for regional airlines to collaborate in a number of areas to save US$64 million a year was barely discussed by a Caricom heads of state meeting. Plans to merge BWIA and Air Jamaica, with British Airways as the 'strategic partner' management interest, failed in 1994, and before the year was out both airlines had been privatized. Only Air Jamaica remained solely in Caribbean hands, bought by Butch Stewart of Sandals Resorts.

The same year, the privatization of the regional state-owned airline LIAT, which provides connecting flights to and between the small islands from Puerto Rico to Guyana, was being discussed at length by Caricom. And while LIAT's debts mounted up, another regional airline, Carib Express, was launched; its majority shares are owned by a Caribbean private-sector group, with British Airways controlling 20 per cent and the governments of the Windward Islands and Barbados 10 per cent.

Foreign interests have continued to proliferate in the air despite the warning of the West Indian Commission's *Time for Action*. As the report put it in its understated style, the 'provision of those services must not become wholly a matter of chance, depending on calculations and decisions made elsewhere in response to considerations far removed from the goals and objectives of West Indian integration'.[26]

The Tour Operators

If foreign airlines decide the routes, the schedules and the prices (flights have never been cheap), the tour operators and wholesalers play another crucial role. Like the airlines, the tour operators are largely foreign-owned. Based in the cities of North America and Europe, they put together the component parts which make up a holiday. They select the flights, choose the hotels, organize ground transportation and day trips. Sometimes these services are sold by travel agents broken into small sectors; more usually they come as one giant prepacked, beribboned offering.

Tour operators deal in volume, negotiating with the airline for 'allocations', seats by the planeload, organizing charter flights and booking 'block off' hotel rooms by the floor. They get good prices for large volume sales and drive a hard bargain for the best deals. Their control over the package holiday means that independent travellers to the Caribbean often find it hard to get an airline seat (the tour operators buy 'allocations' and until they release them, flights register as full).

The mass market tour operators concentrate on the larger hotels, linking them into on-line reservations systems. In the 1990/91 season, for example, more than 200 of the Caribbean's largest hotels tapped into the US wholesalers' tour programmes, of which 33 were in Jamaica, 27 in the Bahamas and 23 in Barbados. Indeed, in such a competitive climate, the smaller hotels have found it difficult to work outside this network, and only in 1995 did the CTO introduce a scheme to link them into a booking system with tour operators.

Tour operators are tough negotiators and put pressure on hotels to increase their discounts, especially in lean years and in the off-season. This is especially true for the smallest hotels, the majority of which tend to be locally owned and can least afford to have their profit margins reduced. Winnie Charles turned her family home into the Golden Beach Hotel on the south coast of Barbados in 1980. Her experience with her 26-room business is typical of small hoteliers. 'Tour operators beat you down. They say they can get their price at another hotel so you have to reduce your rates. Some of them are greedy. We feel the small hotels should all agree to a rate and stick to it but it doesn't happen.'

A 1987 report for the US Department of Commerce pointed out: 'Smaller properties that want to participate (many have no choice since they cannot get their guests in any other way) have to provide rooms at extremely deep discounts.' It also said that hotels which traditionally gave discounts only during the off-season found themselves under pressure even during the peak season. The study found that some tour operators 'will not do business with a hotel that does not give them a quota of rooms at a lower than normal rate during peak periods'.[27]

Like the airlines, the power of the tour operators lies in their ability to direct the flow of the tourist trade. At the same time, they have the power to withdraw it. 'This is an important chain,' says the acting Airtours manager in Barbados, Helen Williams. 'We are in a very powerful position. It's a strong hotelier who turns us down. My job is to make sure that the hoteliers don't go elsewhere.' Airtours, on the other hand, is free to go where it likes. The company, which has a tougher reputation than most other British tour operators, started a programme in the Dominican Republic in 1989, but stopped for what it described as 'purely commercial' reasons. It also expanded to Cuba in 1994, but did not repeat its programme there the next year, again for 'commercial reasons'.

Airtours' first foray into the Caribbean was to Barbados in 1987 when it provided a Caribbean holiday (£299 for 14 nights, room only) for economy-conscious English tourists. Peter Odle, president of the Barbados Hotel Association, had been responsible for first inviting Airtours to Barbados to help boost the summer occupancy rate. 'I cut the first deal with them. We had no summer business.' According to Mr Odle, 'Airtours promised to increase its rates after the first season when it offered dog-cheap rates of US$22–25. Then in the second season, it played one hotel off against another and didn't give an increase. They have no loyalty to anyone.'

While tour operators spread their business into new islands, packaging ever more varied holidays, the financial deals take place in the metropolitan cities. As was pointed out in *The Other Side of Paradise*: 'Owing to the transnational nature of the business, payments for services actually delivered in the Caribbean go directly to the New York headquarters of Sheraton or Hertz, never even passing through agency offices in Jamaica or the Dominican Republic.'[28]

Yet, as a small Caribbean-based travel agent explains: 'Tour operators contract directly with hotels, with airlines and with ground operators. We couldn't do without them. They are the most important people in the business.' And a hotel owner in St Lucia concedes: 'Tour operators are tough. You can't make it without the tour operators because they control the airline seats. You have to court them.'

The Hotels

So if Caribbean hotels depend on foreign-owned airlines and tour operators, who owns the hotels themselves?

In 1989 around 63 per cent of the region's rooms were owned by foreigners. In some countries, the percentage was even higher: St Maarten, Anguilla and the Caymans (82 per cent); Antigua (87 per cent); and Aruba (88 per cent). There has, however, been an indigenizing process in countries like Jamaica and Barbados where there is a high rate of local ownership. This is also true, for very different reasons, in some smaller destinations such as Dominica and St Kitts. At one point in the 1980s, Caribbean governments also owned hotels, but they have since disposed of most of them.

Eight of the world's 15 largest hotel chains and all four of the most gigantic (Holiday Corporation, Sheraton Corporation, Ramada Inns, Marriott Corporation) operated in the Caribbean at the beginning of the 1990s. These companies do not own charming hillside inns; they run large, modern, formatted and computerized citadels. Indeed, despite periods in the 1970s when multinationals took flight, a 1982 study found that the Caribbean region had a larger concentration of multinational-affiliated hotels than any other region in the world.[29]

The story of Paradise Island, off Nassau in the Bahamas, reflects one pattern of hotel ownership: from rich men's retreat to transnational investment. The originally named Hog Island had become a favourite picknicking spot for the Nassau smart set by the time Axel Wenner-Gren, a Swedish industrialist said to be the world's richest man, bought a slice of it in 1939. He dredged a pond to make a lake, cut canals and christened his estate Shangri-La. In 1961 he sold it for more than £3,600,000 to Huntingdon Hartford, the New York railway tycoon, who began a major building expansion by investing US$10 million into Paradise Island.

Twenty years later, there were some 3,000 hotel rooms on Paradise Island. Almost 90 per cent of these were managed and/or owned by five foreign companies. These were Holiday Inn, Club Med, Sheraton and Loews and, above all, Resorts International, the former Mary Carter Paint Company, which had bought most of the island from Hartford in 1966 and came to control 42 per cent of its hotel rooms. By 1985 Resorts International owned four hotels on Paradise Island, the Paradise Island bridge, the Paradise Island airport and Paradise Airlines. At one point, it also owned more than 25 per cent of hotel rooms in the whole of the Bahamas.[30]

This was not the end of the story, for in 1989 Resorts International filed for bankruptcy with debts of US$913 million. Four years later, Sun

International of South Africa acquired 60 per cent of the equity for US$75 million. And in December 1994, Chairman Sol Korzner, whose company also owns Sun City in the former homeland of Bophu-thatswana and 31 hotels and casino resorts in southern Africa, France and the Indian Ocean, announced the opening of Paradise Island's renamed US$250 million Atlantis Resort with 1,150 rooms, 12 restaurants, a casino and the world's largest outdoor aquarium and lagoon. Mega-investment at a global level had taken place over many years.

The sanitized luxury of Paradise Island is one aspect of hotel ownership in the Caribbean. At the other end of the spectrum is the small, locally owned hotel. Yet as the industry expands, the larger hotels arrive, traditionally foreign-owned and foreign-managed. In some cases, the independent, local hotelier finds it difficult to retain a foothold. Occasionally, locals feed off mass tourism, picking up business generated by the big boys, but often the local owner has neither the contacts, the money nor the means to be part of computer tourism.

Local ownership, however, has increased and continues to do so. In 1995, for example, Barbadians owned one quarter of Barbados' luxury hotels, two thirds of the 'A' class hotels and all the apartments and guesthouses on the island.[31]

In Jamaica, with its larger population and more diversified and sophisticated economy, a further process of local ownership has occurred. Local ownership now dominates, at around 90 per cent of the island's 12,000 or so hotel rooms. Leading the way, at an international level, are two Jamaican companies. These have broken the First World's hegemony in mass-market tourism with the successful introduction of the all-inclusive holiday. Butch Stewart of Sandals and John Issa of Super Clubs have spearheaded the development of what has been described as 'the most important innovation in the Caribbean hotel sector during the last decade'.[32]

It is worth looking at Sandals because, like Super Clubs, it is a home-grown marketing success and has been copied all over the region. 'All hoteliers are now calling themselves all-inclusive. When we saw that all-inclusives would grow out of trees, we rolled the dice and said we're going to be at the top of the tree,' says Stewart. Success for Sandals, he claims, comes from value for money. 'We have the biggest watersports business and fitness centres, brand-new restaurants, great entertainment. You have quality choices and with all that you end up with value for money you can't get anywhere else in the world.'

Stewart, originally a businessman with a car parts distribution company, started Sandals in 1981 when he revamped an old hotel in Montego Bay as an all-inclusive couples-only resort. By 1994, the

Sandals chain owned and operated six hotels in Jamaica, two in St Lucia and one in Antigua. Sandals Royal Bahamian and Sandals Barbados were due to open in 1995. By then Sandals had more than 2,600 rooms throughout the Caribbean and in 1994 had been named the world's number one 'independent resort group' by the *Travel Trade Gazette*, an international trade paper.

Stewart's crucial role in Jamaica was highlighted in April 1992 when, at a crisis point for Jamaica's exchange rate, he deposited US$1 million per week into the island's commercial banks at a rate four Jamaican dollars below the prevailing rate. It was a move designed to help prevent the Jamaican dollar's collapse. As a result, other Jamaicans moved their US dollars back into local banks and the currency stabilized. Sandals, according to its own press release, provides Jamaica with 10 per cent of its hard currency.

The enclave culture of Sandals and Super Clubs (and those other all-inclusives, such as Jalousie, which have jumped on the bandwagon of the pioneers) has introduced a new ingredient into the Caribbean tourist cocktail. Not everyone is enjoying the taste (see Chapters 2, 3 and 6), but the tourist establishment has welcomed the likes of Sandals with open arms. As Allen Chastenet, a former director of tourism in St Lucia, puts it: 'All-inclusives have brought security to tour operators and airlines. At the same time, they can also provide an umbrella for small, local developers. Sandals has a US$15 million a year advertising budget. It can help put St Lucia on the map.'

The success of Stewart and Issa has not, until recently, prompted the rest of the Caribbean business community to move into the hotel business. However, Stewart thinks that this will change. 'Traditionally they saw it as for those already established in the trade. They see it as a risk and have been timid, but the younger people are moving into the business,' he says.

Government Ownership

Caribbean governments have also moved into, and out of, hotel ownership. In 1987, regional governments, largely the Bahamas, Curaçao and Jamaica, owned 43 separate properties; their total of some 9,500 rooms accounted for 11.4 per cent of all hotel rooms in the region.[33] In some cases properties were taken into public ownership to save jobs (as in Jamaica and Curaçao) when private-sector interests faltered, or else to create jobs (as in the Bahamas). Yet over the years, management problems made for poorly run hotels and low occupancy rates. Debts piled up and by the early 1990s many of the hotels had either been sold, were up for sale or, at the very least, were being managed by the private sector. Governments were also forced to sell hotels by the privatization agenda of the International Monetary Fund. Under IMF tutelage, Jamaica, which owned 12 hotels at one stage, began to divest through the 1980s, and by the mid-1990s all but one hotel, the Holiday Inn at Montego Bay, had been sold.

In the Bahamas, hotel ownership by the state-run Hotel Corporation was promoted by the administration of Sir Lynden Pindling, the first post-independence prime minister. Its primary aim was to generate employment for the mass of black Bahamians who had voted Pindling into power. Yet its debts became enormous, its profligacy and inefficiency renowned, and alleged corruption endemic (see Chapter 4). Between 1974 and 1993, the Hotel Corporation spent more than US$401 million buying and operating hotels, but by the end of 1994 operating losses stood at more than US$200 million.[34] The new administration of Hubert Ingraham, which came into office in 1992, began to sell off its ten hotel properties, and by the end of 1995 only three Bahamian hotels remained in state ownership.

In Barbados, government ownership of hotels had similarly begun as a way of increasing local involvement in the hotel sector. Heywoods Hotel, for instance, on the west coast was built in the early 1980s by the Democratic Labour Party government. Peter Morgan, the first president of the Caribbean Hotel Association and the Barbados Minister of Tourism at the time, explains what happened: 'The idea behind Heywoods was to create five to six locally-owned and individually managed hotels on a lease-purchase arrangement. Common service facilities and conference rooms would have been used in common to reduce the costs.' Funds were earmarked from the World Bank, but then Morgan's party lost an election. The new administration eventually built the hotel, but by then it was no longer economically feasible, says Mr Morgan. Typically, it was first leased to a Texan management company and then early in 1994 sold to a local company, Barbados Shipping and Trading, for US$17 million, a figure, it was reported, that was largely swallowed up by overdraft payments and repayment of the World Bank loan. It reopened in November 1994 as the all-inclusive Almond Beach Village.

As in the latter days of Heywoods, governments may have owned hotels, but they did not necessarily manage them, preferring to sub-contract management to a private, usually foreign, company. This process also occurred in the private sector. A 1987 survey of hotel ownership in Jamaica, Barbados and Trinidad and Tobago recorded that while 75 per cent of hotels were in local hands, only 31 per cent were locally managed.[35] The pressure to lock into international reservations systems with links to airlines and tour operators in Chicago or London increased the need to franchise management out to foreigners. While ownership appeared to be a necessary condition of control, by itself it was not enough.

Cuba adopted yet another pattern of ownership, the joint venture, as it began its shift away from its socialist model of entirely state-owned and operated hotels. The process began in 1982 when legislation, known as Decree 50, was introduced allowing for joint ventures in all sectors. In 1987 the state agency Cubanacan was formed to attract foreign capital with joint tourism ventures. The collapse of the Soviet Union forced Cuba to promote tourism even more vigorously, and by the early 1990s the joint venture programme was gaining momentum, with companies, mainly from Spain, Italy and Germany, participating in either building hotels or managing them. The Jamaican all-inclusive resort, Super Clubs, also signed up for a joint venture. Favourable terms, including repatriation of profits (in some cases taxes on profits are waived), often as good as in the capitalist Caribbean were part of the deal.

By 1994, *Cuba Business* reported that the 'star' of Cuba's annual tourism convention was Gran Caribe, the state-owned hotel chain which announced that 'it had secured 48 contracts to fill around 2,500 of its rooms with some 100,000 visitors'. Its 1994 capacity of 6,200 rooms would soon be doubled, according to its managing director, through a variety of joint ventures.[36]

In 1994, of Cuba's 20,000 or so rooms of international standard, 1,650 were operated by joint ventures, while 27 of the major hotels were managed by 15 different management chains. Further similar projects were being planned. 'The investment programme extending until the year 2000 contemplates the construction of 27,000 new rooms at an estimated cost of US$2,400 million and an even greater participation of foreign partners,' the Ministry of Tourism reported in 1995.[37] A deal announced in February 1995 committed Cubanacan and Sunrise Ltd of Bermuda to build six new hotels in six years, at a cost of more than US$100 million.

Such ambitious attempts to lure foreign investment into the hotel sector is, however, characteristic not just of Cuba's crisis management, but of the whole region. As has been shown, despite the increase in local ownership, the regional tourist industry continues to rely largely on foreign capital to build and fuel the big hotels which sustain the industry. As Allen Chastenet of St Lucia admits: 'You have to bring in people who can instill confidence into the market place. There has to be someone who can provide that guarantee to tour operators and airlines.' That perhaps explains why, in the conservative political climate of the early

1990s, Jalousie opened for business while the alternative plan for a national park foundered.

That big foreign-owned hotels are a precondition for creating confidence for foreign airlines and foreign tour operators is evidence enough that the region remains partly locked into a pattern of external dependency. Yet choices – the keys to change – remain. Can and do Caribbean governments use tourism as a tool for sustainable development?

Notes

1. *The Voice*, St Lucia, 30 May 1990.

2. *St Lucia Star*, 26 August 1988.

3. Organization of American States, 'Proposal for the Development of the Pitons National Park', prepared for the government of St Lucia Tourism and Co-ordinated Project, Washington DC, 1989 .

4. West Indian Commission, *Time for Action: Overview of the Report of the West Indian Commission*, Barbados, 1992, p. 106.

5. *Ibid.*, p. 105.

6. *Ibid.*, p. 106.

7. Cited in Malcolm Crick, 'Representations of International Tourism in the Social Sciences: Sun, Sex, Sights, Savings and Servility' in *Annual Review of Anthropology*, vol. 18, 1989, pp. 307–44.

8. CTO, Press Release, Barbados, January 1995.

9. R.W. Butler, 'The Concept of a Tourism Area Cycle of Evolution: Implications for the Management of Resources', *Canadian Geographer*, no. 24, 1980.

10. Cited in Tom Barry, Beth Wood and Deb Preusch, *The Other Side of Paradise: Foreign Control in the Caribbean*, New York, 1984, p. 87.

11. Frank Fonda Taylor, *To Hell With Paradise: A History of the Jamaican Tourist Industry*, Pittsburgh, 1993, p. 169.

12. Cited in Kathy McAfee, *Storm Signals: Structural Adjustment and Development Alternatives in the Caribbean*, London, 1991, p. 63.

13. CTO, *Caribbean Tourism Statistical News*, Barbados, 1995.

14. *Ibid*. These figures are based on statistics available in April 1995 and represent a return from 24 countries. Note that some countries, notably the Dominican Republic, include their returning nationals in their stayover arrival figures. Figures for Saba and St Eustatius provided by the Netherlands Antilles Tourist Board.

15. *Ibid.*

16. Economist Intelligence Unit, *Tourism in the Caribbean: Special Report*, London, 1993.

17. International Monetary Fund, *Balance of Payments Statistics Yearbook*, Washington DC, 1993.

18. US Department of Commerce, *Tourism in the Caribbean Basin*, Washington DC, 1993.

19. Victor Curtin and Auliana Poon, *Tourist Accommodation in the Caribbean*, Caribbean Tourism Research and Development Centre, Barbados, 1988.

20. CTO, *Caribbean Statistical Yearbook 1993*, Barbados, 1994.

21. Economist Intelligence Unit, *op. cit.*

22. Curtin and Poon, *op. cit.*

23. Fonda Taylor, *op. cit.*, p. 54.

24. Economist Intelligence Unit, *op. cit.*

25. *Caribbean Tourism Today*, May/June 1993.

26. West Indian Commission, *op. cit.*, p. 111.

27. US Department of Commerce, *op. cit.*

28. Tom Barry *et al*, *op. cit.*, p. 80.

29. Curtin and Poon, *op.cit.*

30. Keith G. Debbage, 'Oligopoly and the Resort Cycle in the Bahamas', *Annals of Tourism Research*, vol. 17, 1990, p. 513 *et passim.*

31. Barbados Hotel and Tourism Association, official figures, 1995.

32. Curtin and Poon, *op. cit.*

33. *Ibid.*

34. *Nassau Daily Tribune*, Bahamas, 31 October 1994.

35. Cited in Curtin and Poon, *op. cit.*

36. *Cuba Business*, June 1994.

37. Cuba Ministry of Tourism, *Tourism Development in the Republic of Cuba*, draft paper, Havana, 1995.

CHAPTER 2

Linkages and Leakages:

The Planning Factor

Keeping the flights full, the hotel lobbies buzzing, the beaches lined with occupied sunbeds, the duty-free complexes crammed with eager shoppers depends to a large extent on the endeavour of local governments. Like unseen, overworked stage managers who have to make sure everything is in place for the showbiz spectacular, the public sector of the Caribbean dances attendance on its audiences for fear the reviews will be poor and that the entrepreneurs – airlines, tour operators, hotel chains, cruise lines – will next year take the show elsewhere.

The burden on Caribbean governments to organize their tourist industries largely on other people's terms was forcefully described by Herbert Hiller, a leading public relations figure in the cruise-ship business who made some innovative suggestions about the region's tourism problems in the early 1970s. He wrote later:

> It takes a particular history to accept that the external manifestations of one's culture are valuable chiefly as ornamentation for hotels designed, constructed, and managed in the interests of overseas profit. In time, however, all successful Caribbean tourism administrators come to accept this about mass tourism, and few can resist giving in. Indeed, they are chosen for their ability to organize the national tourism sector in response to overseas priorities, even if these remain at odds with genuine development, with such objectives as self-resourcefulness, energy conservation, and import restrictions.[1]

Some members of the Caribbean's tourist industry would now argue with Hiller's 20-year-old analysis; others might still agree with it. Whatever the perception, ministers of tourism can rarely afford to let their eye off the ball of customer satisfaction.

First among the priorities, and predicating all tourist activity in the Caribbean, is the safety and comfort of the visitor. These are costly responsibilities. Host governments must create a stable political environment, preferably sympathetic to the countries from which the tourists originate. They must also provide a suitable infrastructure for demanding tourists and shape a financial climate attractive to overseas investors. Places unable to guarantee such conditions attract few tourists.

Keeping the Peace

Tourists must be protected from political upheaval, strikes, or coups. At the first whiff of unrest, both tour operators and governments go on red alert. When a few stones were thrown at the St Kitts parliament building after an unresolved general election in 1993 and a brief state of emergency was announced, cruise ships cancelled instantly. When, in the same year, protesting banana farmers in St Lucia blocked the main road from Hewanorra airport and tourists had to be airlifted to their hotels, the government warned of the negative effect on tourism and pronounced that tourists must not be inconvenienced by local difficulties.

Guided by tour operators, travel agents and governments, tourists react feverishly to bad news caused by any sort of instability, real or imagined. The result is that they stay away; there is, after all, always another beach in another place.

The sort of unexpected and brief flurries of political difficulty experienced by St Kitts and St Lucia caused short-term disruption and short-term loss. More damaging to the region's tourist industries, however, is long-term disaffection. This happens either as a result of the disintegration of civil society, as in Haiti, or because of an externally imposed blockade, as in Cuba.

Tourism in Haiti, for example, has been virtually non-existent since the mid-1980s. First came the rumour that Aids originated in Haiti; then the fall of the Duvalier dictatorship in 1986, a long period of unrest, the election of President Jean-Bertrand Aristide in 1990, the military coup which forced him into exile and subsequent economic sanctions. Those events proved more unattractive to tourists than had the years of the Duvaliers' violent Tonton Macoute excesses. Then, American tourists continued to visit the country, albeit in sheltered enclaves, far from the ugly repression in the slums. When the cruise ships had docked at Port-au-Prince, the squalor had been too distressing for the tourists.

Until the return of President Aristide in 1994, Haiti's Office of National Tourism had a tourism director, six other employees with nothing to do and no brochures. Branch offices in Miami, New York, Montreal and Paris had shut their doors, while hotels had closed (or claimed a less than 5 per cent occupancy rate) and art and craft vendors went out of business. In fact, the whole edifice of tourism was no more.

In contrast, it was not civil unrest which caused Americans to stay away from Cuba but ideological hostility and a trade embargo virtually banning US citizens from travelling there. For similar reasons, Americans also eschewed Grenada during Maurice Bishop's left-wing People's Revolutionary Government (PRG) between 1979 and 1983. Tourist arrivals to Grenada dropped by 25 per cent overall, while the US share of the market decreased by 77 per cent between 1978 and 1982. While some argued that the decline was due more to economic factors than political ones, the pro-tourism PRG claimed that travel agencies in the USA put out hostile information about the left-wing regime. Certainly, the American press followed its own government's anti-PRG line.

Visitors to Jamaica also declined during Prime Minister Michael Manley's first term of office in the 1970s. Hostile reports about Manley's semi-socialist experiments fell foul of US public opinion and the tourists stayed away. As Jamaica's *Daily Gleaner* put it in 1976: 'as naturally as night follows day, American investments for Jamaica dry up; the American press burn us at the stake; our tourist industry, which is almost totally sustained by the American market, begins to die on its feet, and we find that the world has suddenly become a much more difficult place to make our way in'.[2]

Natural as well as political instability also affects consumer confidence. The Caribbean suffers from hurricanes, and, less frequently, from earthquakes and volcanic eruptions. In 1988, for instance, Hurricane Gilbert blew its way through Jamaica just before the start of the tourist season, destroying buildings and infrastructure, with the result that tourists stayed away and tourism receipts for that year dropped by nearly one-third. In some cases, a whole season's income from tourism has been lost in the wake of disasters; and even when stricken areas get back on their feet, it takes time for the international press and the travel trade to note a recovery. In the wake of Hurricanes Luis and Marilyn in September 1995, it was noticeable that the Caribbean Tourism Organization wasted no time in promising that 50 per cent of the region's hotels would be open by the December of that year.

Roads to Development

If the political climate registers calm and the barometer shows no change, the next task of governments is to provide a modern and reliable infrastructure. Investors require that the groundwork is prepared for them. However impoverished the living conditions of the local population, investors need 'modern', Western-style amenities to attract the tourists. As Erik Cohen wrote in 1978, 'a tourist infrastructure of facilities based on Western standards has to be created even in the poorest host countries. This tourist infrastructure provides the mass tourist with the "ecological bubble" of his accustomed environment.'[3]

Such 'ecological bubbles' contain airports, roads, water supply, sewerage disposal, electricity and telephones. These facilities make the tourists' journey not just possible, but convenient and smooth. Police, immigration and customs services, currency and licensing controls must also be upgraded and expanded. All these projects are expensive. Funded partly by aid but also by expensive borrowing, they must all be paid for in the end by local people through some sort of taxation.

Leaders of the tourist industry, both foreign and regional, lobby governments to improve the infrastructure. In St Maarten, for instance, one of the key 'mass tourism' destinations, long-term government neglect has boomeranged on to the hoteliers, and has been one of the causes of low hotel occupancy rates. 'We think all the infrastructural needs should be upgraded to help us with the quality of the product,' says Henk Koek, manager of the long-established Holland House Hotel, on the seafront of St Maarten's capital, Philipsburg.

Of all infrastructural needs, an international airport, which can handle wide-bodied jets from North America and Europe and process jumbo-loads of arrivals, is a priority. The lack of a major airport is one (although not the only) reason why islands such as St Vincent, Montserrat and Dominica have fewer tourists than neighbouring islands such as Grenada or Antigua.

Large-scale investment in the 1960s and 1970s went into building airports for tourism. Funds mostly came from foreign governments and agencies, but the enormous sums of money needed to maintain them must be found by Caribbean governments. The costs are heavy; Grenada's international airport, for example, was built by the Cubans for US$66 million and completed by the Americans for US$19 million. But by 1995, it was receiving an average of only three international flights a day, including charters. A manager for Martinique's international airport has estimated that the arrival of at least six jumbo jets per day or their equivalent are needed to pay for the high running costs.

Airport extensions, anticipating tourism expansion, continued throughout the early 1990s. Massive airport workings in Martinique were undertaken to handle two million passengers a year by 2000, while in the Dominican Republic the newly expanded Gregorio Luperón International Airport opened on the north coast at a cost of US$20 million. Funded by the government and some foreign sources, the airport is designed to handle 1,800 passengers per hour and six planes simultaneously. It has a new taxiway, control tower, two-level passenger terminal, restaurants, shops, car park, and, as the *Santo Domingo News* announced: 'It is forecasted that the new extensions will be able to cope efficiently with the anticipated increase in passengers until the year

2005.'[4] The new airport was opened in 1994 by President Balaguer on the eve of the country's general election as a carefully orchestrated political event. Airports, after all, confer status and represent achievement and modernity.

Hundreds of thousands of Caribbean nationals do not have piped water, but tourists must. Tourists expect unlimited supplies (for those post-beach showers and baths they are estimated to use six times as much water as residents). Yet many parts of the Caribbean have water supply problems, especially in the dry season, which also happens to coincide with the peak tourist season. Local water companies struggle to provide supplies from inadequate storage facilities that were not built to cope with increased demand.

In 1994, a drought in the Eastern Caribbean posed particular problems for island governments. While some hotels made up for the water short-ages by trucking in supplies, this was not always enough. In Grenada, the water problem drove tourists away, according to Augustus Cruickshank, president of the Grenada Hotel Association. He said that the Grenada Renaissance Hotel had been forced to spend thousands of dollars settling law suits brought against it by guests deprived of water. 'If you do not ensure a steady flow of water, there will be a significant decline in the number of visitors coming to Grenada in the peak period,' he warned.[5]

In the same year there were also water shortages in St Lucia although a major US$65 million dam project was under way to ease the problems of both tourists and locals. At one point, Club St Lucia, one of the island's major hotels, had to apologise to its guests for providing no water at night or between 10.00 am and 4.30 pm. In a memorandum it said that the crisis had affected everyone in the north of the island ('those with no water reserves are without water completely') and went on to point out that 'hotels are receiving priority from the government for any possible water distribution'. In other words, tourists came first.

While hotels are built for tourists, at least some features of the infrastructure are in the public domain. Airports are used mainly by tourists, but they also provide Caribbean nationals with direct access to the world. New roads are built to service tourists (the best roads often being the ones from the airport to the hotels) but they are also used by banana farmers, construction workers, teachers and so on. Better water, telephone and electricity supplies, driven by the tourist agenda, are shared by locals, at least by those living in or around the tourist belts.

Whether for tourists or locals or both, building and maintaining an infrastructure are expensive. It is perhaps instructive to examine Jamaica's public-sector expenditure on the tourist industry. In 1992, out of a total budget of more than US$60 million, more than half went to the Ministry of Tourism to support the work of the Jamaica Tourist Board while US$15.7 million went on tourism-related projects such as sewerage works in Montego Bay, Ocho Rios and Negril, city upgrading, water supply, roads, beautification and so on.[6]

To pay for the high operating costs of such tourist management and infrastructural development, governments levy taxes on the tourist sector. As the Caribbean Tourism Research and Development Centre noted in 1988: 'Many Caribbean governments have become increasingly dependent on tourism and tourist-related economic activities as sources of direct and indirect tax revenue.'[7] Apart from direct taxation, there are airport departure and aircraft landing taxes, sales taxes on hotel room occupancy, air tickets and tourist purchases, import duties on goods and services, corporation taxes, and licensing fees, income tax on tourist employees, entertainment taxes, etc.

In Barbados, as in many other Caribbean countries, taxes on goods and services have become the major component of government revenue. Between 1977 and 1987, there was a major shift towards indirect taxation and away from direct taxation; taxes on goods and services grew from 17 per cent of total tax revenues to 31 per cent during that period. At the same time, income from direct taxation decreased.[8] However, in such a tourist-dominated economy as Barbados this strategy made the island even more dependent on buoyant external economic conditions and a healthy tourism 'product'. It also became an added burden on the hotel sector, pushing up already high prices.

Enticing Investors

To compensate for infrastructural constraints and high operational costs governments provide a basket of generous incentives to entice the prospective investor. These usually consist of a variety of tax-free concessions including the right to import duty-free materials and start-up equipment for hotels, exemption from land tax and capital levies, tax holidays, sometimes lasting up to 35 years, and the repatriation of investment and profits. These are considerable inducements.

The introduction of such legislation prompted a tourism take-off in Jamaica and the Bahamas. With Jamaica's Hotels Aid Law of 1944, Montego Bay became a tourist boom town in the post-war years: between 1944 and 1956 there was close to 500 per cent increase in the number of rooms, while in 1958 alone some £2 million of capital expenditure was secured for hotel construction.[9] 'The foreign interests have come down like Philistines in Montego Bay,' a local MP told parliament in 1968, describing the way speculators had forced up land prices and elbowed out Jamaicans.[10]

Foreign investment in the Bahamas was encouraged in the same way when the Bahamas Development Board was set up in 1949 under the control of Stafford Sands, a lawyer, businessman and member of the House of Assembly. The Board's job was to lure tourists to the Bahamas through an expansive and expensive advertising campaign. It proved successful, with tourist figures increasing from some 30,000 in 1949 to 365,000 in 1961.[11] Over the same period, investment in the Bahamas spiralled, with all sorts of speculators swarming into the islands. Perhaps the most spectacular result was the transformation of Grand Bahama from empty scrubland into Freeport, a centre of commerce, industry, hotels and casinos after Wallace Groves, an American lumberman, had been granted 50,000 acres of land to develop into a freeport in 1955.

None of this happened without major concessions and generous conditions handed out by Bahamian politicians to developers. There was no income or corporation tax, capital gains tax, real estate or property tax and no customs and excise duties (except for goods for personal use). Easy terms were available under the Hotels Encouragement Act and lax regulations made banking an attractive proposition. For many years numerous adventurers, tax refugees and crooks basked in this clement financial climate.

When, 20 years after the Bahamas' bonanza, Grenada began to seek private investors in the wake of the US invasion of 1983, the easy terms had a different impact: they drained the government's coffers. Looking back on Grenada in the 1980s, Robert Evans of Grenada's Industrial Development Corporation reflects: 'In the mid-1980s, the government believed that the private sector would solve everything and gave concessions on everything, with the United States making up the shortfall. By the time the US started to withdraw budgetary support, the government had abolished most taxes and had eroded its revenue base.' Governments which dish out concessions also have to expect that investors may abuse the hospitality and disappear on the next plane when the incentives end. Concessions, however, are also not necessarily the determining factor for foreign money. Incentives for hotels had been in place for years, according to Royston Hopkin, president of the Caribbean Hotel Association and Grenadian hotelier, but only a pro-USA government and a new international airport attracted investors to build two new hotels. As a Caribbean Hotel Association draft paper pointed out in 1988: 'Most investors are looking for a stable environment rather than for special deals.' The Economist Intelligence Unit also made a similar point, concluding that 'incentives in the Caribbean would be better aimed at operating costs, which are high, than at capital investment'.[12]

Land and Planning

Strategic planning at a national level is another major public-sector task. Yet, more often than not, the scramble for tourists has seen development determined by short-term fancy rather than a co-ordinated long-term approach. Many countries, as the Economist Intelligence Unit report notes, 'still lack a clear policy and/or development plan for the sector'.[13] John Bell, Executive Vice-President of the Caribbean Hotel Association, pointed out, with reference to St Maarten, that its 'unbridled growth' and lack of long-term planning had had a negative effect. The island, he said, has been 'inundated with the type of tourism which perhaps is not what you would have wanted ... A slower rate of growth could have allowed the infrastructure to have kept pace with that superstructure.'[14]

The spectacular growth of tourism has also affected both the availability and the price of land, not only putting it out of the reach of local people, but also reducing the pool of land for agriculture and other uses. In Bequia, for instance, land sales to foreigners have not only displaced the best agricultural terrain, but through speculation and soaring prices, ownership has become limited to foreigners or the local elite.[15] Similarly, in the British dependency of Montserrat, much agricultural land has become speculative real estate. Land prices have risen dramatically and large tracts have been sold as lots to residential tourists.

Yet in the resort area of Negril on the west coast of Jamaica, a substantial amount of land has remained in local hands. This happened for a variety of reasons peculiar to this part of Jamaica. It was partly because major tourist development in the area never took place, partly because there was a belated reluctance to sell 'family land' and partly because many Negrilian returnees (migrants returning home) realized that they could make money from tourism by renting rooms, leasing land or other business activities. In this way, locals gained an entrepreneurial foothold in the industry.[16]

The overall lack of planning results in spasmodic and unco-ordinated infrastructural development, with governments accepting whatever help and funding is on offer at any one time: an airport from the Canadians here, a road project from the Americans there, a hotel from the British somewhere else. (Dominica's former Prime Minister Dame Eugenia Charles used to say she was a very good beggar.) What development plans do exist are often drawn up by overseas consultants who are unaccountable, who are paid large sums of money to make recommendations and then leave without ensuring any effective follow-up.

A lack of planning regulations, building codes or environmental restraints (see Chapter 5), linked to an obsession with arrival rates, has also seen the unco-ordinated transformation of coastal strips. The south coast of Barbados, for example, between the capital Bridgetown and Oistins briefly became a gold coast when apartments, hotels, bars and fast-food outlets piled in to fill the gaps between the old established hotels. But by the late 1980s, recession, overbuilding, lack of capital and a new trend in down-market tourism had created stretches of abandoned apartment blocks, smashed-up signs, peeling paintwork, 'For Sale' boards, and deserted, locked-up villas. Only tropical vegetation disguised the junk- yard appearance of better days gone before.

Lack of planning combined with high prices put further pressure on the Barbados tourist industry: one side-effect was that tourists spent less time on the island. Such trends produced low hotel occupancy rates and low, if any, profits, especially in the small hotels. As a result, there was no money for refurbishment and upgrading. A recession in the USA in 1991 added to Barbados' plight, and it was eventually forced to seek 'help' from the International Monetary Fund. Barbados appeared to be approaching the vicious circle of tourist decline although more recent figures suggest a certain upswing.

Another constraint working against the adoption of clear, long-term policies is tourism's ambivalent status. Tourism does not always receive the attention it deserves. Firstly, statistical data is not always kept with appropriate attention to detail; nor, despite the work of the CTO, is up-to-date data always available on a country-by-country basis. Such lapses make the work of statisticians and economists difficult. A major study of the economic impact of tourism on Jamaica, for example, concluded that 'in spite of the sector's importance to the economic, social, and environmental well-being of the country, information about the economic impact of tourism has been inadequate to provide a sound basis for policy making. Moreover, tourism does not exist as a separate sector in the National Accounts.'[17]

Secondly, the tourism portfolio is sometimes tied to other ministries, perhaps being attached to the trade and industry ministries. Again, the Minister of Tourism is not necessarily a particularly powerful figure within the Cabinet. And as Jean Holder, the long-serving Secretary-General of the CTO, wrote: 'It is even possible to contest general elections in the Caribbean without either side dealing seriously with national tourism policy.'[18]

The following comments from two Grenadians describe a private-sector view of government's approach to tourism. Royston Hopkin, president of the Caribbean Hotel Association, remarks, 'Government pays lip-service to tourism – it's the only sector that can pull the country round, but there's a very weak ministerial system managing tourism.' At the same time, Richard Cherman, owner/manager of the Coyaba Hotel, complains that the Grenadian government lacks any coherent long-term plans, comparing it unfavourably to the former PRG government (see Chapter 9): 'The PRG was the only government to put in place a proper structure, the only government which had any serious planning.'

The sometimes haphazard organization of the tourist industry also exposes the Caribbean to charges of amateurism which, within a highly competitive and global industry, it can ill afford. As Drew Foster, Chairman of Caribbean Connection, one of the UK's leading tour operators, points out: 'The governments have to understand that tourism is a major industry. It's such a major part of the economy, but it doesn't get the money, the effort, the time. It's not necessarily run by professional people. I don't think that most governments and their officials understand the operational side of tourism.' Foster also alleges that politicians use tourism for political gain. 'The politicians tell their tourist boards that they need an increase of two or three per cent in arrivals; the tourist boards come to us and say they'll give us the money for a marketing plan. But we don't need to do it at that time. It's numbers, numbers, and percentage increases all the time.'

Within the Caribbean national tourist industries are organized in a variety of ways. Some countries run tourism from a ministry, headed by the minister and staffed by civil servants. These are often countries with more 'centralized' traditions, such as the Bahamas, or those with small, underdeveloped tourist industries, such as Dominica and Guyana. Others have set up tourist boards, run by a director of tourism, who reports to the Minister of Tourism responsible for policy. These boards, made up of a mixture of public- and private-sector interests, are usually responsible for marketing and promotion and 'product development'.

The private sector has latterly sought, and won, a more central role, especially within the Anglophone Caribbean. Yet the relationship between the public and private sector remains fraught with certain tensions. Most significantly in Barbados, but also in some other countries, the private sector has been dominated by whites, or at any rate, the lighter-skinned. That racial underpinning has expressed itself with the key jobs in tourism, both at home and overseas, sometimes being dominated by whites. In the past, tourism ministers, too, tended to be light-skinned. As the Barbadian General-Secretary of the Caribbean Conference of Churches, Edward Cumberbatch explains: 'You have perceptions in the hotel industry that whites want to be handled at the top by whites.'

He said this in February 1994 during a disruptive dispute between the then Prime Minister, Erskine Sandiford, and the Barbados Tourism

Authority (BTA) over the appointment of a new chief executive officer. The Authority had refused to endorse Sandiford's choice, the acting chief executive officer, Tony Arthur, and three ministers had resigned. Later, Sandiford sacked all but two members of the BTA. Some people had said that Arthur had been rejected because he was 'not a good mixer' or 'too African in appearance'.[19]

Whatever the truth, considerable damage had been done to the country's tourist industry by this period of indecision and internal wranglings, which had been going on for some years. In 1993, a commentator in the *Sunday Sun* wrote: 'The political tinkering and fooling around have cost the country an incalculable fortune. The appointment of incompetents to strategically vital positions of import-ance cannot be afforded any longer.'[20] When Arthur resigned only one year after his appointment, the new Tourism Minister, Richard Chelten-ham, soon to resign himself, said the morale of the BTA staff had been 'shattered completely' by the changes. 'No attention was paid what-soever to ensuring that this winter would be a successful winter and that Barbados' tourism business was attended to,' he claimed.[21]

Missing Links

One overall effect of the weak organization of the tourist industry has been to enable foreign capital to make further inroads at the expense of a sustainable development strategy. This was critically summed up by Professor Dennis Conway of Indiana University in 1989:

> *Government passivity or lack of foresight has left the tourist capitalist sec-tor virtually a free-for-all. The tourist sector has been either completely dominated by foreign capital or managed by foreign institutions in cooper-ation with local mercantile capital. Both of these interests, foreign and local, are committed to maintaining dependence on imported technology and imported goods and services, a major influence on the minimal level of intersectoral linkages between tourism and other economic sectors in Caribbean countries like agriculture and light industry.*[22]

One of the distinctive features of the Caribbean's tourist industry is the extent to which hard-earned foreign exchange is depleted by a high import bill for goods and services. In most of the Caribbean, the level of what are known as 'leakages' is very high, averaging at around 70 per cent, which means that for every dollar earned in foreign exchange 70 cents is lost in imports. In the Bahamas, a senior tourism official suggested in 1994 that the leakages for that country might be as high as 90 per cent. More diversified economies such as Jamaica's have been more successful in blocking the leakages. The Organization of American

States assessed Jamaica's leakage at 37 per cent in 1994, a far more respectable figure than is usual in the region.[23]

In 1988, the Caribbean Tourism Research and Development Centre admitted in a report on economic development and the tourist industry that 'food and most finished goods required by hotels to satisfy tourist demand must, at present, be brought largely from the outside, with considerable leakage of foreign exchange'. It went on to say that: 'While a certain amount of foreign exchange leakage is inevitable in tourism, much can be done to improve the Caribbean's capability to supply a greater part of the goods and services required by tourists from internal sources.'[24]

Jean Holder of the Caribbean Tourism Organization, too, points out that the Caribbean has 'failed miserably to maximise the possibilities for supplying the tourism sector' from local and regional goods and services.[25] Holder attributes this to policy failure by the public sector and a lack of confidence by the private sector so that ultimately buyers do not know what is available and sellers do not know what is required.

The other side of the economic coin to leakages is known as 'linkages'. These are the ways in which the tourist industry utilizes locally produced goods and services rather than importing them. Maximizing the linkages minimizes the leakages of foreign exchange. This process also lessens the dependence of tourism on outside factors while stimulating local economies and 'people development' and encouraging a greater sense of self-determination. In 1992 the West Indian Commission's *Time For Action* urged that 'agriculture, manufacturing and tourism be developed on a symbiotic basis'.[26]

While the underproduction of the manufacturing sector for domestic use is one example of how the leakage problem impoverishes the Caribbean, nowhere can this process be better seen than through the lack of interaction between agriculture and tourism. While some islands, such as the dry coral territories of Aruba and Anguilla, would find it difficult to become fertile vegetable gardens, many now unproductive islands have long histories of agricultural production, from sugar to cotton or from sugar to coffee and citrus and, more recently, bananas. The land is fertile and versatile.

Yet in the dining rooms of many Caribbean hotels, where millions of meals are consumed daily, the tourists do not eat the mangoes and breadfruit, citrus and bananas of every Caribbean yard. They drink orange juice from Florida, eat a banana from Colombia or stab at pineapple chunks from Hawaii. Only perhaps in countries like Jamaica, or perhaps for different reasons Dominica, can it be reasonably claimed that local products dominate tourist dining tables. 'There is now more traditional Jamaican food in hotels than ever before. You'll find yam on hotel menus as easily as you'll find Irish potatoes,' says Lionel Reid, president of the Jamaican Hotel Association, who claims that Jamaica's tourism industry is almost self-sufficient in food and only imports choice cuts of meat. The change, he says, occurred in the 1970s when the Manley government set up the Agricultural Marketing Corporation to help farmers find local markets for their crops.

But such initiatives have been, and are still, rare. The explanation lies rooted deeply in the history of Caribbean agriculture rather than in the culinary tastes of tourists from Texas or Toronto, however conservative those may be.

Centuries of slavery and colonialism imposed an export imperative on the region; the raw materials of the land, primarily sugar, were exported in bulk to fuel Europe's industrial revolution. Away from the plantations, slaves with access to 'provision grounds' grew their own food when their labour was not required on the estates. They grew it for their own use and sometimes to take to market; but this was marginal, subsistence agriculture and labour was always monopolized by the plantation system.

Neither emancipation nor independence changed this pattern of one-crop dependency, only the crop changed. The dominant crop is nowadays more likely to be the banana than anything else, but it is primarily for export, while 'provision' farming remains largely unorganized and practised very much on traditional lines. Farmers grow yam and dasheen and a small selection of seasonal fruit and vegetables for family use or for taking to market.

In his study of agricultural diversification in the Windward Islands, Mark Thomas found that Ministries of Agriculture had little marketing experience. 'Successful crops in the Windwards have always been introduced as estate crops and smallholder production has followed, once post-harvest and marketing arrangements were established by the companies and exporters associated with the estates.'[27]

Such systems have not fitted easily into satisfying the requirements of luxury hotels with *nouvelle cuisine* menus. Agricultural practice in the Caribbean has been slow to respond to the needs of the region's growing tourist industries. As Chester Humphrey, a Grenadian trade unionist, points out, 'The government can't expect farmers to automatically develop the linkages with tourism because for 500 years they have been trained in a culture of export agriculture.'

The result has been that the hotels and restaurants of the Caribbean have depended heavily on imported food. Unable to rely on local supplies, the crates and containers of pineapples, concentrated fruit juice, canned tomatoes, iceberg lettuces and Californian melons pour into the islands. For the food and beverage managers of the region's hotels, it is easier and cheaper to import than to search for local supplies.

Reflecting the region's agricultural history, the fundamental problems of buying local include low volume, erratic supply, high prices, seasonality and, sometimes, poor quality. Club St Lucia, for example, is one of St Lucia's largest hotels, providing more than 800 meals three times a day. Among its daily requirements are 3,000 oranges, 150 dozen eggs and 300–400 heads of lettuce. St Lucian farmers and co-operatives cannot supply this amount. 'It is just not economically sound for the hotel to use local oranges at 25 cents each for juice, especially when they are only available for three months of the year,' said Bill Stewart of Club St Lucia.[28]

The needs of tourists are a further discouragement to the local agricultural market. 'If you didn't provide what the tourist wants, you'd get so much hassle. We would have so many problems if we didn't provide beef and lamb. We had a beautiful seafood buffet, but many people wouldn't eat it,' says hotelier Peter Odle, president of the Barbados Hotel Association. Farmers complain that the hotels tell them that their guests only have a fish-and-chip palate.

So the entrenched conservatism of the package tourist provides a justification for hoteliers to sidestep the problems associated with local purchasing. 'To satisfy their demands the hotels and restaurants must, of necessity, buy the imported Grade A beef, "Irish" potatoes and the variety of cheeses, condiments, jams and jellies that their customers automatically expect to see on the menu.'[29] It is the excuse in any case that some hoteliers and chefs seek, especially those from Europe or North America. Chefs trained in Switzerland may not recognize Caribbean vegetables or even if they do they may have no idea how to cook with them. Despite a tightening-up of import regulations, vegetables not normally associated with the Caribbean such as broccoli, cauliflower and courgettes appear on import lists.

The emphasis on export agriculture has continued despite tourism. Once again the demands of foreign capital dictate the direction of policy. In fundamental terms, the Caribbean produces what it does not eat, and eats what it does not produce. Crucially, the decades in which the tourist industry grew to maturity were also years when the banana, in particular in the Windward Islands, was riding high; spurred on by high prices, farmers cultivated every gap and hillside. However, by the late 1980s when the future of the secure preferential market in Europe was beginning to look increasingly doubtful, governments were seeking to diversify their agricultural programmes. Yet the tourist market on the doorstep was ignored. Instead, in 1988 the Organization of Eastern Caribbean States embarked on a US$6.2 million programme, funded by the US Agency for International Development and called the Tropical Produce Support Project. The emphasis, once more following in the footsteps of colonial economics, was on production and marketing for export.

Despite aid money, extra-regional exports from the Organization of Eastern Caribbean States increased very little during the early 1990s. 'Farmers were so secure with bananas that they didn't bother with other commodities. It took them a little while to change,' explains Stephen Fontinelle, St Lucia's Director of Agricultural Services. Dame Eugenia Charles, then Prime Minister of Dominica, has another explanation; she believes that bananas are 'man's work' and male farmers do not like dealing with non-traditional 'women's crops' such as passion fruit.

Meanwhile, questions were increasingly asked as to why some of that money, expertise and effort could not be turned towards exploiting the tourist market. An editorial in *Focus on Rural Development* demanded: 'Are we so stuck on developing exports for extra-regional markets, where we are at a comparative disadvantage, that we are overlooking a burgeoning market on our own doorsteps?'[30]

Against this background of tradition and ideology – neither aspect determined by the needs of the Caribbean but rather by outside forces – another factor has worked against the development of effective local tourism/agricultural linkages. During the 1980s agricultural output continued to decrease as a percentage of Gross Domestic Product in almost all Caribbean countries. Agriculture and fishing decreased from 12 per cent of GDP in Barbados in the mid-1970s to 4.5 per cent in 1989, while Jamaica recorded a decrease from 8.2 per cent to 6.2 per cent.

The general decline in agriculture has, in turn, upgraded tourism; the incentives, the talk and the excitement have all been at the expense of agriculture. Benny Langaigne works for Grencoda, a development organization based in Gouyave, on the west coast of Grenada, where tourists are rarely seen except in passing minibuses *en route* to the north coast attraction of Caribs' Leap. 'We are concerned about the dominant trend which is to use tourism as the motor of the economy and downplay the significance of agriculture. This results in a lack of concentration in agriculture,' he says. 'Instead, the more energetic people are drawn away from farming and into being a taxi-driver or a security guard at a hotel. The average age of the Grenadian farmer is now 55–60.'

The shift is perhaps inevitable. As Jean Holder has said: 'People cannot be kept in agriculture as labourers by preaching to them about the virtues of agriculture in the country's needs. People are kept in agriculture by revolutionising agriculture and creating conditions that can compete with other sectoral activities.'[31] The problem is that this has not happened. Agricultural work remains for the most part badly paid, physically hard and subject to climatic and market risks.

Making Connections

Throughout the Caribbean governments have articulated the problem of the leakages and the need to create backward linkages. Yet there appears to be little action to help farmers or small traders to revolutionize their methods: to learn about the necessary packaging, transport, marketing and delivery processes for the tourist industry. In any case, small farmers have little access to credit to help them expand and be more efficient.

The exceptions have been Jamaica and Grenada (see Chapter 9), where developments were led by government initiatives. By the early 1990s, however, it was left to Grenada's non-governmental organizations to propose reforms to encourage such linkages. The report of a Grencoda workshop, for example, held in May 1993 to review and evaluate events in Grenada since 1989 stated: 'A specific area for collective enterprise and collaboration between all bodies – government, church, private sector, NGOs – was identified as the necessary and overdue marriage between tourism and agriculture.'[32]

In Grenada, any linkages between agriculture, agro-processing, fishing or manufacturing and tourism that do exist have tended to develop from individual initiative. Joseph Gill, a former civil servant in the Agricultural Extension Department, started the Wharf Agricultural Produce Co-operative with four other farmers in 1986; they cleared 80 acres of Crown land to grow a variety of vegetables, sugar, tree crops and to keep livestock. 'Sixty per cent of our income comes from the tourist trade,' explains Gill. 'We supply yachts and the supermarkets and marketing board with melons, squash and vegetables. The yacht people take great pleasure in buying our fruit.' But the co-operative has only a ten-year lease, and a proposed hotel development on nearby Hog Island has threatened their land. 'We're living in limbo now. We can't raise funds from the bank with a short lease like this.'

Grenada's agro-processing industry, which had begun to develop under the PRG, has also been in decline. Cecile Lagrenade's business at St Paul's on the lush hillsides above St George's was started as a cottage industry in the late 1960s by her mother; it produces jams and jellies from nutmeg, guava and limes. Lagrenade buys from 35 farmers, employs 17 people at the factory, and dozens of vendors sell her gift baskets to tourists. It seems a small but efficient business, but hers is the only one of its kind in Grenada. 'After 1983, people lost sight of agro-processing,' she admits. 'The PRG's agro-processing business was leased to a Jamaican who couldn't make a go of it.'

Similar problems exist throughout the agriculturally rich islands of the Eastern Caribbean. In St Kitts, for example, Euphemia Weekes, of the non-governmental Inter-American Institute for Cooperation in Agriculture, observes, 'there are no plans for linking tourism and agriculture. It happens spontaneously. The problem is about information flow between farmers and hotels.' And in St Vincent, the Director of Tourism, Andreas Wickham, concedes: 'It's a real problem. I can't think of any concerted programme to ensure that the leakages are being reversed.'

Yet, there are some signs of progress. In St Lucia the government and the private sector are beginning to work together to improve the linkages question. 'There is a need for government to play a role to transform agriculture,' says Charles Cadet, chairman of the St Lucia Marketing Board. 'We need to intensify agriculture. Everyone must change. We need to be more disciplined to reduce costs and increase production.' There, the Ministry of Agriculture has also begun working with the Hotel Association on a strategy, an input and output model, to gauge demand for commodities.

Regina Paul, the Chief Agricultural Planning Officer, admits that there have been few co-ordinated policies. 'We never insisted that we have a local product to sell. Now this is gaining momentum. There has to be a clear vision for the way forward.' One farmers' co-operative which is helping to making the linkages work is the Sunshine Harvest Fruit and Vegetable Farmers' Cooperative. I met Dr Josephine Rickards, a former English vet, who is marketing officer for the co-operative, on the Castries dockside where she was waiting to get clearance for a consignment of watermelon off a boat from Trinidad. She said that the co-operative of 66 farmers had been set up because the market had been 'disorganized', with hotels buying imported goods from the Marketing Board rather than going to individual farmers. 'We try to co-ordinate production and marketing,' says Dr Rickards. 'If we don't have the produce, we buy from other farmers or bring in from Caricom. We protect our farmers' interest by holding the market for them and satisfying the demand of the hotels.'

Dr Rickards would like to see the government help with developing technology in agriculture and providing good support systems. Regina Paul agrees that the system of monitoring crop production and licensing imports has to be better organized. 'We need to get our end more synchronized and share information with the farmers. The two sectors of tourism and agriculture never got together in the past. There is a recognition for the need to have linkages now.'

In 1994, the St Lucia Hotel Association and the Ministry of

Agriculture launched an 'adopt a farmer' pilot programme with the two largest all-inclusives on the island, Sandals and Club St Lucia. 'Farmers will interact directly with hotels and provide from a list of items. Farmers can then borrow against this agreement,' says Hilary Modeste, president of the Hotel Association, which initiated the programme.

One rare example of a government/farmer/hotel link-up which shows signs of proper planning has been set up in the small Leeward Island of Nevis where three local groups, the Nevis Growers' Association (vegetables), the Nevis Livestock Farmers' Cooperative (meat) and Daly Farm (poultry) are trading with the 200-room Four Seasons Resort under the guidance of a task force set up by the Ministry of Agriculture and the Caribbean Agricultural Research and Development Institute. The task force's role is to plan and organize vegetable production 'avoiding any gluts and scarcities', to provide seeds and technical information for farmers, to forecast production, to regulate imports and, most importantly, to act as a negotiating agent between the farmers and the hotel. It offers the farmers a guaranteed market and in return demands high standards.

Sales started in January 1991 and since then the project has grown from 20 to 80 farmers. In 1993 it recorded a turnover of more than EC$500,000 (US$1 = EC$2.70). 'We started with providing six crops and now we provide 38 different items,' says Daniel Arthurton, the co-ordinator of the task force. 'We supply 100 per cent of the eggs required, 35 per cent of fruit and vegetables, 15–20 per cent of fish. We are fine-tuning constantly. Four Seasons now come and ask us to try and grow different varieties. It's a tacit understanding that they will take our produce if quality standards are maintained.'

According to Arthurton, the effect of the project has been to change not only incomes, but also attitudes. 'Some farmers have now decided to go into commercial large-scale production with drip irrigation and production extended all-year-round and not just the rainy season.' Nevisian farmers have learned another way of production which generates its own homegrown success from the tourist industry.

Mechanisms for stimulating tourism's linkages with the wider economy are also missing. Within the manufacturing sector, for example, the constraints on developing this linkage were described in a 1991 report from Caricom's Export Development Project. It described how regional manufacturers had limited marketing and sales expertise and little experience of competing within an international market; they also had a reputation for sub-standard products and unreliability. Small-scale businesses and high prices also compounded their problems along with hoteliers reluctant to change their long-time business practices of buying from Florida suppliers. The study revealed a high correlation between hotel ownership and local purchasing, with local hoteliers more likely to buy local. In the smaller countries with largely foreign-owned hotels, local manufacturers, inhibited by a lack of raw materials, and marketing and capital restrictions, have great difficulties in competing for hotel contracts.

Cuba's larger industrial base would suggest better opportunities for fostering linkages. Yet the enclave nature of Cuba's tourist industry has limited that potential. Until 1995, foreign tourists with US dollars could not patronize private restaurants which dealt only in pesos, nor could they buy Cuban goods produced in the private sector. The result has been that most of the hard currency earned from tourism has remained in circulation within the tourist sector, hence minimizing the trickle-down effect. There are, however, opportunities for Cuba's manufacturing industries to supply the tourism sector with such items as furniture, mattresses, linen and building materials. But quality is again a problem; Fidel Castro once noted that the standard of work in Cuba's elevator factory was not good enough for luxury hotels.[33]

The Ripple Effect

The essential fact about the economic benefits of tourism is that the more goods and services an economy can supply, the greater the proportion of tourist expenditure will remain within the country as income. Conversely, those countries that are heavily dependent on imports will have less income after all costs have been deducted. There are, however, different methods of working out the relationship between cost and benefit. One method is called the ripple or 'multiplier' effect, which is the degree to which tourism expenditure filters through an economy and thus contributes to income and employment.

In the Caribbean different experts have come up with different results. One report by H. Zinder, undertaken for the US Agency for International Development and produced in 1969, put the tourism multiplier for the Eastern Caribbean at 2.3. This meant that for every US$1 spent by a tourist some US$2.3 would be added on average to the national income. Later economists would criticize the Zinder report for using a suspect methodology and for producing misleading figures. Another study, in 1989, by John Fletcher, an economist in the Management Studies Department of the University of Surrey, produced very different results. Looking at selected countries, including those in the Caribbean, Fletcher estimated the tourism income multiplier for Jamaica at 1.23, the Dominican Republic at 1.20, Antigua at 0.88, the Bahamas at 0.79, the Cayman Islands at 0.65 and the British Virgin Islands at 0.58. Only two

South Pacific states recorded lower multipliers.[34] The debate on the 'ripple' effect was reopened in 1994 with a report about the impact of cruise ships on Caribbean economies (see Chapter 7).

Fletcher is now trying to take his research on economic impacts in a different direction, believing that much of the information provided to tourism ministries is out-of-date and therefore unhelpful. Fletcher, a pioneer of input/output models, has begun to work on computer models for two countries in the Caribbean, St Lucia and Bonaire. He provides the software and data for ministries of tourism to use themselves. 'It is a planning tool,' he says, which will show the impact of tourism on an economy as a whole and indicate the different patterns of expenditure. Data can be fed in annually to reveal the effect on income, both direct and indirect, how and where each sector spends its revenue and so on.

Meanwhile, small islands, with small populations and few natural resources, generally score lowest on the multiplier scale. In contrast, the Jamaican tourist industry's high score on Fletcher's multiplier reckoning reflects such factors as a relatively large population and land mass, high local ownership of hotels, a steady growth rate in tourist arrivals, and, importantly, a relatively low leakage rate. Tourism's contribution to GDP accounted for 13.3 per cent in 1992. The Organization of American States study of Jamaica's tourist industry found that total foreign exchange earnings from tourism totalled J\$23,179.1 million (US\$1 = J\$22) in 1992, while the total of direct and indirect imports in the sector was J\$8,583.9 million. Net foreign exchange earnings stood at J\$14,595.2 million, which meant a total retention factor of 63 cents for every dollar of foreign exchange earnings.

Those relatively healthy figures, however, disguise other problems. Despite its mature, large and what many see as an energetic tourist industry, Jamaica remains vulnerable. Firstly, it remains heavily dependent on the economic climate in the USA in terms of tourist arrivals and fluctuations in the exchange rate. It also has much poverty, a severe balance-of-payments deficit and a huge foreign debt. These difficulties contribute to volatile and sometimes violent social conditions, which create problems for its image as a relaxed holiday playground (see Chapter 4).

The Jamaican government's task has been to balance the needs of its people, its poor crowded into city slums or scattered on rural hillsides, with the requirements of a rapacious tourist industry. The answer, for Jamaica, as elsewhere in the region, has been to turn to tourism as a generator of jobs, whether at the airport, in the hotel bar, duty-free shops, construction sites or on the beach. That has offered one way of easing those burdens.

Notes

1. Herbert L. Hiller, 'Tourism: Development or Dependence?' in Richard Millett and Will W. Marvin (eds), *The Restless Caribbean*, New York, 1979, p. 53.

2. Cited in Frank Fonda Taylor, *To Hell With Paradise: A History of the Jamaican Tourist Industry*, Pittsburgh, 1993, p. 184.

3. Erik Cohen, 'The Impact of Tourism on the Physical Environment', *Annals of Tourism Research*, vol. 5, 1978, p. 215.

4. *Santo Domingo News*, Santo Domingo, 20 May 1994.

5. *Barnacle*, Grenada, vol. 4, no. 2, 1994.

6. Organization of American States, *Economic Analysis of Tourism in Jamaica*, Washington DC, 1994.

7. Caribbean Tourism Research and Development Centre, *Caribbean Tourism – Economic Development, Tourism Management*, Barbados, June 1988.

8. Ransford W. Palmer, 'Tourism and Taxes: the Case of Barbados' in Dennis Gayle and Jonathan Goodrich (eds), *Tourism, Marketing and Management in the Caribbean*, London, 1993, p. 58.

9. Fonda Taylor, *op. cit.*, p. 163.

10. *Ibid.*, p. 176.

11. Philip Cash, Shirley Gordon and Gail Saunders, *Sources of Bahamian History*, London, 1991, p. 292.

12. Economist Intelligence Unit, *Tourism in the Caribbean: Special Report*, London, 1993.

13. *Ibid.*

14. Caribbean News Agency, 7 February 1995.

15. Neil Price, *Behind the Planter's Back: Lower-Class Responses to Marginality in Bequia Island, St Vincent*, London, 1988, p. 206.

16. Lesley McKay, 'Tourism and Changing Attitudes to Land in Negril, Jamaica' in Jean Besson and Janet Momsen, *Land and Development in the Caribbean*, London, 1987, p. 132.

17. Cited in Organization of American States, *op. cit.*

18. Jean Holder, 'The Caribbean: Far Greater Dependence on Tourism Likely', *The Courier*, no. 122, Brussels, 1990.

19. *Caribbean Contact*, Barbados, March/April 1994.

20. Cited in Graham Dann and Robert Potter, 'Tourism in Barbados: Rejuvenation or Decline?' in D.G. Lockhart and D. Drakakis-Smith (eds), *Island Tourism: Problems and Perspectives*, London, 1995.

21. *Caribbean Insight*, London, April 1995.

22. Dennis Conway, 'Tourism and Caribbean Development: Opinion Aside, What is Needed is Measurement and Appropriate Government Management' in Gayle and Goodrich, *op. cit.*, p. 174.

23. Organization of American States, *op. cit.*.

24. Caribbean Tourism Research and Development Centre, *op. cit.*

25. Jean Holder, 'The Caribbean Tourism Organization's Role in Caribbean Tourism Development Towards the Year 2000' in Gayle and Goodrich, *op. cit.*, p. 217.

26. West Indian Commission, *Time for Action: Overview of the Report of the West Indian Commission*, Barbados, 1992, p. 99.

27. Mark Thomas, *Agricultural Diversification: the Experience of the Windward Islands*, Institute of Development Studies, University of Sussex, 1989.

28. Caribbean Farmers Development Company, *Focus on Rural Development*, St Lucia, no. 3, 1992.

29. *Ibid.*

30. *Ibid.*

31. Jean Holder, 'The Caribbean', *op. cit.*, p. 78.

32. Grenada Community Development Agency, communiqué, 1993.

33. Derek R. Hall, 'Tourism Development in Cuba' in David Harrison (ed.), *Tourism and the Less Developed Countries*, London, 1992, p. 117.

34. John Fletcher, 'Input-Output Analysis and Tourism Impact Studies', *Annals of Tourism Research*, vol. 16, 1989, pp. 515–29.

CHAPTER 3

From Banana Farmer to Banana Daiquiri:

Employment

For every new hotel room in the Caribbean, roughly one more new job is created. In a region beset by chronically high unemployment, any job, even though low paid, seasonal, unskilled and with few prospects, might seem welcome. For as Jean Holder, Secretary-General of the Caribbean Tourism Organization, states, employment in tourism is 'the difference between social order and social chaos'.[1] Tourism provides not just direct employment in hotels, casinos, restaurants, shops and transport, but also indirect employment in the services and industries spawned by the industry. It also fuels a peripheral 'informal' economic belt where the poor and unskilled strive to earn an income from selling or providing services to tourists on a casual basis.

Whether tourism is an efficient generator of jobs is a matter of debate, but what is significant is that the Caribbean relies on a strategy that equates jobs with tourism. On the tiny island of Aruba, for instance, the pursuit of tourism brought unemployment down from 40 per cent in 1985 to virtually zero a decade later. The assumption that tourism will provide, reflects the region's dependency on tourism; at the same time it highlights the lack of alternative forms of employment, especially in the smaller islands.

This view finds telling expression at the formal opening of a new hotel. The gala occasion where government bigwigs, local celebrities, airline executives, hotel owners, public relations officers and tourist board officials rub shoulders for cocktails and long speeches is not only used as a demonstration of faith by the investors in the stability and well-being of the country, but also provides an opportunity for local politicians to celebrate the biggest job creation scheme since, quite possibly, the opening of the last hotel.

When the Rex Grenadian Hotel opened in December 1993 in appropriate style, the then Prime Minister Nicholas Brathwaite was there to savour the moment; his speech revealed the extent to which Grenada has come to rely on tourism. Pointing out that some 150 people were to be employed at the 212-room hotel – the island's largest – he indicated that 'workers must regard themselves as stake-holders with everything to lose if the venture fails'. The Rex, owned and managed by Marketing and Reservations International, had instantly become one of the island's biggest employers. The local newspaper *Grenada Today* pointed out that more than 75 per cent of the hotel's staff had been previously unemployed and had no experience of hotel work.[2]

In one generation, the coming of tourism has changed the pattern of employment and the structure of communities for ever. Peasant economies have been moulded into service sectors where cane-cutters become bellhops and fishermen are turned into 'watersport officers'. Where statistics exist, the slide away from agriculture into the service sector in the last 30 years (and in some islands in the last 15 years) looks dramatic. Rural communities, first dislocated by migration, now find that the young move to the tourist, coastal areas looking for casual work in the way that in other parts of the world they drift to the cities. Traditional life-patterns are altered as women become wage-earners, often for the first time, in the hotel sector where the demand for domestic work is high. Economic interests become more stratified with the higher-class locals identifying with the tourist interests and better able to exploit the opportunities offered by foreign capital and personnel than the unskilled majority.

Throughout the Caribbean, up to one in six workers finds direct employment in tourism, more than in any other region of the world according to the World Travel and Tourism Council. Accurate figures are hard to come by, but the Caribbean Tourism Organisation estimates that in 1994 tourism provided direct employment for 216,000 people in the region, with some 580,000 gaining indirect employment from the industry.[3]

In general, it is the countries with the most 'mature' tourist industry, the biggest hotels and the least diversified economies which are most dependent on tourism employment. The mass tourism of the Bahamas, for instance, supports 45,000 jobs, representing 35 per cent of formally employed labour. In more diversified economies, such as the Dominican Republic, Barbados and Jamaica, the figures are lower despite the importance of tourism to the economy as a whole. For example, 71,710 Jamaicans were employed full-time by the tourism industry in 1992, which amounted to some 8 per cent of the total workforce.[4] In contrast, work generated by tourism in countries such as Trinidad and Guyana has made, to date, little impact on employment figures.

In the hotel sector, Caribbean nationals are largely concentrated in unskilled jobs. Until very recently, they tended not to be in the top jobs. Middle management posts are now often held by Caribbean nationals, while white-collar jobs in the front-office and sports sections of hotels are sought after by the school-leaving children of the local middle class. Most hotel work, however, is relatively low grade: the security officers at the gate, bellboys in the foyer, 'room attendants' servicing the bedrooms, gardeners sprucing up the foliage, cooks, barmen, waitresses in the restaurants and bars, watersport 'officers' and deckchair attendants. Many of these workers remain unskilled and untrained. Sometimes it appears that tourism is used as a desperate measure to soak up the unemployment rates of the unskilled. Or even as Derek Walcott put it:

These were the traitors

who in elected office, saw the land as views
for hotels and elevated into waiters
the sons of others, while their own learnt something else.[5]

For a region steeped in poverty, there is no shortage of recruits for such jobs. Supply in most cases, in fact, far outstrips demand, although in some islands such as Antigua, St Maarten, Aruba and the US Virgin Islands, a labour shortage has required migration (particularly by women) from other islands to fill the jobs at the bottom of the pile. In Aruba, labour has even been brought in from the Philippines. Tourism still offers, as Gordon Lewis wrote almost 30 years ago, opportunities 'at once more comfortable, more exciting and more socially prestigious than work in the agricultural sector'.[6] In larger hotels with high occupancy rates, a (rare) all-year-round clientele and trade union representation, employees may be reasonably well paid; a 'room attendant' with good tips can make more in the peak season than a shop assistant or a clerical worker.

A long-standing trade union movement within the hotel sector has helped to improve wages and conditions, especially in the more mainstream resorts. Indeed, one reason given for the reluctance of investors to buy into the Caribbean is what they consider to be high labour rates. According to the Economist Intelligence Unit, total payroll and related costs were 13 per cent of room revenue in the Caribbean in 1990, compared to 6.1 per cent in Africa and 9.2 per cent in Latin America. Only Europe and North America had higher costs.[7]

However, for most hotel employees, especially in the smaller establishments, both the perception and the reality of the industry entail seasonal work, low wages, poor conditions and scant security. Yet for both men and women, any sort of paid employment offers a certain status, an opportunity for a guaranteed income, however small, which is not subject to the sun, rain or a fickle market. For women, hotel work is regarded as suitable employment since it takes place in 'respectable surroundings' and is an extension of traditional domestic skills. Indeed, women switch to hotel work from domestic service as 'helpers' because of higher pay, regular hours and better conditions despite the disruptions to family life caused by shift work.

For similar reasons men see employment in the tourist trade as preferable to traditional work in fishing or agriculture. A young man from Bequia explained: 'Man, when I working in de hotel in de harbour last year, even though I getting paid really bad wage I at least know dat each week I gonna get dollar for pay for food and thing. An when I finish work I know I ain't hafi think about going fishing or nutting.'[8]

Indeed, one of the few surveys into worker attitudes in Caribbean hotels found a high 'worker satisfaction' rating. Of 654 hotel employees interviewed in 1990 at 12 of the larger hotels (including six all-inclusives) in Jamaica's main resort areas of Montego Bay, Ocho Rios and Negril, almost every worker felt 'very positive' about being part of the tourist industry. 'The hotel workers in these larger hotels have a strong tourism self-image and feel a sense of pride in being part of a vital industry,' commented the survey done by the Jamaican pollster, the late Carl Stone.[9]

Most of the interviewees also enjoyed their work: they liked working with people, dealing with foreigners, learning about foreign countries, learning useful skills, getting basic training and experience. The job satisfaction was far higher than that for the Jamaican labour force as a whole: 87 per cent compared to 61 per cent (in the 1982 national work attitudes survey). Of those who did not like their work, most complained of unfair accusations of stealing guests' property, management harassment and poor relations with other workers.[10]

In contrast to the high rate of job satisfaction, there was general dissatisfaction in relation to other criteria. Except for employees at the all-inclusive Sandals resort, workers complained of 'relatively low wages and meagre benefits' and did not believe that 'they were getting a fair share of the benefits'. At Sandals only 35 per cent felt that they did not receive fair shares, but 73 per cent of other hotel workers said wages and benefits were low. The resentment of these workers was fuelled by the belief that the hotels were making hefty profits. Grassroots opinion supported the view of workers: asked whether they thought hotel workers got full benefits from tourism, between 70 and 78 per cent of respondents outside the industry said they thought wages and benefits were very low.[11]

It is the small resorts with the smallest hotels, often locally owned and staffed, which for the most part pay the least and offer the least job security. The bottom end of the market is also less efficient in creating jobs. On Bequia, for example, where there are only small hotels and guesthouses, in some establishments in the early 1980s not only was pay very poor (a day's wage for a waitress was only twice as much as the price of a beer), but sackings were common. Local employers would dismiss staff for 'being too familiar wid tourists', 'not showing respeck and manners', and for 'taking nah pride in dey job', knowing that there was a ready supply of labour available.[12]

Trade Unions

While 'mass' tourism tends to trigger a range of social and cultural problems, the biggest hotels appear to offer the best pay and best conditions. One reason for this is that a well-organized trade union movement has operated in the hotel sector for some 30 years and has, on occasions, used its muscle. (This is not the case in Cuba where hotel workers were still paid in pesos by a government agency in 1995 while the hotels paid the agency in US dollars. There were, in effect, few incentives except for dollar tips.)

Where trade unions have established a foothold in the hotel sector, in particular in the English-speaking Caribbean, they have often managed to negotiate reasonable wages and conditions. In Antigua, for example, where the first agreement was made with 13 hotels in 1962, the Antigua Workers' Union (AWU) now negotiates with 106 hotels and guesthouses and, according to Keithlyn Smith, the AWU's General-Secretary, represents most of the island's 6,000 hotel workers. It negotiates three-year agreements which set wage rates (for three grades of hotel) and conditions. Agreements include clauses on equal pay, maternity leave, redundancy payments, holiday and sick pay. In 1994 the AWU was negotiating a pension for its members. In Grenada, where unions have been involved in the hotel sector since the birth of the union movement on the island in the 1950s, workers have negotiated similar clauses including pensions and profit-sharing. Similar union agreements exist in the Bahamas.

One important issue that aggravates relations between management and union is that of job security – or rather the lack of it. Throughout the region, workers are laid off in the summer months, the traditional low season. This period may last as long as seven months, and most workers will have no unemployment benefit. More recently, seasonal contracts and an overall cutback in staff have been introduced, according to union leaders. 'In the past, there was a core of permanent staff who were added to in the season, but now a lot of properties are not adding to the core,' says Le Vere Richards, assistant general-secretary of the Barbados Workers' Union. Another method that hotels in Barbados have intro-duced to reduce the wages bill during tough times was to use non-union labour by contracting out hotel services such as gardening and cleaning.

There is little unions can do when recession hits the industry, although hotel employees are the first to suffer. As competition intensifies, demand shrinks and costs rise, the labour force is reduced. In 1991, hotel workers in the Bahamas lost their jobs when US tourists, affected by the slump at home and the effects of the Gulf War, began to cancel their holidays. At Resorts International, 130 workers were laid off; at Nassau Beach, 106; at Holiday Inn, 63; at Sheraton British Colonial, 44; at Sheraton Hotel on Paradise Island, more than 100. By May of that year, some 1,500 workers had lost their jobs with many more on short time. Workers marched through Nassau in protest at the job losses, and Leonard Archer, secretary-general of the Trade Union Congress, said that the unions would 'close the whole damn country down' if any more workers were sacked.[13] In the event, job losses slowed down for a time.

During industrial disputes in the hotel sector, governments intervene by issuing appeals to settle, warning of the consequences of upsetting the tourist industry. In December 1993, at the start of another tourist season, a two-year wage freeze in Barbados imposed by the International Monetary Fund's structural adjustment programme had run its course but no agreement had been reached with the hotel workers on a gains-sharing scheme. When the Barbados Workers' Union called out its 6,000 hotel workers on a three-day strike, the then Minister of Tourism, Evelyn Greaves, appealed to both sides to reach an agreement to end the crisis in a crucial economic sector.

Another feature of hotel employment which affects job security is that the larger hotels tend to change hands, and this often means changing 'chains'. When this happens, there is no guarantee that staff will be kept on: new employers find it more convenient to 'train up' new employees rather than take over staff not trained in the 'culture' of the new management. When Sandals took over Cunard's La Toc Hotel in St Lucia in 1993, for example, many of the 300 or so workers were allegedly either not re-employed with the new company or were offered jobs in lower positions and at lower rates.

The Informal Sector
Beyond the hotels, restaurants and casinos, an unknown amount of 'indirect' employment is generated by the tourist industry, especially in agriculture and handicrafts, transport, construction (in the boom hotel-building years) and some manufacturing. The extent of this employment

depends on how effective the linkages are between the different sectors of the tourist economy (see Chapter 2).

Taxi-drivers are a major feature of Caribbean tourism. It sometimes seems that every middle-aged man with a car and a driving licence turns to taxiing, waiting at hotel entrances, airports, cruise-ship terminals and town squares, often for hours between jobs. Those with minibuses may get a job with the cruise ships, ferrying groups on island tours. Scaramouche, the singing taxi-driver in Grenada, is one such guide. A veteran calypsonian, who talks nostalgically about the days when calypsonians learned their trade in Port of Spain's Nelson Street, he sings to his clients, improvising flattering calypsos about their personal charms. In general, the familiar complaint of taxi-drivers is of slow times and of too many drivers chasing too few tourists.

Other paths for small-time entrepreneurs are to gain a foothold in the accommodation sector. Many of the small hotels and guesthouses (often converted family homes) in the Caribbean, like those along the south coast of Barbados, dotted around the St George's basin in Grenada and at Negril in Jamaica, are owned by women. In the same way as women have gained hotel jobs as an extension of domestic work, running a guesthouse has historically eased the way for lower-middle-class women to become financially independent.

Yet most of the employment generated in this area is limited to family members helping out in a largely informal way. While this sector offers some opportunities for the small business class, the high costs and lack of access to credit mean that their profit margins are slight and their financial base shaky. As one St Lucian small hotel owner complains: 'The government has no policy on tourism for locals – their attitude is that they prefer outsiders because they bring in money.'

In the hinterland of the formal tourist industry hundreds of thousands of Caribbean men, women and children earn a living in the markets, on the street or the beach. Every day, all over the Caribbean, vendors cluster in the public spaces anxious to sell to tourists as they leave the controlled, private zones of their hotels. Like the women who walk two miles up the sun-baked hill to the tourist look-out of Shirley Heights in Antigua, a supply of T-shirts on their heads; or the Haitian vendors in St Maarten with their paintings in cramped side-streets; or the Grenadians who cruise the beaches for the chance to sell jewellery, straw hats, T-shirts, imported Taiwanese tat or finely crafted sculpture. Or the small boys in St Kitts with a plastic bucket of peanuts; or the women who braid hair in Jamaica or cook chicken on coal pots in Tobago; the boys who shine shoes in the Dominican Republic; or the young men in most places who offer their services as guides or as suppliers of casual sex.

The vendors are survival strategists. However their income is earned, it makes an unquantifiable financial contribution to families and communities. Yet the vendors are more marginalized than formal-sector employees and are sometimes under threat from the tourist authorities who want to 'tidy them away' or eliminate them altogether. This is nothing new: Jamaican accounts mention Kingston's streets teeming with beggars, unofficial tour guides and vendors selling liquorice seeds and postcards in the early years of the twentieth century. In response, extra police were sent out to patrol the streets, and magistrates fined and imprisoned the 'harassing' masses.[14]

The modern tourist industry has introduced less punitive, if sometimes as restrictive, methods to curb the vendors. As tourism has become more organized, the fortunes of the vendors have changed. While, in theory, more tourists mean more customers, the freelance hustlers sometimes find that as the tourist trade expands and as the big hotel chains and large-scale businesses move in, their opportunities are reduced. Responding to the perceived holiday needs of the tourists rather than the economic needs of locals, official policy towards the 'informal sector' is often to tighten up its operations.

Sosúa, on the north coast of the Dominican Republic, became a tourist area during the 1980s, in particular after the 1983 opening of the international airport at nearby Puerto Plata. The numbers of street and beach vendors increased as the town experienced a tourist boom, but when the formal sector of large hotels, villa conglomerates and smart restaurants arrived in town, the vendors found that the places where they were used to working were no longer available. Signs saying 'vendors prohibited' began to spring up. Some of the vendors even believed that eventually they would be forced out of business.[15]

Even if that does not happen, unofficial vendors and guides discover that as their numbers increase, the tourist establishment can no longer afford to ignore them. The occasional vendor who walks the beach or the guide who hangs around the beauty spot becomes a 'problem' as numbers increase and officials worry that they are harassing tourists. One by one, the islands of the Caribbean have responded in the same way by organizing vendors, demanding that they purchase a licence and take a 'course' in tourism awareness and eventually restricting them to corners of the beach or to special booths or plazas in urban areas. They are dusted down, spruced up and educated in the ways of the tourist.

In some instances, this process has caused offence and contributes to the resentment that tourism has caused among local populations (see Chapter 4). The issue of the beach as a function of the tourist industry rather than as an intrinsic part of local life has caused particular controversy. In the 1980s, Jack Dear, the chairman of the Barbados Tourist Board from 1981 to 1986, was instrumental in, among other things, restricting beach vendors to booths for the first time. Mighty Gabby's popular calypso of the time, entitled 'Jack', expressed the popular sentiment of distaste for the new regulations. One verse went:

> I used to sell coral and lime
> But Jack insists that is a crime
> Now when I see the police face
> I run in haste with my briefcase

The vendors who tend to like the system least are the beach boys who cruise the beaches with an eye to selling to the tourists whatever is available. 'I work this beach and can make a lot of money doing this,' says Pine Boy on Rockley Beach, a popular south-coast stretch in Barbados, while keeping a look-out for patrolling police and wardens. 'I can get you anything and sell you anything you want – mainly smokes, sometimes aloe, sex.' He and his friends occupy the less picturesque end of the beach, hanging out by an abandoned guesthouse around the back of a beach bar where they fill discarded bottles with the juice of aloes which they sell to the sun-bathers as an 'after-sun gel'.

But not all vendors dislike the changes, even though they have to pay rent for a beach booth. Some, especially the older women, who no longer want to walk the beach, prefer the new system. Heather, a middle-aged woman, has been braiding hair at Rockley Beach for seven years. She charges US$40 for a full braid (with your own choice of coloured beads) which takes two hours. She is quite happy with her patch alongside the other vendors selling clothes. 'People come from all over and ask for me,' she says proudly, producing a book of photographs of her crowning glories fading behind cellophane. She has been on a course, she says, where 'they told us how to behave to tourists and how to dress nice'. On Barbados' posher west coast, the elderly women selling strips of chiffon beachwear along the beach from the exclusive Sandy Lane Hotel complain that the tourists are 'haughty and puffed up', but they are glad to have a permanent pitch and not to have to walk the beach any more.

In Grenada, where the industry is less 'mature', the process of containment is still incomplete and the vendors walk the three-mile stretch of Grande Anse Beach. Ras Ian (to rhyme with lion) is a wiry veteran beach vendor with a licence to sell coral jewellery. As a young man, he was in the militia during the PRG and spent some time in prison between the murder of Maurice Bishop and the US invasion. Seven days a week, he walks Grande Anse beach with a board hung with coral and seedpod earrings. He can make around US$80 on a good week, he says, which is better than agriculture.

By 1994, the government was already planning to move the itinerant beach vendors to a specially constructed trading area behind the beach. Ras Ian claims that since he was harassed by hotel managements for trying to sell to the guests, he would not mind selling from a booth. However, he envisages difficulties in working with other vendors in a confined space. 'It might make people jealous and create nastiness. On the beach you are free up to move.'

At the same time, a somewhat similar process was under way in Dominica whose fledgling tourist industry was beginning to experience similar conflicts of interest. There, a growth in tourist arrivals, mainly from the cruise ships, meant a steady stream of visitors to Trafalgar Falls, the twin waterfalls at the head of the Roseau valley. With this increase in tourist traffic, the young and unemployed men from the village of Trafalgar had begun to offer their services as guides, escorting people from the car park area to clamber up to the hot springs pool at the base of the larger waterfall.

Congregating around the car park where the minibuses and taxis dropped off the tourists, they became more obtrusive as they competed for guiding jobs. Other locals who had invested money and skills to be professional guides were discomfited by the 'pirate' guides, some of whom it was claimed were aggressive, offered drugs to tourists and abused the women visitors. The Trafalgar guides, who denied that they behaved badly, recognized the opportunities to make money from the tourists but had neither the skills nor resources to do it within a more formal framework. As a result their presence tended to create problems for everyone.

In response, a plan to regularize their position (to train some of them, to give them official status) was under discussion. What had happened was all too familiar: the inability of the tourist industry to retain an 'informal' relationship between host and guest as numbers increased. The shift is from a personal engagement to an economic contract.

Throughout the Caribbean, the need to contain the vendors and the guides, the unofficial face of tourism, illustrates the region's fundamental unease about encounters between host and guest. Implicit in the thinking of the establishment is that the vendor could pose a threat to the tourists' well-being and, essentially, to the region's economic survival.

'Smile Please'
It is not just the freelance vendor whose behaviour creates unease within the industry. It is the whole range of encounters experienced by the

guest, from the first exchange at the immigration desk. The holiday brochures put a euphemistic gloss on sometimes indifferent service, for instance, by describing it as a 'laid-back attitude to service' which reflects 'the slow pace of life', and tourists are urged to enjoy it as part of the atmosphere. Yet at a more profound level, the issue is not just about different approaches to service, but also about the unequal and racist historical relationship between blacks and whites. The parameters of this issue have to some extent been ignored by tourism administrators. Instead, the problem of the encounter has been approached pragmatically, as an educational exercise in which the burden and learning process have been placed on the Caribbean national rather than on the tourist. As a poster in Dominica in the early 1980s put it: 'SMILE. You are a walking tourist attraction.'

The failure of the Caribbean population to be 'nice' to all tourists at all times, with its implications for the tourist industry, is the reason for the concern. Criticism of poor 'attitude' is common in newspapers and the radio, including phone-ins, and is identified by Caribbean nationals as much as by expatriates although the tone of the upbraiding is different.

In 1994, the newspaper *Caribbean Week* carried an article entitled 'Smile Please', by the columnist Garry Steckles, an expatriate Englishman. He described how a tourist leaving Golden Rock airport in St Kitts gave a hefty tip to two young porters who had carried her bags for a couple of minutes. 'In return, she didn't get as much as smile or a nod, much less a thank you,' wrote the indignant Steckles. He continued: 'And as the two youngsters wandered off counting their money, I was left pondering, not for the first time, how long we in the Caribbean are going to be able to keep attracting visitors while so many people working in the tourist industry seem to have a totally indifferent attitude toward the people who are providing them with a living.' Steckles went on to argue that until the Caribbean learnt to provide pleasant, efficient and courteous service, the future of its tourist industry would be in doubt.[16]

Two years earlier, in the same newspaper, came another article on the same subject. This time it was written by Peter Morgan, who had been Barbados' first Minister of Tourism. Morgan wrote:

> In small communities, which most of our Caribbean islands are, everyone is involved in tourism whether they believe it or not or like it or not because it is the total impression of his or her vacation which decides a person whether or not they plan to return. The price might be right, the climate perfect, the rum just what the doctor should have ordered but, above all, if a person doesn't feel welcome then he is not coming back.[17]

With the Caribbean in open competition with the rest of the world, the region's tourist establishment is sensitive to criticism, such as the verdict of the Economist Intelligence Unit: 'Given that the Caribbean is expensive, second-rate service simply will not do.'[18] The remedy is, according to the mandarins of the Caribbean's tourist industry, professionalism and excellence. 'The day of the enthusiastic amateur is over,' wrote John Bell, executive vice-president of the Caribbean Hotel Association,[19] while management consultants call for 'high service performance' and 'customer-friendly personnel'.

Some experts have identified cultural conflicts as the problem. Peter Goffe, for example, a Jamaican-born academic, defines in consultant-speak what he calls a 'service performance gap' caused by 'mismatched cultural values' which occur when foreign multinational managers trained in an 'efficiency' culture are in charge of a local staff who do not share such goals.[20] Indeed, the prescriptions for change require the adoption of a new culture, of new business practices.

The view of another outside 'expert' was expressed in a consultants' report on Dominica's service sector submitted to the Ministry of Finance and Development in 1991. A summary of the major findings concluded: 'Poor worker attitudes manifest themselves in a variety of ways – lack of concern about punctuality, absenteeism, low productivity, an acceptance of underemployment, low career expectations and a failure to accept responsibility for problem solving.'[21] These attitudes, surmised the report's authors, would have a particularly detrimental impact on productivity and profitability in the services sector.

A New Slavery?

The legacy of slavery underpins much of contemporary Caribbean culture and the expression of it pervades many aspects of tourism. It is a thread which, significantly, Jean Holder of the Caribbean Tourism Organisation identified, when he wrote: 'there appears to be a deep-seated resentment of the industry at every level of society – a resentment which probably stems from the historic socio-cultural associations of race, colonialism and slavery'. He adds that the Caribbean is 'forced to choose between an industry it "deep down" does not really want, and the economic fruits of that industry which it needs and which, it seems more and more, only tourism will provide'. Holder concludes that significant numbers of employees 'are not proud of what they do, and harbour resentments rooted in the inability to distinguish between service and servitude'.[22]

Many of the 'problems' associated with the tourist industry stem from slavery and colonialism, this folk memory lingering in the shadow of every encounter: that black people have served white people for hundreds of years and that before they did it for a wage, they did it under servitude. As Maurice Bishop, the former Prime Minister of Grenada, said in a speech to regional policy-makers on tourism in 1979:

> It is important for us to face the fact that in the early days and to some extent even today, most of the tourists who come to our country happen to be white, and this clear association of whiteness and privilege is a major problem for Caribbean people just emerging out of racist colonial history where we have been so carefully taught the superiority of things white and inferiority of things black.[23]

Indeed, tourism in its early days rekindled memories of slavery. In Jamaica, for example, the best jobs in Jamaican hotels had been reserved for white Americans, while black Jamaicans were left with the most menial tasks. The predominantly American tourists brought their own racist attitudes and behaviour on holiday with them, and Jamaicans often found themselves unwelcome on the beach or in hotels, treated as dehumanized curiosities and exotic objects in the tourist literature. In Cuba, the resort area of Varadero, which was developed from 1880 by the textile magnate Dupont, banned native Cubans. Thus tourism began to marginalize Caribbean peoples in their own countries.

Service in turn-of-the-century Jamaica had also left much to be desired. One visitor commented that the hotel staff behaved 'as if it were gall and wormwood to their haughty souls to have to wait upon the white person'.[24] Those early travellers referred to the generous hospitality of the white planter class, but in contrast, the black Jamaican offered little but discourtesy, being 'unpleasantly familiar and cheeky'. From the outset, there were the echoes of slavery in the dynamics of the tourist industry; indeed, the languid behaviour of black hotel employees evoked the passive resistance practised in slavery.

Indeed, it should be no surprise that whenever there are conflicts between locals and often foreign management (less often, between locals and tourists) this underlying feeling is articulated. In a letter to an Antiguan newspaper, a member of staff at a restaurant complained about poor working conditions: 'how are we to work right through the day from 7.00 am until 3.30 pm with only one meal on empty stomach; ARE WE SLAVES?'[25] In Bequia, staff expressed their grievances about their subservient role at work by asking: 'Dey think we is still slaves?'[26] A nurse training for her new job at a Grenadian hotel describes how the staff have to eat their lunch under a tree, 'like we were back in massa's time'.

This connection between slavery and tourism was made by the Trinidadian-born writer V.S. Naipaul, who argued in the 1960s that the

Caribbean had this time *chosen* its path to a 'new slavery'. In *The Middle Passage*, he wrote: 'Every poor country accepts tourism as an unavoidable degradation. None has gone as far as some of these West Indian islands, which, in the name of tourism, are selling themselves into a new slavery.'[27]

About the same time as Naipaul, the Martiniquan polemicist Frantz Fanon wrote in *The Wretched of the Earth* that tourism recreated the labour relations of slavery and the colonial situation. More directly than Naipaul, Fanon blamed the local bourgeoisie as the enablers of this 'new slavery': 'the national middle class will have nothing better to do than to take on the role of manager for Western enterprise, and it will in practice set up its country as the brothel of Europe'.[28]

Jamaica Kincaid's satire on Antigua, *A Small Place*, argues that the hotel school taught Antiguans how to be good servants. 'In Antigua, people cannot see a relationship between their obsession with slavery and emancipation and their celebration of the Hotel Training School (graduation ceremonies are broadcast on radio and television).'[29]

In the 1990s the argument has been picked up and developed by Hilary Beckles, professor of history at Cave Hill, the Barbados campus of the University of the West Indies. In his analysis of the relationship in Barbados between the white business elite, the state and the people, he has called tourism the 'new plantocracy'. 'The new financial tourism base means that the state has become the overseer,' says Beckles. 'The feeling is that black people are more marginalized now, that there is a return to colonialism. Because whites own all the land, commerce, and have all the major duty-free outlets and now the sea ports – the same group is in control. In tourism, blacks have no status in terms of decision-making.' In neighbouring Antigua, opposition politician and journalist Tim Hector observes a similar pattern. 'In the beginning a tiny, foreign élite in ownership and management, controlled sugar. In the end a tiny, foreign élite, in ownership and management, controls tourism. Slavery or wage-slavery that has been our lot.'[30]

Training

Cultural attitudes, racism, patterns of control and ownership have all contributed to the perceptions of many black Caribbeans that they remain bunched at the bottom end of the tourist industry with few opportunities for career advancement.

Another reason is that training has traditionally been the industry's poor relation. Until recently, training a well-equipped and finely tuned army of employees has remained a low priority, with money more likely to be budgeted for upgrading buildings than people's skills. The

Economist Intelligence Unit found a 'lack of investment in training facilities, shortage of experienced trainers and an uncoordinated approach to training in the region'.[31] There were not enough systematic and effective training schemes to go round at all levels, whether for graduate managers or chambermaids. According to the Caribbean Hotel Association's John Bell, training at all levels needs to be 'dramatically upgraded' and 'significantly enhanced and expanded' if the Caribbean is to be successful 'in the twenty-first century crucible of increasing international competition'.[32]

Sixty students a year graduate from the University of the West Indies degree course in hotel and tourism management. They spend the first year at one of the three University of the West Indies campuses before moving to the College of the Bahamas, Nassau. Since the course began in 1978, some 300 students have graduated from the College. However, according to Ainsley O'Reilly, the head of department, courses are undersubscribed and there is a 25 per cent drop-out rate. 'We don't get the numbers we should. There is still a stigma attached to the industry and then lay-offs also cause young people to doubt.' Only a handful of men take the course, which causes problems in the market, says O'Reilly, because there is still prejudice against appointing women to top jobs.

There are also some twenty hospitality schools throughout the region offering a variety of courses of different scope and quality. These implement some vocational education and industry-based programmes. Antigua, for example, has a government-funded Hotel Training Centre, which opened in 1980. It offers a one-year course in basic skills, including a two-month hotel attachment. At a more sophisticated level, Jamaica has the Tourism Action Plan Ltd, a joint venture between the public and private sectors. In the first year of its human resources programme in 1993, more than 1,000 tourism workers participated in a variety of training programmes. Yet Jamaica's first hotel school was only opened in 1969 and at that time its students had to sit external exams set by the American Hotel and Motel Association.

'Training is a very new concept within the region – general managers don't see it as important as marketing. There is a lack of formally trained people,' admits Antiguan Shirlene Nibbs, director of training and curriculum development of the Antigua-based Caribbean Hospitality Training Institute (CHTI). The CHTI is the training arm of the Caribbean Hotel Association and was set up in 1980. Its role to professionalize and regulate training on a regional basis is crucial. By the end of the 1980s, the CHTI was running 130 to 140 weeks of courses annually for more than 2,000 hotel workers in three different languages.

According to Ms Nibbs, the private sector has been more proactive in providing training than the public sector, where 'human resource development is secondary to providing tourism infrastructure'. Yet even within the private sector, 'training is very spotty – some hotels understand the training role and have a training manager. Even then when you examine what they have to offer and ask, is the training beneficial, are there proper systems in place, generally speaking the answer is no.' In both sectors, training programmes are often badly co-ordinated and duplication occurs. In the public sector, Shirlene Nibbs pinpoints groups such as immigration and custom officers, national tourism office staff and even government ministers as being in need of training.

Shirlene Nibbs has 45 trainers working with her in a 'travelling university'. This provides short-term, custom-built courses on food and drink, front-of-house, accounting, management skills and customer-related work. The CHTI works with local hotel associations to plan the courses, which are part-funded by American Express.

One aspect of these courses which reveals the complicated cultural imperatives of working life in the Caribbean is that trainers do not take courses on their home ground (a fact which increases the CHTI's budget). According to Ms Nibbs, this system has been adopted because students are more receptive to outsiders than to their own people. Being unreceptive to instructions from superiors and the inability to make decisions and to 'manage' are two major problems throughout the Caribbean. Ms Nibbs explains:

> Firstly, there is a lack of skills and knowledge and on top of that is the syndrome common to small communities of finding difficulty with decision-taking. For example, two maids from the same village work at the same hotel. When one is promoted over the other, problems arise. We try to equip the supervisors to manage and to explain that it is critical that they disconnect their personal life from their professional one.

Wilfred Fletcher is general manager of the small Caribees Hotel, perched on a hillside outside Castries in St Lucia. Fletcher, a St Lucian, who was formerly assistant general manager at the much bigger La Toc Hotel, agrees that workers find responsibility difficult; because of community and family ties they find it hard to reprimand other workers. 'This is a culturally embedded attitude. I've found it difficult myself when I've known someone on a personal level. You have to learn that you have to make decisions and that those decisions are fair.' Tyrone Maynard, president of St Lucia's National Workers' Union, which represents a majority of the island's hotel workers, emphasizes that the cultural norm makes for difficulties and resentment when a local person climbs up the career ladder. 'It's difficult for that person to get respect,' says Maynard. 'If you play with pups, you get fleas.'

The Expatriates

While there is no significant disagreement between Caribbean nationals and expatriate experts about the need to improve 'standards' in the tourist industry and to increase the numbers of skilled and trained locals, some Caribbean nationals do not believe that the industry is creating structures to secure their employment at senior levels. In many hotels throughout the region, it is not unusual to find that the general manager, the food and beverage manager, the accountant and the executive chef are white expatriates from Europe or North America, who have progressed across the Caribbean in a series of career moves.

'Not enough is done to secure posts for St Lucians,' claims Fletcher. 'There is no infrastructure in place to show that there are opportunities for progress.' His own training was 'mediocre', he says; he had been on a two-month training programme in the UK, but the more long-term training that he had hoped for never happened. 'I would have liked to have been given the opportunity to go on for a degree.'

In St Lucia, with its estimated 90/10 split between expatriates and locals in senior positions, Claudius Quashie, personnel manager at Club St Lucia, believes that a proper 'understudy scheme' in which Caribbean nationals shadow the expatriates and eventually step into their shoes should be put in place. In theory, everyone with a work permit should have a national working beside them, but this does not happen. This situation, says Quashie, accounts for the gaps in middle-management expertise. Labour regulations generally demand that jobs are advertised in the local media and that if no suitable local applicant is found, an expatriate can take the job. In some cases, the advertisement has been deliberately phrased so that it is the expatriate who gets the job.

In Antigua, where there are few locals in hotel management positions and where in any case 35 out of the 37 major hotels are foreign-owned, there is a similar problem, according to Keithlyn Smith of the Antigua Workers' Union:

> The government closes its eyes to the work permit situation. The Labour Code states that a local must understudy an expat, but this is ignored. It's becoming worse and worse. For example, in a recent dispute at St James' Club, the Antiguan chef was made redundant while the foreign one was kept on. There was no understudy scheme, no provision made for succession. The reason given was that the 'native was not as capable' – they always say that.

In 1994, there was only one black general manager (Audrey Ballantyne of the St James' Club) of Antigua's luxury hotels and, by the end of the year, she had been sacked, according to an article entitled 'The Tourism Week Massacre'.[33]

The hotel sector has argued that short-term work permits create more expense for employers and virtually ensure the employment of expatriates seeking a sinecure in the sun. A similar view is expressed by the Caribbean Tourism Organization's Jean Holder, who argues that there are no gains from employing 'untrained, unqualified and inefficient personnel simply because they are nationals, or to satisfy a political objective'.[34] Those within the tourism establishment are irritated by what they see as the oversensitivity of nationals. 'Tourism is an international industry; it's an advantage to have an infusion of new blood,' retorts Allen Chastenet, former Director of Tourism for St Lucia. Others call those who complain about the job situation 'obsessed and xenophobic'.

The work permit situation has its own negative knock-on effect. Firstly, it creates tensions between the expatriate staff and the local staff. 'Expats come with ideas that we are swinging in a few mango trees,' says Tyrone Maynard. 'They push their weight around; they are very young, it may be their first job and they are under pressure from absentee bosses who are looking to make profits. That creates tension and insecurity.' The presence of expats at management level further emphasizes the 'mismatched cultural values'.

The casual enforcement of the work permit legislation suggests to local workers that there is a glass ceiling in the hotel industry. While Shirlene Nibbs and her trainers at the CHTI are busily trying to convince students that 'if you have the skills and the ability, you can reach any level', there is a deep-rooted sense that this is not the reality. As a result, admits Ms Nibbs, the industry does not attract the best candidates: 'People don't have role models, so the brightest don't go into tourism.' Her own family had experienced the doubtful reaction of neighbours: '"How can you allow your daughter to go into that business?", they said.'

The ambitions of the Caribbean middle classes have been directed into becoming economists or lawyers, not food and beverage managers. This is another legacy of colonialism and the result is a small pool of local management material. Greg Glace, the St Lucian owner and manager of the Islander Hotel in St Lucia, says: 'The government should push tourism; the kids are just not coming into the business. Sometimes I see no end in sight. It's shameful to have to advertise and get an expat.'

The CHTI is working to counter these attitudes, to promote the idea that tourism is for high-flyers rather than the unskilled, to insist that tourism does not end with carrying bags or serving banana daiquiris. The

Caribbean nationals at the sharp end of the industry, who try to make it work, are anxious to create a new set of images about tourism. They want to portray a modern, efficient, go-ahead environment offering a variety of jobs and an iconography that makes tourism everyone's business. At the same time, they are fighting to overturn negative images of tourism, the mindset replay of colonial relationships where smiling waiters and limbo dancers attend to the needs of white foreigners, not in great houses but in marble-lobbied hotels. Experiences at the College of the Bahamas suggest that this remains a problem.

Where role models of successful locals exist, this has helped to dissolve the problems surrounding the host community's workers. This view is held by Peter Odle, of the Barbados Hotel Association: 'The confidence is slowly coming. It shows in the way guys approach me. Our education is beginning to work. The idea of service and not servitude is filtering through. Tourism used to be for the lower classes, but now it's everyone at every level and that has made a tremendous difference.' This is reinforced by Le Vere Richards of the Barbados Workers' Union who believes that the 'attitude' problem was decreasing with the increase in black tourists, local people using the hotels and more Caribbean nationals in senior positions in the industry. 'The workers in the industry don't go along with the colonial concept of service any more. A lot of our workers travel and they see that in other countries the waiters are white.' In Jamaica this change in perception was achieved in the late 1970s by promoting holidays for Jamaicans within Jamaica. As a result, hotel waiters, for example, began to understand that not all tourists were white and that the needs of a Jamaican holiday-maker were no different from those of a foreigner.

Tourism Awareness

While foreign management technique experts and commentators have probed the 'attitude' problem and training schemes are belatedly work-ing with the hotel sector, tourist boards throughout the region have been busy launching 'tourism awareness' programmes for the population at large.

The Caribbean's generic message 'Be Nice to Tourists' is not just directed at hotel employees, but at customs and immigration officers (the 'welcoming committee'), taxi-drivers (the 'service ambassadors') and at market women, beach vendors, farmers and schoolchildren. The whole population, charged with a responsibility towards the tourist, is encour-aged to feel part of the tourist industry. A television advertisement put out by Barbados' Government Information Service in February 1994, entitled 'Tourism and You', featured two men playing dominoes on a beach. 'We need all the tourists we can get,' said the first character. 'We all got a part to play,' he continued. 'But I never come in contact with tourists,' said the second man. 'You'll get your chance,' says the first man. 'If they come and talk with you in the street …. Make them feel at home.'

The 'tourism awareness' programmes are basically aimed at educating local populations into understanding the nature of the tourist industry. At best, they open up a debate about the nature of tourism, discuss how tourism can be used for sustainable development and explain what opportunities exist for careers within tourism, not just as waiters and bellboys but as architects or interpreters. At worst, they crudely promote the idea that tourists' needs are paramount: in other words, Be Nice to the Tourist.

With a varying degree of success, intensity and sophistication, the word is being taken into every corner of every island, into schools, villages and rum shops by television, newspapers, car stickers and posters. What is publicly acknowledged, however, is always the positive side of tourism. In Dominica, for example, where serious attention to tourism development is a recent phenomenon, children from a primary school in Roseau came up with this calypso:

> We will always give our best
> At a reasonable price
> Give good service
> To Mr Tourist.

St Lucia has the most extensive tourism awareness programme in the Eastern Caribbean. The slogan 'Let's be the best' is found on bumper stickers, posters and T-shirts and is highlighted on television and radio slots where profiles of local success stories in the tourist business are publicized. Yet the public awareness programme only began in 1992 and before that there was nothing. Agnes Francis, formerly in charge of tourism awareness in St Lucia's Board of Tourism, tells how a survey had been conducted at the beginning about perceptions of tourism. 'People didn't understand their role in tourism; they didn't know how to get into it. They thought it was just about hotel work,' says Ms Francis. To counter this, the tourism awareness programme was launched along with a parallel programme for primary schools, based on the book *Hello, Tourist!*. Schoolchildren work with the book, submit material and are sponsored by a hotel which then invites the whole class to spend a night there.

Hello, Tourist!, probably the first of its kind in the Caribbean, was originally used in St Croix in 1977. It was adapted for St Lucian children

15 years later (funded by American Airlines, American Express and the public and private sector of St Lucia). 'We have so few resources,' says Agnes Francis. 'Every little thing helps.'

Hello, Tourist! explains that tourists are not necessarily all rich ('Mr and Mrs Brown saved US$3,000 over a 10-year period so they could celebrate their silver wedding anniversary in St Lucia'), or indeed, particularly nice ('They may be insensitive or rude; they may drink too much and be unruly'). It points out that tourists, who come in all colours, ages and sizes, want to holiday somewhere clean and friendly and that they are interested in things that St Lucians might take for granted. It emphasizes the ways that tourism benefits St Lucia and why St Lucia needs tourism. Using the image of a money tree which nourishes the island with jobs, it says: 'We must nurture the roots, fertilise them with the pride we feel about our island by keeping it clean, by not acting rude, by making sure we don't pollute our beautiful water, by smiling and being friendly.' And it concludes with a long list of jobs which are connected, either directly or indirectly, with tourism.[35]

A somewhat different approach is applied in the Bahamas where the Bahamahost programme has been used to train workers for nearly twenty years. 'We didn't say you have to be nice to the guests,' explains Beverly Saunders, co-ordinator of the Bahamahost programme ('Bahamahost serves with dignity and pride') and manager of the Ministry of Tourism's industry training unit. 'We went back to basics. We said let's look at ourselves as individuals and instill our own values system, to have a positive attitude about the industry and to show that it does offer viable career choices.' There was also a need, adds Ms Saunders, to teach Bahamians about their country, a subject ignored by the colonial educational system.

The Bahamahost programme was started in 1978, only a few years after independence, and there are now 14,000 graduates, including teachers, bankers, as well as those directly connected with tourism. Students attend a series of lectures in subjects such as the history of the Bahamas, effective communication, culture and folklore and basic first aid, and take an exam at the end. Participants are told: 'Our aim is to increase the awareness of the importance of tourism to our economy and to set the stage for attaining the highest level of customer service satisfaction in the world.'

Ms Saunders and her team also train tourism managers, and in 1994, they won the contract to train the senior expatriate team of Sun International, then about to take over Paradise Island. 'Expatriates have skills,' she says, 'but they need to understand the Bahamian psyche.' The Bahamahost programme should be mandatory for expatriate management, reported the Bahamas Tourism Task Force of 1993 in a check-list of initiatives drawn up by the Ministry of Tourism.

The new professionals like Shirlene Nibbs and Beverly Saunders are helping to make workers feel positive about tourism. A poem entitled 'Tourism' by Augustus Saltibus, of the kitchen department in Club St Lucia, catalogues the island's problems with the banana industry and appeals for support for the tourist industry. This is the last verse:

> De Tourism Ministry appealing
> To all ah we
> Bar man, Chef Compton, T John
> Make this a priority, Lucians in majority
> Who really love their Country
> And of course their family
> Support the Tourist Industry.

Public Opinion

Much of the debate at an intellectual level has been about the disputed economic benefits of tourism (see Chapters 1 and 2). What ordinary Caribbean citizens, outside the industry, feel about the costs and benefits is even more difficult to assess. Commonly held assumptions are that it is foreigners and local entrepreneurs who benefit. Such views have not changed much through the century, given this comment from a Jamaican newspaper in 1904: 'All de storekeepers dem in Kingston and de big tabern-keper, dem is de one dat get de money out of dem . . . dem is not going to do anything fa we, but take picta and laugh at we. Chu! me bredder, only de buckra [whites] dem will profit.'[36]

One of the few objective polls that has sought the views of ordinary people was conducted by Carl Stone in three Jamaican tourist resorts, Montego Bay, Ocho Rios and Negril, in 1990. Polling 662 citizens, who included vendors and higglers, small business people, workers in small hotels, taxi-drivers and residents not involved in the tourist industry, Stone asked them: 'Do you feel that people like yourself benefit from tourism in this town?' The small business people and taxi-operators were most satisfied: 75 per cent answered 'yes', with 25 per cent saying 'Yes, but benefits could be better.' Hotel workers also overwhelmingly (98 per cent) saw tourism as beneficial, although 68 per cent of them said the benefits could be better. Vendors and higglers were less satisfied: 32 per cent of them had a negative view and saw tourism as only benefiting the big hotels and the business élite. Two-thirds of the residents unconnected with the industry saw it as largely beneficial. As Stone concluded: 'Grass roots criticisms of the industry tend therefore to centre most on who gets what benefits from the industry, while accepting the industry as being something positive and beneficial.' What the survey discovered, moreover, was that the benefits were seen mainly as economic, while the negative aspects of tourism were associated with its social impact (see Chapter 4). As Stone observed, 'policy makers in the area of tourism and hotel development often ignore the views of both small business interests in the industry and the average citizens in the resort areas whose lives have been greatly affected (positively and negatively)' by tourism.[37]

In Bequia, attitudes are also divided between those who appear to benefit from tourism and those who do not, according to Neil Price in *Behind the Planter's Back*. While there is a general sense that it brings employment, those with enough resources to open their own small businesses also see that foreign capital is a necessary condition of growth. However, the community is aware that foreign investors do not reinvest their capital in Bequia and that the government has largely abandoned its control. Among the lower classes, feelings are similar to those of turn-of-the-century Jamaica: 'Dem rich honkies done take all dey money back home for make more .... And dey de only people de bank prepare for give loans to .... Dey ain't for give nutting back to de island or de people of Bequia. It just de same as robbery.'[38] For them, tourism means a shortage of affordable land and housing, inflation and a decline in wage labour opportunities.

The 'All-inclusive' Controversy

The rise of the all-inclusive resort throughout much of the Caribbean in the late 1980s reawakened many of the hostile sentiments of the 1970s about tourism. While the all-inclusive has been around since that time in the form of Club Med, whose self-supporting little empire in the sun somehow seemed tucked away and a law unto itself, the increased number and the distinctive vigorous marketing of the all-inclusives, led by the Sandals group, have triggered new waves of resentment.

Opinion in the islands which had experienced all-inclusives set off publicity in the islands which did not yet have all-inclusives. Those which were about to get all-inclusives were adamant that they were monitoring the situation carefully. Tour operators, on the other hand, see them as a gift. 'They are marvellous from our point of view,' says Drew Foster of Caribbean Connection. 'It's a very simple package. But it's a problem for the image of an island. For example, St Lucia is now thought of as an all-inclusive destination. There has to be a balance.'

In 1994, eight out of St Lucia's 12 major hotels were all-inclusive. According to the Tourist Board, the invasion of the all-inclusives had 'just happened', the latest development being the arrival of the Sandals chain, taking over from two formerly non-all-inclusive hotels. Hilary Modeste, head of the St Lucia Hotel Association, claims that the arrival of Sandals has done a lot for St Lucia, as it maintains a high occupancy rate and therefore a high level of staffing.

While for the tourism establishment, all-inclusives are an expression of the industry's confidence and are pivotal in contributing to economic growth, the perception at grassroots level is the opposite. Public opinion, including those in indirect employment such as taxi-drivers and vendors as well as people working in local restaurants and small hotels, is often bitter about the glittering ghettos that have opened in their midst. They appear to further corral the tourists, offering everything bigger and better than anywhere else and for free because the tourists have already paid back home and have 'left their wallets behind'.

Dissent about all-inclusives has united St Lucia. A popular perception is that it has not just been the informal sector and the poor who have lost out in the scramble for dollars, but also the local élite who normally reap the benefits from tourism. In St Lucia local restaurant owners with significant clout in the community reported a substantial downturn in business. Together with the vendors and the taxi-drivers, the entrepreneurial class has also felt threatened. The economic fall-out from the all-inclusives has fuelled a social response (see Chapter 4). As a result, a leading St Lucian concludes: 'I used to welcome tourists, give them a lift if they looked lost, extend my hand of friendship. Nowadays when I see them with their plastic wrist-tag, I pass them by.'

In Jamaica, where all-inclusives have been around longer, Carl Stone provided some evidence of grassroots perceptions about all-inclusives. The popular view was that they were 'big money spinners for the big hoteliers, but stumbling blocks in the path of the small interests in tourism'. Only a small minority believed that they had made a very positive contribution to the development of the area, while 11 per cent believed that their impact was all negative. The positive respondents said that all-inclusives created new employment and that they earned dollars for hotels and the country; the negative respondents said that all-inclusives took business away from local entrepreneurs, that tourists spent nothing in Jamaica and remained isolated from the people.[39]

The truth, according to the 1994 Organization of American States' analysis of Jamaica's tourist industry, lies somewhere in between. The Organization of American States obtained financial statements from 11 out of Jamaica's 19 all-inclusive hotels in its detailed survey. It drew some interesting conclusions about the role of the all-inclusives compared to other types of accommodation. Firstly, it found that 'all-inclusive hotels generate the largest amount of revenue but their impact on the economy is smaller per dollar of revenue than other accommodation subsectors'. Secondly, it concluded that all-inclusives imported more and employed fewer people per dollar of revenue than other hotels. This information confirms the concern of those who argue that all-inclusives have a smaller trickle-down effect. However, thirdly, in terms of direct impact, all-inclusives made the largest contribution to GDP, with the biggest non-all-inclusives second.[40]

Carl Stone's survey also looked at the all-inclusives' finances, but from different angles and in a smaller sample. It analysed the foreign exchange contribution made by six all-inclusives (four Sandals and two of the Issa group) and six non-all-inclusive hotels (among them Trelawny Beach and Holiday Inn) during the 1989–90 financial year. According to Stone, all-inclusive hotels in the sample lodged 81 per cent more US dollars per room than the other hotels. Sandals averaged US$51,100, the two Issa hotels US$45,800, and the non-all-inclusives US$27,000. One non-all-inclusive, Half Moon, however, came out top, just pipping Sandals Negril for highest per room contribution.[41]

While received opinion is that all-inclusive tourists spend little money in Jamaica, Stone's poll found that, in fact, they spend more on local shopping than guests in other hotels. However, they spend more in hotel shops and less with small shopkeepers and vendors (whose goods Stone suggested sometimes lack variety and quality) than guests in non-all-inclusives. The survey did not inquire about expenditure on taxis, tours or restaurants: all areas that all-inclusive guests traditionally eschew.

Stone was enthusiastic about all-inclusives. He said that they represented 'the strongest component of the Jamaican tourist industry'. Far from being an obstacle in the path of progress of small business and vendors, 'these hotels have assisted the expansion of the tourist market in various important ways'. Stone believed that public education was needed to 'dispel and remove the many myths surrounding the all-inclusive hotels and to turn widespread ambivalence about all-inclusive hotels and their value into a more positive and supportive body of public opinion'.

If the jury still appears to be out on the economic impact of all-inclusives in particular and tourism in general, there is much less ambivalence about the industry's social impact on the region as a whole.

Notes

1. Jean Holder, 'The Caribbean: Far Greater Dependence on Tourism Likely', *The Courier*, Brussels, no. 122, 1990.

2. *Grenada Today*, Grenada, 11 March 1994.

3. *Caribbean Insight*, London, April 1995.

4. Organisation of American States, *Economic Analysis of Tourism in Jamaica*, Washington DC, 1994.

5. Derek Walcott, *Omeros*, London, 1990, p. 289.

6. Gordon K. Lewis, *The Growth of the Modern West Indies*, New York, 1968, p. 140.

7. Economist Intelligence Unit, *Tourism in the Caribbean: Special Report*, London, 1993.

8. Neil Price, *Behind the Planter's Back: Lower-Class Responses to Marginality in Bequia Island, St Vincent*, London, 1988, p. 175.

9. Carl Stone, 'A Socio-Economic Study of the Tourism Industry in Jamaica', *Caribbean Affairs*, Trinidad, vol. 4, no. 1, 1991, p. 12.

10. *Ibid.*

11. *Ibid.*

12. Price, *op. cit.*, p. 224.

13. *Caribbean Insight*, London, June 1991.

14. Frank Fonda Taylor, *To Hell with Paradise: A History of the Jamaican Tourist Industry*, Pittsburgh, 1993, p. 119.

15. Brian M. Kermath and Robert N. Thomas, 'Spatial Dynamics of Resorts: Sosúa, Dominican Republic', *Annals of Tourism Research*, vol. 19, 1992, pp.173–90.

16. *Caribbean Week*, Barbados, 14 May 1994.

17. *Caribbean Week*, 4 April 1992.

18. Economist Intelligence Unit, *op. cit.*

19. John Bell, 'Caribbean Tourism in the Year 2000' in Dennis Gayle and Jonathan Goodrich (eds), *Tourism, Marketing and Management in the Caribbean*, London, 1993, p. 229.

20. Peter Goffe, 'Managing for Excellence in Caribbean Hotels', in Gayle and Goodrich, *op. cit.*, p. 150.

21. Dorothy Riddle and John Jay, *Dominica's Service Sector: Overview and Assessment*, Dominica Ministry of Finance and Development, 1991.

22. Holder, *op. cit.*, p. 74.

23. Maurice Bishop, 'Opening Address, Regional Conference on the Socio-Cultural and Environmental Impact of Tourism on Caribbean Societies'. Grenada, 1979, mimeo.

24. Fonda Taylor, *op. cit.*, p. 90.

25. *Outlet*, Antigua and Barbuda, 9 July 1993.

26. Price, *op. cit.*, p. 224.

27. V.S. Naipaul, *The Middle Passage*, London, 1962, p. 210.

28. Frantz Fanon, *The Wretched of the Earth*, London, 1967, p. 123.

29. Jamaica Kincaid, *A Small Place*, London, 1988, p. 55.

30. *Outlet*, 14 October 1994.

31. Economist Intelligence Unit, *op. cit.*

32. Bell, *op. cit.*, p. 229.

33. *Outlet*, 21 October 1994.

34. Jean Holder, 'The Caribbean Tourism Organization's Role in Caribbean Tourism Development Towards the Year 2000' in Gayle and Goodrich, *op. cit.*, p. 215.

35. *Hello, Tourist!*, Project St Croix, US Virgin Islands, 1977.

36. Fonda Taylor, *op. cit.*, p. 110.

37. Stone, *op. cit.*

38. Price, *op. cit.*, p. 214.

39. Stone, *op. cit.*

40. Organization of American States, *op. cit.*

41. Stone, *op. cit.*

CHAPTER 4

'Like an Alien In We Own Land':

The Social Impact

The winning calypso of the 1994 Carnival King competition in St Lucia was 'Alien'. Sung by the Mighty Pep and written by Rohan Seon, a teacher at Derek Walcott's old school St Mary's College, it was an enormously popular hit, played continuously on local radio and heard on buses, in rum shops, offices and homes throughout St Lucia during the carnival period.

Calypso is a vehicle for social change and political protest and, like any good calypso, 'Alien' touched a chord with St Lucians by articulating strong feelings against the dominance of all-inclusive resorts on the island. According to the calypso, all-inclusives are 'buying up every strip of beach, Every treasured spot they reach.' The chorus line, 'Like an alien, in we own land', was particularly cheered by St Lucians because all-inclusives, unlike other types of hotels, restrict the entry of non-residents to those who can afford expensive day passes, thus effectively barring the majority of islanders from the premises.

This is part of the calypso:

All-inclusive tax elusives
And truth is
They're sucking up we juices
Buying up every strip of beach
Every treasured spot they reach.

Some put on Sandals
Exclusive vandals
It's a scandal
The way they operate
Building brick walls and barricades
Like a state within a state.

For Lucians to enter
For lunch or dinner
We need reservations, passport and visa

And if you sell near the hotel
I wish you well
They will yell and kick you out to hell.

Chorus:
Like an alien
In we own land
I feel like a stranger
And I sensing danger
We can't sell out whole country
To please the foreign lobby
What's the point of progress
Is it really success
If we gain ten billion
But lose the land we live on?

The popularity of 'Alien' had also been fuelled by a dispute between Ronald 'Boo' Hinkson, a well-respected St Lucian musician, and the all-inclusive resort Sandals La Toque. Hinkson had gone to Sandals one evening in late 1993 to drop off two friends at the resort when a security guard demanded to search his car, saying that the procedure was company policy. Hinkson refused to give his permission, was held against his will, and as a result sued the company for wrongful imprisonment.

Echoing the words of 'Alien', Hinkson expressed his outrage at what had happened at Sandals in an open letter to the Minister of Tourism, Romanus Lansiquot: 'No matter how many jobs, airline flights or US dollars Sandals brings into this country, they cannot buy the authority to trample on the rights and human dignity of the St Lucian people.'

A similar episode from another island touched the same nerve. The Prime Minister of Antigua, Lester Bird (a man of enormous height and girth), was apparently barred from the all-inclusive Club Antigua in 1994 when a zealous security guard, not recognizing him, refused him entry because he had no pass. The opposition newspaper *Outlet* (usually no friend of Lester Bird) commented:

Antiguans and Barbudans who literally give millions of dollars to these very all-inclusive hotels in customs duties and taxes, do not, cannot, will not, and must not be asked to accept by those to whom we give, that we are not allowed in these halls, except accompanied by a trailing Security Guard. There was a time, in the long and far off times, when people of this country had to have a pass to be out of doors after the ringing of a Church bell at night. We overcame that. We did not overcome that in those long and far off times to have it reimposed in another form in these present times.[1]

81

The calypso and the treatment of Hinkson and Prime Minister Bird raise particular issues about Caribbean tourism and its social impact on the region. For a start, they reflect the region's distaste for a tourism which denies Caribbean peoples access to parts of their own country. Echoing a widely expressed view, one St Lucian who has lived in Europe for 20 years would never go back because 'I can't walk along the beach in my own country.'

In theory, there is no such thing as a private beach in most of the Caribbean since all land up to the high-water mark is public in law (the conformation of many Caribbean beaches, however, means that there is often only a narrow strip between sea and high-water mark). Yet in practice, access to the beach has been, and in some cases remains, restricted. While popular sentiment endorses claims such as 'the beach is the birthright of the people' made by Grenadian politician George Brizan, more and more hotels are on the best and most accessible beaches, yet access to the beach is barred by hotel security. Even when access is not forbidden, some locals, especially older ones, often feel uncomfortable or unwelcome sharing the sea and sand with tourists.

As a result, on many islands there are beaches such as Friar's Bay in Antigua or Pigeon Point in St Lucia which have become refuges for local people, where they go for a barbecue or a family outing away from the hotel strips. In the 1970s, the Jamaican authorities fought a rearguard action to protect local access by putting up signs saying, 'Reserved as a Public Bathing Beach'. However, such beaches were not usually the best spots as those were 'reserved' for the tourists. By that time, a contributor to the *Gleaner* wrote, 'The day could come when the ordinary Jamaican doesn't know what a good beach looks like.'[2]

The restrictions, either by design or by effect, on locals sharing beaches with tourists are part of a strategy to 'safeguard' tourism for the visitors. Within the hotel grounds, the tourists' environment can be controlled, but the beach remains, in law at least, a public space. Yet with the arrival of tourists, this area also becomes part of the holiday-maker's sphere of influence. As a result, not only do casual vendors tend to be restricted (see Chapter 3), but local behaviour begins to be scrutinized and contained.

One of the major strategies used by tourism officials has been to employ wardens and/or police (and in a few cases the military) to patrol the beaches. In Barbados, the issue became hot in the early 1980s when Jack Dear, the chairman of the Barbados Tourist Board, was responsible for introducing wardens to the beaches. 'There was a problem of beach harassment, mainly sexual, in which women were called lesbians if they rejected the beach boys,' says Dear. 'The situation got worse and worse and became a major issue for the industry. My solution was to get them off the beach. Some people who cursed me then went on themselves to impose control.' The introduction of wardens (who 'want the women, too', according to the beach bums) and, later, the police to Bajan beaches did not make Dear popular. His critics promptly interpreted the new policy as a means of keeping black Barbadians off the beach. Again, a calypso sums up local sentiment of the time. This one, famously called 'Jack' begins:

I grow up bathing in sea water
But nowadays that is bare horror
If I only venture down by the shore
Police is only telling me I can't bathe any more

And the chorus includes the lines: 'I want Jack to know that the beach belong to me/That can't happen here over my dead body/Tell Jack that I say that the beach belong to me.'

In Cuba it is not just access to beaches that has caused dismay among local people. There, the re-emerging tourist industry has practised a virtual economic and social apartheid, barring Cubans from restaurants, bars, nightclubs, hotels and 'dollar' shops, unless accompanied and paid for by foreigners. 'It's disgusting. We are second-class citizens in our own country. And for what? The US dollar, the symbol of our old imperialist enemy,' one Cuban cabaret dancer told a journalist.[3]

While locals may feel corralled and controlled, tourists sometimes behave as if they own the place. Many, for example, like photographing the local 'scene' although guides ask them not to take pictures of people without first asking permission. In more remote islands such as Dominica, tourists cannot resist taking 'picturesque' images of market vendors, women washing clothes in the river, or of the indigenous Caribs. Local people are not greatly thrilled by this intrusion.

The effect of strangers, with and without cameras, invading the domestic and working lives of Caribbeans is difficult to calculate. Many locals, especially in non-tourist-driven areas, continue to live and work as they always have done. What is clear, however, is that tourists are not always treated with the flattering cheeriness demanded by both tourist boards and tourists. As the British novelist Martin Amis wrote in an essay on St Lucia: 'The street-wanderers of Micoud regard us with ambiguous levity. We stop for a can of orange juice and are unsmilingly overcharged. Although you wouldn't call them hostile, they are no more friendly than I would feel, if a stranger drove down my street in a car the size of my house.'[4]

The fishing communities of Les Saintes, the group of tiny islands off the coast of Guadeloupe, have experienced the daily arrival of day-tripping tourist groups since the 1960s when the airstrip first opened. According to one anthropological essay on the community, those Santois who could not profit from the tourists first treated them with 'total indifference'. This attitude changed to hostility when the islanders realized how insular and isolated they were, cut off from the modern, developed world of the visitors. Tourism, concluded the anthropologist, had made them envious of life outside Les Saintes.[5]

Bad Influence?

Caribbean intellectuals express concern about how the ethics of materialism transfer to the resident population. Tourists parade their wealth before people whose experience of First-World lifestyles are perhaps second-hand and received through media images. Tourism, they argue, promotes hedonism and superficial experiences; it does not build self-confidence and discipline. Such thinking is also part of a broader analysis which blames tourism for undermining national identities (see Chapter 8) and for the spread of a general malaise within Caribbean societies.

Central to this idea is the so-called 'demonstration effect' in which tourism is said to create a demand for Western lifestyles and attitudes. In pre-war Jamaica one observer noted that Jamaicans 'assume the bovine loud aggressiveness of the tourist manner'.[6] In this context, the supposedly malign influence of tourism ranges from the corruption of local youth, changes in consumption (burgers and supermarkets rather than bammies and coalpots) to the mimicry of Western styles of entertainment and architecture. While this demonstration effect is in part a consequence of tourism, other factors exist alongside tourism: the emergence of a Caribbean middle class, travel, contact with relatives abroad and, more recently, widespread access to North American media.[7]

But tourists get the blame, especially when there is stress and economic hardship. Grenada's rudderless politics since the US invasion in 1983 has had its effects. 'The poor now see that there is no one out there seeking out their interests, therefore they become mercenary too,' says Robert Evans of the Industrial Development Corporation and a former technical manager of the airport under the People's Revolutionary Government. A Rastafarian called Ras Herb notices a similar effect among his own community. He describes another Rasta, who lives around the tourist area of Grande Anse beach, as follows: 'living among the tourist and other people in that area, has made him hook on worldly materials and fantasy. To "I", he is an exaggerator, and inciter and one who will always make a talk for food.'

Joseph Antoine, a Grenadian community worker, has also watched the way tourism has changed communities. He believes that tourism has serious social implications:

> When people move to tourist areas, there is a break up of community and family. People then start turning away from traditional foods – they begin to think that bottled drink is better. Then people want to sound like tourists, too. Tourism 'demotivates'; only a small percentage benefit. Unless tourism is tied to aspirations of political development; anything else leaves people deficient.

Tim Hector, Antiguan journalist and politician, blames the nature of tourism in Antigua for similar negative effects. In *Outlet* newspaper, he wrote:

> And where sugar was succeeded by Princess Tourism, the fragility of the industry, and the industry itself has introduced new social relations. Where sugar brought people together, working together on large estates, tourism brings people together at hotels, without it seems, the same social bonding. Everyone is on his own. Imitating the life-style of the holidayers whom he or she serves. More and more tourism alienates. Especially when tourism is in foreign hands.[8]

A more extreme description of how tourism corrupts comes from Gerardo Mosquera, the Cuban art critic, who has watched Cuba realign itself with foreign investors while holding on to a centralized economy. This contradictory situation creates such ironies as doctors working as hotel waiters: a paradox beyond the imagining of the rest of the Caribbean. Yet that is the extent to which the Cuban population can enjoy the fruits of tourism, according to Mosquera. 'The Cuban people have had to confront neoliberal policies without even having the option of legally participating in the informal economy. This curious mixture of "socialist" fundamentalism and "neoliberalism" has created corruption, widespread theft, marginality, the black market, mass exodus, and *jineteo* [prostitution] as survival strategies,' he wrote.[9]

For the rest of the Caribbean, imitating the tourist culture is a legacy of colonial history. Aspiring to imitate others, labelling others as better, led to V.S. Naipaul's concept of the 'mimic-men', his contemptuous put-down of the region's psyche. One way in which such insecurity expresses itself is in the observance of public prudery and respectability.

Outward propriety reflects both the Caribbean's conservative (and religious) mores and its sense of history. While elegant French tourists on St Martin go barefoot as an expression of tropical hedonism, for the Caribbean, bare feet are an image of poverty; going barefoot has connotations of struggle and slavery, not of carefree indulgence. Conversely, to be well-dressed is a mark of social status and economic well-being.

This contrast in economic and cultural values between host and guest is expressed at a public level in dress, exemplified by the padded shoulders and high heels of the bank clerk changing the travellers' cheques of tourists dressed in sarongs and sandals. In an attempt to assert its own values and to 'protect' its people from tourist values, most Caribbean countries issue a 'dress code'; this implores visitors to observe local customs while reassuring them that locals are not out to spoil their fun.

The St Kitts tourist magazine, for example, has a section entitled 'Proper Attire' which advises: 'By all means go native while you are here, but please understand that to us "native" means no short shorts, bikinis or bare chests in public places. In the pursuit of fashion, please remember to dress conservatively. Beach attire is just that and is not considered appropriate for around town, in shops and stores, or in restaurants.' Barbados takes a more jokey approach with drawings of a woman tourist in a bikini pushing a supermarket trolley, with a caption: 'When you're in town or just shopping around don't be confused. You may be a peach but leave swimwear for the beach.' Beneath a drawing of a fat male tourist in a shop, is the caption, 'We know your business and we know that you're cool but please leave exposed tummies for around the pool.'

The 'rules' also extend to the beach where nudity is unacceptable (there are exceptions in Guadeloupe, Les Saintes and Martinique, St Martin and in Negril, Jamaica) and topless bathing is frowned upon. In Cuba, however, whether Cubans like it or not, beach nudity has become the norm with larky holiday competitions involving 'waggling willies' and wet T-shirts. In more restrained Barbados, meanwhile, wardens and police enforce the dress code on the beach by clapping their hands loudly in disapproval whenever they see a naked breast.

Sex Tourism

Distaste for beach nudity may, in part, be an expression of religious propriety, but it also underpins the region's attempt to discourage what is seen as unwelcome foreign sexual mores. A report by the Caribbean Tourism Research and Development Centre in 1980 concluded that: 'There is a general feeling that tourism corrupts the moral values of the youth and that a lot of tourists have sexual relations with the local population. Respondents are also of the opinion that tourist sexual values are loose compared to those of local people.'[10]

While it is certainly true that older Caribbean people hold more 'old-fashioned' views than most Western tourists about public codes of

behaviour, it would be fanciful to think that Caribbean sexual convention, let alone the behaviour of the majority of Caribbean men, owes
much to traditional 'family values'.

Tourists whose expectations of the Caribbean are of one long
bacchanal are rewarded by the behaviour of dollar-seeking locals, who
cannot afford to be bothered too much by stereotyping. This goes as
much for the bored singers who mouth 'No Woman No Cry' at
American cruise tourists eating pizzas on St Maarten's casino-packed
beach front to the 'professional' hustlers of Montego Bay cruising the
beaches for single white women. The tourist industry supplies whatever
is required and by whom: by the women who have fun learning to
'wine' in hotel dance lessons ('learn to reggae with Errol') or by the
groups of middle-aged men who paw proprietorally their teenage
'acquisitions' in the bars and hotel foyers of the Dominican Republic.

While much sex tourism in the Caribbean, especially that between
local men and women tourists, exists within an informal framework,
more formal prostitution has become a matter for concern, especially in
the Dominican Republic and Cuba. There is also evidence of traffic in
prostitutes, notably from the Dominican Republic, to other islands and
to Europe, and some participation of organized crime in prostitution
networks. The situation is such that in 1994 the Caribbean Conference
of Churches (CCC) set up a regional arm of the Ecumenical Coalition
for Third World Tourism. General Secretary of the CCC, Edward
Cumberbatch, says that he is determined that the Caribbean should not
go the way of Asia, in particular in the proliferation of child prostitution
and crime.

At a deeper level, local dislike of sexual relations between locals and
tourists has less to do with sexual puritanism (although gay and lesbian
tourists do not get much encouragement) than with the realisation that
poor locals, whether men or women, are being racially and economically
exploited by tourists. Their availability is made more seductive by
received images, laced with racism: the 'exotic', easy 'native' woman
with a hibiscus behind her ear; or the beachboy whose sexual prowess
has been defined by white culture. It is also resented that the only
encounters that most tourists have with local people are either as waiters
or beachboys. There are no representations of 'ordinary' people in the
tourists' experience. As one Barbadian advertising executive says:
'Tourists only meet beach boys, therefore the idea of a Barbadian man is
restricted to that image.'

Such perceptions are encased in a familiar cultural currency. In a short
story published in the Barbadian magazine *Bim* in 1969, a character says:
'I was a Barbadian, a man of the tropics, wild, untamed, supple, POTENT

– what every northern woman wishes for. It was a generally accepted idea among us men on the island that the only thing that women from Canada, England and the States came down to the West Indies for was to sleep with the Natives.'[11]

In the English-speaking Caribbean, unofficial anecdote dates it all from the planeloads of French-Canadian women who visited the Caribbean on charters in the early 1960s. Nowadays, the beach boys are jokingly called 'The Foreign Service' and the practice of male prostitution is known as 'Rent a Rasta'. Public opinion still maintains that French-Canadian women remain the most available for sex, although the British and Germans are also on the beachboys' agenda (with Americans, according to one study, being the least approachable).

Like many other aspects of the tourist industry, the beachboy phenomenon is based upon the dependency of the host. Young men, usually poorly educated and unemployed, offer their sexual services in return for money or temporary support to affluent, often middle-class, white women tourists, whose age and marital status are pretty well irrelevant. While it might not be called prostitution, the contract has a barely disguised financial basis, with the tourists providing meals, drinks, transport, money and clothes in exchange for sex.

The beach is usually the territory for the initial encounter. The men hang out at the scruffier ends of the tourist strips; if they have something to sell so much the better. In Barbados the beach bums sell aloe, good for sunburn, which they use as a way to introduce themselves. 'I work this beach,' boasts one Bajan hustler, proud of his ability to get anything any tourist wants to buy. 'I can make a lot of money doing this. Lots of the tourists buy sex – they have to give the boys for their time. I can get anything you want – drugs, except heroin; even boys, for US$500.' If they have nothing to sell except themselves, they adopt approaches such as a request for a cigarette or a pick-up line such as 'you lookin' lonely'.

A satirical book called *The How to Be Jamaican Handbook* describes the 'North Coast Hustler' and his way of life. 'He is easily recognizable. Almost inevitably, he wears locks, has a trim figure (quite often with a few knife scars), carries an ornately carved stick and is a walking collection of gifts from happy clients: chains, rings, Gap and Banana Republic jeans and T-shirts, and Nike, Adidas or Reebok sneakers, as well as Sony Walkman or ghetto blaster ....' The description continues:

> *The hustler, enigmatic behind mirrored glasses, sits and 'grooves' waiting for two teachers from Iowa eager to see the 'real Jamaica' to pass by where-upon our hero will grin and say 'Greetings to the daughters'. Such an ethnic introduction works wonders and the women are soon asking the locks-*

*man about Bob Marley who was, of course, his 'personal idren' [brother]
.... He casually tosses his locks and the goosepimples begin for the
Iowans. Soon they are off, listening to learned discourses on Rastafari, an
invitation to a fish and bammy feed. They drink it all in, enthralled.
Excitement .... Can the Big Bamboo be far behind?*[12]

This account is a recognizable parody of reality. It illustrates the
calculated nature of the hustler's role, it understands that the tourists do
not recognize this (at first they are just responding to 'native friendliness')
and ultimately it evokes the *frisson* associated with a holiday romance and
a dreadlocked boyfriend.

What the account does not point out is that these encounters reverse
more conventional gender roles and also confuse race and class roles.
Within Caribbean societies, a lower-class male would never be invited
by a middle-class woman for a drink in a hotel, but women tourists do
not observe (or care about) such prescriptions. From the beachboy's
point of view, as one study in Barbados put it: 'The mere presence of the
beachboy on tourist premises thus represents a personal triumph in
having overstepped such racial boundaries.'[13]

From the woman's point of view, a black boyfriend, however
temporary, offers more than a 'holiday romance'. It gives her power over
a man in a way she does not have in New York or Manchester. Her
economic power means that she can choose to treat him sympathetically
or contemptuously. As one Antiguan tour representative puts it: 'She
takes him home from the disco by taxi but she'll only give him the
money for the bus the next morning.'

For the beachboy, however, each 'client' represents more than a
means of survival and a triumph over the racial/class system of his island.
It also represents temporary access to the First World. In one of the more
closely observed accounts of sexual tourism in the Caribbean, Neil Price
describes the patterns of this transaction in Bequia, where relationships
with white women offer the possibility of escape from the restrictions
and frustrations of island life. As one young man, who had been in serial
relationships with young Italian women visitors, says: 'If a girl done love
you, she gonna do everything she can for get you to be near her. For
dese Italian girls wid rich family, it possible dat dey gonna get enough
money for give I a ticket to Europe .... Man I just waiting ....'[14] The fact
that the ticket to Milan was a daydream did not deter the young men of
Bequia.

The impact of their behaviour on their own community, however,
was disruptive. Firstly, relationships between women tourists and locals
were resented by local women and provoked tensions between partners.

Secondly, Price noted that disputes broke out between the youths over women, while relationships between young men and the older genera-tion became tense. One man who had been seen sleeping on the beach with a tourist had caused his father embarrassment: 'De way he done carry on is just worthless. He ain't got not respeck, and he making so I done lose my own respect in de village ....'

In the Spanish-speaking countries of the Caribbean it is often young women who serve the tourists, although male prostitution also flourishes. This is particularly true in the Dominican Republic, with its reputation for 'dusky beauties'. The Dominican Republic has now joined Thailand and the Philippines on the list of countries known for their exploitative sex industries. There, young women from impoverished homes provide 'fun' for ageing Europeans while stylish boys ply the beach for sex with either men or women. Most worrying for those campaigning against sex tourism are the growing numbers of children in the Dominican Republic who are involved.

Mark Connolly, an international consultant on children's rights, went to Sosúa and Boca Chica, two beach resorts in the Dominican Republic, to investigate the sexual exploitation of children. He had been told that in the northern resort of Sosúa, where the T-shirts are printed with 'Jump 'em, Pump 'em and Dump 'em', 'most of the households probably have at least one kid who has sold his/her body for dollars'.[15]

By talking to both Dominican adolescents and European tourists in Sosúa and Boca Chica, Connolly concluded that the sexual exploitation of both girls and boys was condoned 'and most likely promoted' by the government, tourist services, travel agencies and hotels. For example, in Boca Chica, most hotels and other rented accommodation allow guests to take visitors into their rooms. One real estate company, which rented out condominiums mainly to single European men where 'almost every-one had young kids' in their rooms, said that children could also be 'delivered' to the condo as part of the rental deal.

In Cuba, too, there is sex tourism. Before the Revolution, Cuba was known as the 'brothel of the Caribbean'; after 1959 both tourism and prostitution virtually disappeared. Now, with more tourists and more hardship, sex tourism is back. A 14-year-old boy writing in the Spanish newspaper *El País* said that it seemed that most of the tourists in Cuba went there for sex. He ended his letter, 'I believe that one of the principles of the revolution was to eliminate prostitution.'[16] However, according to Cuban's weekly youth magazine *Juventud Rebelde*, prosti-tution is a reflection not of economic desperation, but of moral laxness. An article entitled 'Flowers of Fifth Avenue', a reference to the young women who hang around a street in Havana's Miramar district, endorsed the official line. 'More than 60 per cent of them are working or studying and none of them are prostituting themselves to eat daily or have a roof over their heads.'

At Cuba's 15th annual tourism convention, held in the beach resort of Varadero in 1994, Tourism Minister Osmany Cienfuegos did not ignore the prostitution problem. He blamed foreign tour operators for projecting a distorted image of Cuba for their own propaganda: 'Our women are not a commodity,' he said. President Castro also warned: 'We don't want the image of a country of gambling, drugs and prostitution: we want the image of a country with a high cultural level, a healthy country both morally and physically, an organised country that looks after the environment.'[17]

Yet in every hotel lobby in Varadero and Havana, there are young women holding stilted conversations with middle-aged European men, while, wherever there are tourists, teenage 'escorts', known as *jineteras*, in lurex and hotpants, hang around discos to be picked up for a meal or a dollar or two. 'The only thing that's a bargain here is the sex,' says an octogenarian German. That was the case in Haiti, too, before Aids became the ultimate deterrent to the sex industry. The dramatic decrease of US visitors to Haiti in the winter of 1981–82 from 70,000 to 10,000 was seen as the direct result of the US medical establishment's pronouncement that Haitians were one of the four Aids high-risk categories. When lurid press reports in the US press suggested that Aids originated in Haiti, Haiti's considerable sexual attractions dissolved overnight.

Aids has joined sexual impropriety, materialism and envy, changing values and tensions within the community to build an undesirable picture of the social impact of tourism. Jamaica, for example, recorded its highest incidence of Aids in the western parish of St James, the area encompassing the tourist belt of Negril. There, 112 out of every 100,000 persons were HIV positive, according to the Ministry of Health in 1994, which had introduced a health programme among prostitutes. As the Cuban historian Juan Antonio Blanco told *Time* magazine in 1993, 'Tourism is a sort of chemotherapy. You have cancer and it's the only possible cure, but it might kill you before the cancer does.'[18]

The Drugs Connection

For many Caribbean islands, drugs just as much as sex tourism have threatened local communities. Among the thousands of T-shirts on sale in every cruise port is one of a puny camera-laden male tourist and a Rastaman holding a large spliff; beneath the picture is printed 'different island, same shit'. Tourists attract drug-sellers (most will be offered drugs, mostly ganja, but everything is available) although the exact links between drugs and tourism are more complex and difficult to disentangle.

The most obvious connection between tourists and drugs consists of locals supplying tourists with their holiday highs. It is a largely peripheral and small-scale business. However, at a more general level the Caribbean's tourist trade provides an infrastructure in which the drug trade can flourish. The daily network of planes and cruise ships makes trafficking easy with large numbers of tourists, crews and officials constantly on the move. Hotels and good telecommunications make life convenient for the traffickers and their agents in their own secretive sub-cultures.

Since Havana's heyday in the 1950s, those behind the drug trade and other illegal activities have seen the Caribbean as a useful transit point and as a launch-pad to the USA. The routes for the huge drug traffic from Latin America, in particular cocaine from Colombia, have been through the small, scattered, ill-policed and underpatrolled islands of the Antilles. The deserted islets, coves and cays of the Grenadines, the Bahamian Out Islands, the Virgin Islands and many other spots are ideal for drug drops, by sea or air. The Florida coast (40 miles away at its nearest point from the Bahamas) can be reached 'before a milk shake melts' in a fast motorboat, so streamlined that it is called a 'cigarette' boat.

The US Department of State Bureau of International Narcotics Matters (INM) publishes an annual country-by-country summary of the Caribbean's drug activity. Its assessment often mentions the way that tourism facilitates drug trafficking. In the Eastern Caribbean, for example, its 1994 report revealed that:

> sophisticated and organised drug rings from South America are making use of the traditional advantages the area has to offer: geographic location, easy navigation, inadequately patrolled coastlines and waters, an ample network of airline and cruise ship connections, a large and mobile volume of tourists, as well as the inherent difficulties of policing a group of island mini-states.[19]

Barbados was one of the Eastern Caribbean's islands to receive a critical report. 'Transshipments of cocaine increased in 1993; available evidence suggests that crews and passengers of cruise ships bring both marijuana and cocaine into the country and assist in transshipping cocaine to the US Virgin Islands and Puerto Rico, from which it reaches the US mainland by commercial airliners.' The situation in St Lucia had also worsened, according to the report, as tourist numbers increased, with cocaine smuggled in by 'yachts, fishing boats and cruise ship and plane passengers'.

Nowhere in the Eastern Caribbean escaped censure although Dominica, the US State Department said, had a lower incidence of drug activity. Its 1995 report made particular reference to Antigua, St Vincent and the Grenadines, and St Kitts, where allegations continue to be made that senior officials 'are knowledgeable of or allow drug activities to continue, regardless of official policy'.[20] In St Vincent, the presence of Italian investors in two tourism projects, which are both being handled by the Prime Minister's Office rather than by the Ministry of Tourism, has given rise to many rumours.

Behind the movement of drugs are the drug cartels. Tourism coexists with organized crime in a kind of symbiotic relationship, and the US State Department reports also emphasize this link between tourism, money-laundering and offshore banking. In 1994, for example, it was reported: 'Money laundering fostered by the off-shore banking and casino and resort industries on Aruba, Curaçao and St Maarten flourishes on these islands. Aruba and Curaçao have also witnessed an increase in such drug-related crime as shootings, robberies and murders between rival drug gangs vying for territory.'[21] What is good for casinos is good for organized crime.

By the 1990s, it was thought that other countries which had formerly been riddled by money-laundering corruption had to a large extent cleaned up their act. But not before enormous sums of money had been laundered and island states corrupted. In 1989, *The Economist* reported that some US$20 to US$30 billion in drugs money had been laundered through the Cayman Islands in that year alone. In another British dependency, the Turks and Caicos Islands (again a tourism and financial centre), Norman Saunders, the chief minister (1980–85), and two government members were arrested in Miami by undercover FBI agents. Accused of bribery and drug-smuggling offences, Saunders resigned. He was convicted and served eight years in prison, but was back in politics in 1995, winning a seat in that year's general election.

British lawyer Barry Rider, Dean of Jesus College, Cambridge, and a former head of the Commonwealth Secretariat's commercial crime unit, says the institutions of some Caribbean countries have been so effectively penetrated by the vast amounts of money generated by organized crime that they could be described as criminal states. Aruba, for instance, fits this description, with drug cartels moving there in the 1990s attracted by its rapidly developing tourist industry. In February 1993, slot-machines shipped from the US Virgin Islands to Aruba were found to contain millions of dollars in secret compartments. 'There is concern that drug money is "integrated" into the Aruban economy through real estate purchases,' the INM observed in 1994.[22]

Organized crime is efficient, says Dr Rider. 'It tends to be conservative and protects those it has corrupted.' It operates best where it can work unhindered, undetected and in conditions of political stability. This, he concludes, is one reason why Jamaica has not been infiltrated by organized crime (it has its own 'Yardies' in any case): its politics are too volatile. Organized crime does not like, and will not allow, petty crime or political violence to get in the way of its activities.

In some cases, a busy tourist industry can offer a suitable cover for criminal activities; it can also provide opportunities for investment. When the drug cartels looked for avenues to invest their billions, they found plenty of opportunities in the tourist industry where they could use their laundered money in legitimate operations.

Perhaps one of the most telling examples of how tourism can provide an ideal cover for corruption is the Bahamas, close to Miami and Atlantic City, where casinos and real estate development flourish. This happened both before independence, when the so-called Bay Street Boys, the white merchant élite, ruled, and also afterwards during the premiership of the multimillionaire Sir Lynden Pindling.

When in 1967 Pindling (who later was himself the subject of a corruption investigation) set up a commission of inquiry into the running of the casinos and to investigate whether any politician had received any financial reward from their operation, the main accusation concerned Sir Stafford Sands. The report stated:

> *The fee of £200,000 which Sir Stafford Sands was paid so promptly for his work in obtaining the Certificate of Exemption for the Amusements Company, was, even by Bahamian standards, out of all proportion to the legal services which he rendered .... The enormity of the fee demanded and the speed and manner with which payment was effected .... leave us in no doubt that he was selling his services primarily as an influential Member of the Executive Council and not as a lawyer.*[23]

One of the central contentions of the commission was the recurring and numerous conflicts of interest in which consultancies were granted in exchange for an exemption certificate to operate a casino. Indeed, running through many deals made for all sorts of tourist activities in the Bahamas, and indeed in other countries, is a common factor: local politicians and foreign developers fostering close relationships. In many cases, says Barry Rider, politicians have been badly advised, weak and easily 'captured, unaware that they were being corrupted'.

By the 1980s, Lynden Pindling himself was under investigation. The charges, relating to allegations made in the *Wall Street Journal*, were that Pindling and other top officials had been paid by Robert Vesco, the fugitive financier, and Colombian cocaine boss Carlos Lehder to allow drug smuggling into the USA through the Bahamas. A royal commission confirmed the claims but could not prove the charges against Pindling, who survived the scandal. Two Cabinet ministers, however, resigned. One was Kendal Nottage, Minister for Youth, Sports and Community Affairs who became a front for Salvatore Caruana, a member of the American mafia. Caruana 'loaned' Nottage US$400,000 to buy the Islander Hotel in Freeport; the loan was only to be paid back if the hotel was sold. Meanwhile, Nottage and his wife set up front companies for Caruana.[24]

Such activities were typical of the evidence that emerged from the commission's 500-page report which records a hugely complex catalogue of shady business deals, in which millions of unaccountable dollars changed hands. What is relevant here is that most of the deals involved real estate or airlines, hotels or villas, casinos or catering firms, each one an intrinsic part of the tourist industry. In 1994, three state-run corporations, hotel, airline and telecommunications, were subject to another commission of inquiry probing the workings of the corporations during the Pindling regime. Further sleazy evidence of unaccounted-for financial transactions on a grand scale also characterized the hearings of this inquiry.

The international network of organized crime is such that it was not surprising that Sol Korzner of Sun City resort, southern Africa, allegedly involved in money-laundering activities, moved into the Bahamas in 1994. In a legitimate operation he bought Paradise Island Resort in Nassau (see Chapter 1).

Casino Economies

Gambling, as well as drugs and sex, is part of the package of alien and undesirable imports which is seen to undermine the moral well-being of the Caribbean people. While this view is largely church-based, a broader coalition has expressed unease about the economic and social consequences of casinos (gambling on horses and the lottery is considered a separate issue and more acceptable).

A regional conference on the socio-cultural and environmental impact of tourism on Caribbean societies held in Grenada in 1979, during the days of the PRG, drew its own conclusions about gambling. It recorded that gambling was not 'productive', that professional gamblers spent money only in the casino and that there was a 'high correlation between gambling and organised crime'. The 'gut feeling' of the conference was that 'gambling is not considered necessary or desirable' nor a useful extra 'attraction' for the tourist industry. It recommended that 'great caution' should be exercised by governments in deciding their policy on gambling.[25]

Yet by 1993, there were casinos in 13 Caribbean territories, including the Dutch Antilles, Antigua, the Bahamas, Haiti, Guadeloupe, Martinique and the Dominican Republic. The Bahamas, Aruba and St Maarten, in particular, have built their tourist industries largely on the back of their casinos.

The pressure to introduce casinos into other territories has grown. The classic approach is for a developer to agree to build a hotel only if a casino licence is included in the deal. The St Lucia government, for example, turned down a casino-hotel complex on Pigeon Point causeway only after churches and other island organizations campaigned against it in the early 1990s. Guyana, whose tourist industry barely exists, was approached almost immediately after a tourism ministry opened in Georgetown in 1993 by Arubans and Jamaicans wanting to open a casino. That offer, too, was turned down.

In Barbados, attempts to introduce casinos have been rebuffed for many years. 'We don't have casinos in Barbados,' said the Permanent Secretary in the Ministry of Tourism in February 1994, 'but tomorrow is another day.' Indeed, less than one year later, the new Barbados Labour Party government of Prime Minister Owen Arthur announced a commission of inquiry into casino gambling but later accepted its recommendations against the introduction of casinos.

At an economic level, casinos provide employment and government income. Whether they boost tourist arrivals is another question, although by the 1990s the casino culture appeared to be expanding all over the world. A survey by the US travel industry found that 22 per cent of potential US travellers planned casino vacations in 1995, up from 14 per cent in 1994.[26] Cruise ships, too, have casinos, an important attraction, and extra competition for hard-pushed land destinations (see Chapter 7).

By 1995 there was evidence that opposition to casinos was fading. In St Croix, US Virgin Islands, a non-binding vote in November 1994 produced 58 per cent in favour of casino gambling on a turnout of less than half the electorate. This reversed an anti-gambling referendum vote held two years earlier. Since then unemployment had risen, real estate prices had dropped and opinion was swinging in favour of casinos. The president of the Chamber of Commerce, for example, had campaigned in favour, and developers, waiting in the wings, indicated that at least three large hotels with casinos would be built once legislation was in place.

There have been similar developments in Jamaica. Hotels have installed games rooms with computer-simulated versions of casino games, while yet-to-be-built resorts are planned with casinos. Even Cuba, as it expanded its mass tourist base, relaxed its anti-gambling laws when in 1994 a cruise ship, the *Santiago de Cuba*, operated the first casino in Cuba since 1959. The ship, jointly owned by Italian investors Havana Cruises and the government enterprise Havanatur, began its day trips with gaming tables and one-armed bandits open once outside territorial waters. There, Cubans with dollars gambled alongside foreigners. Once the gambling headquarters of the Caribbean, Cuba was being lured back into the world of blackjack by tourist demand and joint-venture enticements.

Street Crime

Tourism also creates conditions which attract crime in the street as well as in boardrooms, in particular when First-World wealth meets Third-World poverty. Crime directed against tourists, largely robbery and mugging, is a feature, often drug-related, of tourism in the Caribbean. (Tourists also commit crimes – again, much is drug-related.)

A survey of residents in three Jamaican resort towns revealed that sex and crime were seen to be two of the negative effects of tourism. Pimps, hustlers and prostitutes were mentioned by 17 per cent of those in Negril, by 14 per cent of Montego Bay respondents and by 13 per cent in Ocho Rios. Drugs were even more of a tourist-related problem cited by 25 per cent of respondents in Montego Bay, 22 per cent in Negril and 11 per cent in Ocho Rios.[27]

It is the fear of being a victim of crime that bothers tourists. Drug dealing, political repression and institutionalized corruption have less impact on arrivals than the one-off shooting of a tourist or serial muggings. In fact, the overall level of crime against tourists in the Caribbean has remained small. According to the Consumers' Association magazine *Holiday Which?*, the Caribbean did not feature in the top ten of 'thieving' destinations. The region, however, came fifth below Gambia, Morocco, Malaysia and Latin America as a destination where tourists had felt threatened or shaken (but not hurt).[28] More official perhaps is the consular travel advice issued by the UK's Foreign and Commonwealth Office in London. This is issued for tourist destinations as a guide to tourists and as an insurance for the Foreign Office. The threat of a travel advisory hangs heavy over Caribbean tourist boards. At the beginning of 1995, Trinidad and Tobago joined Jamaica and Barbados as the only Caribbean countries handed the travel industry's yellow card.

In 1993, a travel advisory for Barbados was issued as 'a precautionary measure', according to the British High Commission in Bridgetown:

> *Like many holiday resorts elsewhere, Barbados has experienced an*
> *increase in crime such as muggings, and visitors are advised to take sens-*
> *ible precautions at all times, e.g. not to carry jewellery when visiting*
> *secluded areas. They should seek and take local advice about which areas*
> *might at any given time be considered more dangerous than others, in par-*
> *ticular in relation to travel in open vehicles to the more remote areas. They*
> *should pay attention to security at night in all parts of the island.*

The advisory does not, in fact, suggest any alarming local conditions, and its advice could, one would think, apply to just about anywhere.

Tourism attracts crime, while at the same time crime repels tourists. High crime levels within communities and, in particular, against tourists strike horror in the hearts of tourism officials, especially when the reports are given high-profile coverage in the international press. Throughout the region, increasing crime rates are discussed at conferences and work-shops, with demands for government to take a stand against criminals and with calls for the execution of convicted murderers. The tourist industry knows that flurries of cancellations, especially from the ultra-sensitive US market, come swiftly in the wake of gruesome crime reports.

The few available figures of crime against tourists appear very selective and give little impression of the true situation. In Jamaica, for example, in 1992 around 1,500 tourists (0.02 per cent of the island's 1.5 million visitors) reported crimes against them; Bonaire reported 755 thefts (of which 9 per cent were against tourists); while Guyana said there had been 32 incidents, mainly larceny, against its small number of visitors, who are, in any case, mainly business people.

In the 1980s, while the Bahamas was at its most drug-dominated, Inter-pol rated it as the tenth most crime-ridden country in the world, the second for rape and the sixth for murder. With large proportions of young men unemployed and drug-addicted, a 1984 government-sponsored report stated that a 'severe drug problem exists in government corporations, hospitals, major hotels, a number of banks, restaurants, industrial corporations at Grand Bahama, government ministries, fast food businesses and night clubs'.[29] Yet in the Out Islands of the Bahamas far away from Nassau and Freeport, there is so little crime that in some hotels tourists cannot lock the door to their room because they are not given a key.

Jamaica in particular, with more than 600 murders a year, continues to suffer from high rates of drug-related organized crime, political violence and gang shoot-outs by hardmen from the yards of Kingston. From time to time such activity spills over into the tourist areas, especially the resorts of Ocho Rios, Montego Bay and Negril. In 1992, a German tourist and a Dutch tourist were shot dead in separate incidents on the north coast. Then, in February 1994, two middle-aged Americans were robbed and shot while rafting on the peaceful Rio Grande river. This incident was particularly damaging to the Jamaican tourist industry, for rafting down the Rio Grande is one of the island's most popular and imaginative tourist attractions.

The response from the local tourist leaders was characteristic. Hotelier Butch Stewart of Sandals said that crime, if left unchecked, would destroy the tourist industry, and the Jamaican Hotel and Tourist Association demanded 'swift and decisive punishment' for those convicted of such 'heinous acts'.[30] In a flurry of activity, the government announced that armed military patrols would guard the resorts. Some hoteliers did not welcome these moves, arguing that soldiers and guns sent out 'the wrong message' to holiday-makers, while others said that crime had dropped and that the gun-toting officers had not worried the tourists. (Mr Stewart's own long-term solution to the problem has been to make his hotels all-inclusive resorts so that his guests have no need to move beyond the well-patrolled perimeter fences of his properties.)

By 1994, public opinion against the crime rate in Jamaica was giving rise to even greater agitation. Agreeing that Jamaica's reputation had been tarnished by its high murder rate, Tourism Minister Carlyle Dunkley announced another initiative to tackle security: this time a joint police and military task force set to work to round up drug dealers and illegal vendors.

Such attempts to contain violence against tourists lie at the more extreme end of the crime and tourism spectrum. Most Caribbean islands do not experience anything like the violence of Jamaica although many other islands are experiencing higher crime rates than ever before. In June 1994, the St Lucia Tourist Board held a meeting in the wake of increased crime levels against tourists. 'I perceive a real threat overhanging the industry in St Lucia right now,' said chairman Stephen McNamara. 'It is important the country as a whole appreciates the danger we face and the danger presented to the tourist industry by what is going on.'[31]

In Grenada, the Tourist Board called for stiffer penalties for crimes against tourists when one cruise line threatened to stop calling at St George's because of passenger harassment by vendors. One official said melodramatically: 'Tourism is Grenada's lifeblood and anyone found tampering with it must be treated harshly ... it should be treated like treason.'[32]

Despite growing alarm about crime, the first regional conference on crime and tourism in the Caribbean was not held until 1993. The conference concentrated on the practical difficulties involved in protecting tourists given the limited resources of police and judicial systems. The problems ranged from inadequate policing and police training to poor hotel security. Another difficulty is that even when a crime against a tourist is reported to the police, it rarely comes to court because of a backlog of cases. Grenada, for example, has introduced night sittings of magistrates' courts to try and deal with this and has also changed the law to give beach security officials powers of arrest.

One of the most pressing concerns at a sub-criminal level involves what is commonly called 'harassment'. A survey of 500 tourists departing from Barbados in 1994, for instance, found that 53 per cent reported harassment. Of these, 49 per cent were harassed on the beach, 42 per cent in the streets and 8 per cent in their hotels. The most common form of harassment was by vendors (71 per cent), followed by drug-sellers (29 per cent); verbal abuse was mentioned by 14 per cent and sexual harassment by 7 per cent. While vendors can be more easily brought under official control (see Chapter 3), harassment by, for example, beachboys is trickier to deal with. In 1994, the Caribbean Tourism Organization commissioned a study to determine whether legislation was required so that harassment could be legally codified. It also recognized that in taking that approach it created the potential for 'developing laws for the protection of tourism'.[33]

What tourist boards and hoteliers appear to ignore in their demands for greater punishment and tightened-up security is the connection between socio-economic change and crime. Yet the contrast between the conspicuous consumption of hotel life, economic stress and poverty beyond the security gate presents fundamental questions about the impact of the tourist business. As Jean Holder put it:

> As Caribbean countries become more dependent on tourism, as other economic sectors fail (putting more and more people out of work), as wealth and poverty are brought into greater proximity, the levels of crime due to need or greed, and harassment of visitors by hard-selling vendors, can be expected to increase.[34]

An even more forthright view was provided by Orville Durant, Commissioner of the Royal Barbados Police Force. At a crime and tourism conference, Durant pointed out that the Caribbean was a 'post-colonial society' in which no recognition had been given to the problems and needs of such a society. The emphasis of the tourist industry was, he said, 'only in terms of increasing the numbers of visitors without any regard to the negative impact of that increase on the society, particularly where legitimate alternatives are limited and balanced economic development is non-existent'.[35]

The calypso 'Alien', with its chorus of frustration and loss:

> *What's the point of progress*
> *Is it really success*
> *If we gain ten billion*
> *But lose the land we live on?*

is a succinct enough popular interpretation of Durant's analysis and Holder's warning to suggest that the social impact of tourism needs to be handled with particular care.

Notes

1. *Outlet*, Antigua and Barbuda, 14 October 1994.

2. Frank Fonda Taylor, *To Hell with Paradise: A History of the Jamaican Tourist Industry*, Pittsburgh, 1993, p. 171.

3. *The Independent*, London, 5 August 1991.

4. Martin Amis, 'St Lucia' in *Visiting Mrs Nabokov and Other Excursions*, London, 1994, p. 72.

5. Jean-Luc Bonniol, 'Perceptions of the Environment in a Small Island Community: Terre de Haut des Saintes', in Yves Renard (ed.), *Perceptions of the Environment*, Caribbean Conservation Association, Barbados, 1979, p. 66.

6. Fonda Taylor, *op. cit.*, p. 153.

7. See Robert Potter, 'Urbanisation in the Caribbean and Trends of Global Convergence-Divergence', *Geographical Journal*, vol. 159, 1993, pp.1–21.

8. *Outlet*, 11 March 1994.

9. Gerardo Mosquera, 'Hustling the Tourist in Cuba', *Poliester*, London, vol. 3, no. 10, 1994. *Jinetear*, literally meaning riding or jockeying, is the slang term used in Cuba for providing services, particularly sexual, to tourists.

10. Cited in Peggy Antrobus, 'Gender Issues in Caribbean Tourism'. Paper given at conference on Tourism and Socio-Cultural Change in the Caribbean, Trinidad, 1990.

11. Paul Layne, 'Sunny Barbados', *Bim*, vol. 13, Barbados, 1969, p. 48.

12. *The How to be Jamaican Handbook*, Kingston, 1992, p. 40.

13. Cecilia Karch and Graham Dann, 'Close Encounters of the Third World', *Human Relations*, vol. 34, no 4, 1981.

14. Neil Price, *Behind the Planter's Back: Lower-Class Responses to Marginality in Bequia Island, St Vincent*, London, 1988, p. 231.

15. Mark Connolly, 'Sex Tourism and Children in the Dominican Republic', paper for Defense of Children International, New York, 1992.

16. *El País*, Madrid, 8 November 1993.

17. *Cuba Business*, London, June 1994.

18. *Time*, New York, 6 December 1993.

19. Bureau of International Narcotics Matters, *International Narcotics Control Report*, Washington DC, 1994.

20. Bureau of International Narcotics Matters, *International Narcotics Control Report*, Washington DC, 1995.

21. Bureau of International Narcotics Matters, 1994, *op. cit.*

22. *Ibid.*

23. Philip Cash, Shirley Gordon and Gail Saunders, *Sources of Bahamian History*, London, 1991, p. 300.

24. *Sunday Times Magazine*, London, 29 September 1985.

25. Regional Conference on the Socio-Cultural and Environmental Impact of Tourism on Caribbean Societies, 'Recommendations', Grenada, 1979.

26. *Caribbean Week*, Barbados, 7–20 January 1995.

27. Carl Stone, 'A Socio-Economic Study of the Tourism Industry in Jamaica', *Caribbean Affairs*, vol. 4, no. 1, 1991, p. 8.

28. *Holiday Which?*, London, 7 May 1991.

29. *Sunday Times Magazine*, *op. cit.*

30. *Barbados Advocate*, Barbados, 15 February 1994.

31. Caribbean News Agency (CANA), Barbados, 23 June 1994.

32. CANA, 18 April 1994.

33. CANA, 14 September 1994.

34. Jean Holder, 'The Caribbean Tourism Organization's Role in Caribbean Tourism Development' in Dennis Gayle and Jonathan Goodrich (eds), *Tourism, Marketing and Management in the Caribbean*, London, 1993, p. 215.

35. Orville Durant, paper delivered at conference on Crime and Tourism in the Caribbean, St Lucia, 1993.

CHAPTER 5

Green Crime, Green Redemption:

The Environment and Ecotourism

When Christopher Columbus went ashore on Crooked Island, Bahamas, in October 1492 he wrote:

> Here and in all the island everything is green and the vegetation is like April in Andalusia. And the singing of the birds is such that it would seem that a man would never wish to leave here. And the flocks of parrots that darken the sun, and birds of so many kinds so different from our own that it is a marvel! And then there are trees of a thousand kinds all producing their own kind of fruit, and all wonderfully aromatic ...[1]

Four hundred years later, a Victorian traveller, E.A. Hastings Jay, described his first sight of a tropical beach at Hastings, Barbados: 'There were the cocoa-nut palms, with clusters of green cocoa-nuts, growing all along the sea-line out of the soft, white sand, with beautiful rainbow colours in the water as it moved lazily backwards and forwards, glittering in the brilliant sunlight.'[2]

And so it remained. Accounts by visiting Europeans, whatever their purpose in the region, continued to marvel at the Caribbean's pristine physical beauty in diaries, letters, travelogues and novels, straining for the words to describe that beguiling landscape. In the 1940s, the US war correspondent Martha Gellhorn passed through the British Virgin Islands, and came across a cove which was 'a place where nothing had changed since time began, a half circle of white sand, flanked by huge squarish smooth rocks, the rocks overlapping to form cool caves and the water turquoise blue above the furrows of the sandy sea bed'.[3] Returning many years later, she found her cove 'full of sun-tanned bodies and ringed by boats, from swan yachts to rubber Zodiacs, and there were bottles and plastic debris on the sea-bed and picnic litter on the sand for the rich are as disgusting as the poor in their carelessness of the natural world'.[4] The magic had become tainted. Yet it is that Caribbean canvas, brushed blue for the sea and sky, green for vegetation and yellow for sand, so conveniently splashed with hummingbirds and hibiscus, coconut palms and sunsets, that tourists have come to expect. Those well-edited images of the Caribbean environment are what tourists want; they go to the Caribbean for its climate, sea and beaches, not for its mountains and rivers, its cities or ruined battlements. Such demand has put its coastlines under enormous pressure.

The sort of tourism that now dominates the Caribbean, as Martha Gellhorn noted, has redefined its physical landscape. It has brought about the region's second invasion of land-snatchers; first it was the planters who changed the natural environment when they cleared the land for sugar-cane (islands now almost treeless, like Barbados and Antigua, were once shaggily forested). This time it has been the coastline which has been cleared. And it is the tourists who are feeding off the land and water.

The coastal clearances have usually been along white sand beaches, on ancient and ground-down coral, predominantly on the west and sheltered littoral away from the rougher Atlantic shores. Large concrete hotels have been built close to the high-water mark, groynes and piers erected, marinas for yachts and deep-water harbours for cruise ships constructed. The great wetlands of the Caribbean have been grubbed out by developers eying their proximity to some of the region's best beaches. In Jamaica, Montego Bay's international airport was built on a wetland, while at nearby Ocho Rios, 40 acres of swamp were turned into a resort with 4,000 beds and a cruise-ship pier.[5] In a generation, the land and seascape have been transformed: the bays where once local fishermen pulled in their seine nets, where villagers went for a sea-bathe or where colonies of birds nested in mangrove stands now provide for the very different needs of tourists. The impact has been dramatic.

These transformations have been superimposed on a fragile environ-ment particularly vulnerable to change. As the Caribbean Tourism Organization's Jean Holder warned in 1988: 'Our tourism product is our environment. We therefore destroy our environment at our economic peril.'[6] Yet serious damage has been done and continues to be done. According to Calvin Howell, director of the Caribbean Conservation Association, 'We are a very fragile area and the environment is tourism's resource. However, there are countless examples throughout the region to suggest that there is a tendency to overlook the well-being of the environment in order to maximise the tourist dollar.' Significantly, he adds, 'it is hard to find examples of good practice in the region'.

Paradise Lost
The catalogue of environmental destruction directly attributed to the growth of the tourist industry is long. It includes the erosion of beaches, the breakdown of coral reefs, marine and coastal pollution from

watersports, the dumping of waste and the non-treatment of sewage, sand-mining and the destruction of wetlands and salt ponds. In many cases, the impact is interrelated, locked into a chain of tourist development where short-term gain takes precedence over long-term protection. For example, a hotel cuts down coastal trees to improve the view from its bedrooms; this accelerates coastal erosion and sand loss; then, when a jetty is built for a new dive shop even more sand is lost because sand from the newly shaped beach is washed on to the coral reef. The result is two-fold: the sandy beach has become smaller and the marine environment has been spoiled. And what the tourist came to enjoy no longer exists in its pristine condition.

For the Caribbean's smaller islands and communities, the greater the numbers of tourists the greater the pressure on the physical environment and the greater the demands on limited resources. Yet as we have seen, the major thrust is always to increase visitor arrivals.

At some point the 'carrying capacity' threshold of a tourist spot is reached. This is the point, according to the World Tourism Organization, 'when negative factors start to operate'. It is a vague enough definition, but it is at that point that the tourists vote with their feet and go elsewhere.

'However tolerant local inhabitants will be, it is clear that the tourist who has a choice, will not put up with litter, beach erosion, water pollution, dead coral reefs and other fall out from environmental neglect,' Jean Holder told a London audience in 1993 in a paper on the compatability of conservation and economic growth. Invoking the Butler tourism-cycle model (see Chapter 1), he spoke of the last phase of the tourism model, the point of self-destruction: 'As the place sinks under the weight of social friction and solid waste, all tourists exit, leaving behind derelict tourism facilities, littered beaches and countryside, and a resident population that cannot return to its old way of life.'

Barbados, and in particular its south coast, has at times seemed to be closest to that mark. Even without tourists, Barbados is densely populated. In 1995 its population was just over a quarter of a million, the majority of whom live along the narrow coastal strips of the south and west coasts (roughly one-sixth of the island). These two coastlines are also the heartland of the tourist industry, adding almost 400,000 stayover visitors and the same number of cruise passengers per year to the resident population.

The result has been overwhelming pressure on the tourist zones, especially the south coast from Oistins in the south-east to Bridgetown. And despite a new sewage plant for the south coast and attempts to stem coastal erosion, tourists have moved away. Tourist arrivals started to show a decline first in the early 1980s and again from 1989 onwards. Yet the acting Minister of Tourism insisted in 1994 that 'there has been a negligible impact of environmental degradation. We have been committed from day one to quality tourism.'

It is not, however, just the cheaper end of the tourist market which poses a threat to the environment. In an attempt to attract the high-spending, up-market tourist, Barbados fell in love with real estate and golf, a game which not only claims agricultural land but uses 600,000 gallons of water per course per day. The Royal Westmoreland Golf and Country Club, a US$400 million residential and tourist resort, is the island's largest private investment. A 27-hole course is due for completion by 1996 despite the further strains on the environment.

While Barbados' 'mature' tourist industry has been forced to examine the reasons behind its environmental decline and address them with a regeneration project (albeit still on the drawing board), the region as a whole pays lip-service to the environment, allowing its degradation to continue largely unchecked and unmanaged just so long as tourist arrival figures look good. Yet as the West Indian Commission's *Time for Action* put it: 'We cannot assume automatic victory in our battle against environmental degradation of our tourist destinations in the region.'[7]

One of the worst offenders in its abuse of the environment is Antigua and Barbuda. This twin-island state, which is heavily dependent on tourism, promotes itself as 'the heart of the Caribbean'. As the official blurb has it: 'With 365 powdery white sand beaches (one for every day of the year), a wide variety of hotels and other accommodation, a fascinating history and warm, friendly people, the islands offer an exotic and unspoilt paradise in the Heart of the Caribbean.'[8]

One of the busiest stretches of coast is the sandy sweep of Dickenson Bay and nearby Runaway Bay. There, hotels, including the all-inclusive Sandals (opened in 1993), and restaurants edge the beach, facing seas used by scuba divers and snorkellers, windsurfers and waterskiers. Some locals, however, who are familiar with the recent history of the area have been reluctant to swim in its murky waters, complaining of itchy skin and, during some months of the year, peculiar smells.

The cause may lie close by. Behind the beach on a spit of land that divides Dickenson Bay from the more southerly Runaway Bay is a former salt pond, part of an expanse of wetland called McKinnons Saltpond. Wetlands, such as salt ponds, lagoons and mangrove stands, have several important functions: they are wildlife habitats, the nesting grounds for birds; mangroves also act as nurseries for reef fish and lobsters; and they filter and collect the rainwater run-off which damages coral reefs and sea grass meadows. The tangled root structure of mangroves finally holds the land together and so functions as the last line of defence against the sea, providing protection against land erosion, sea surge and storm damage.

McKinnons Saltpond in Antigua was no exception, even if it had earlier been subjected to damage from oil spills from a now abandoned refinery. Yet like thousands of other stretches of mangrove thoughout the Caribbean, the attractions of unused land close to stretches of fine sandy beach were too great a temptation for developers to ignore. In the mid-1980s, the St John's Development Corporation, a statutory government body, and an Italian investment company planned to build condominiums and a marina on land that included the salt pond. However, before this could happen, an environmental impact assessment was made which recorded, among other things, that the condition of the reef at that point was 'fair' and that the salt pond prevented the outflow of polluted fresh water into the two bays. It recommended various remedies to limit the environmental damage that would be incurred by the Marina Bay Condominiums project.[9]

However, the report was shelved and the project went ahead. Part of the pond was reclaimed by dredge-and-fill methods and the condominiums were built. Within a few years the impact of these changes had been felt: divers confirmed that there was dead coral on the reef, fewer fish, turbid water and patches of dead sea grass around the dredge channel. The salt pond that had become a swamp also suffered. Its mangroves began to die because untreated sewage from some of the hotels was periodically emptied into the swamp. For several consecutive summers following the draining of the pond, thousands of fish died from lack of oxygen, their bodies rising to the surface of the rotting swamp. To solve this problem, the government pumped sea water into the swamp. The 'diluted' sewage spilt out of the swamp and ran down on to the beaches before escaping into the sea to join the frolicking tourists.

The destruction of Antigua's wetlands triggered a broader environmental decline. The removal of sand from beaches for use as construction material has a long-term impact beyond the specific act of vandalism. The worst incidences of sand-mining have been in Barbuda, according to Edward Henry, the curator at the Antigua Museum and a founder of the Environmental Awareness Group, the island's only environmental watchdog. Where there used to be miles of 'pristine sand', says Henry, beaches have just disappeared, their sand shipped to places like the Virgin Islands to build other beaches.

In 1993, two sand-mining companies, part-owned by Lester Bird, Prime Minister of Antigua and Barbuda, and former Agriculture Minister, Hilroy Humphreys, were found guilty of breaking an injunction which forbade them from mining sand in Barbuda. According to a local newspaper report, in four months in 1993, the companies mined 114,000 tons of sand, which were sold for EC$15.4 million.[10]

Sand-mining has also started in Antigua, mainly on the southern and western coasts, causing erosion, bare rocks and damaged reefs. 'The long-term effect of sand-mining could be devastating if we have a hurricane or a tidal wave. But more immediately, apart from erosion, the ground water supply becomes brackish, contaminated with the removal of sand,' says Henry. A pure water supply has already been damaged in Barbuda.

In Tobago, the surge in sand-mining coincided with the expansion of tourism in the 1980s. Both the airport extension and the deep-water harbour at the island's capital, Scarborough, were constructed with sand from local beaches. Local naturalist David Rooks points out, 'The beaches are Tobago's tourism mainstay, take them away and your tourist goes away.... Furthermore, the sand contains micro-organisms, so without the sand another part of the food chain has gone.' Goldsborough beach, for example, has already shown the effect of mining: the sand is black, the beach has narrowed and it is littered with dead and rotting plants and trees. 'No one, tourist or local, goes there any more,' reported a local newspaper.[11]

A Sick Sea

Beaches are destroyed not only by sand-mining, but also by coastal erosion. Wave motions move sand along coastlines and replenishment occurs naturally. But this equilibrium has been disrupted on many Caribbean beaches by groynes and piers, built to trap the movement of sand. On the west coast of Barbados, some beaches have been reported as receding at a rate of 1.5 metres per decade.[12]

Those sandy beaches are made up of coral, thrown up on the coastline from the continuous erosion of the reefs which ring Caribbean islands. When the Caribbean archipelagos were created, colonies of corals were formed just below the surface. The coral comprises millions of living polyps which depend on specific environmental conditions to survive; these include warm, clear and unpolluted water, strong wave action, oxygen and plenty of sunlight. In return, coral reefs provide an important barrier against coastal erosion and in themselves create a source of food for both humans and marine life.

Globally, 90 per cent of reefs are said to have been damaged. The reefs of the Caribbean are no exception; overfishing and tourism have become the coral reefs' greatest enemies. All over the Caribbean, environmentalists and divers have reported tales of reef abuse: snorkellers and scuba divers break fragile branching coral with their flippers and kill the marine life by spearfishing; tourists destroy the shallow, exposed coral by walking on it in plastic sandals (the Buccoo Reef in Tobago); sailors in dive boats and yachts let their anchors drag over the coral, ripping it to shreds (US Virgin Islands) and dump their garbage overboard to further damage the reefs (the Grenadines); fishermen either dynamite the reefs or overfish them, their catches of lobster and conch going to feed tourists (US Virgin Islands); souvenir shops loot the reef for stock, loading their shelves with shells, dead coral and seahorses (Bahamas); and beach vendors sell the rare black coral made into earrings (Grenada) and the backs of endangered turtles (Barbados).

From the land, the reefs are also under threat as they become smothered by sediment from run-off caused by rainforest clearance or from the destruction of mangroves and salt ponds for hotels and marinas (Jamaica); from airport construction (Bequia) or dredging to build marinas (Rodney Bay, St Lucia); from sewage plant leakage (Buccoo, Tobago); or from soil erosion and excessive use of agricultural chemicals (most territories).

Other enemies of the reefs are the anchors of cruise ships. In the Cayman Islands a local scientist reported in 1994 that more than 300 acres of coral reefs had already been lost by the action of cruise-ship anchors in George Town harbour. At the same time, the Cayman Islands, with some of the best reefs in the Caribbean, announced plans to expand its facilities for cruise ships by adding shallow-water moorings. Its chosen site was a hitherto untouched bay off Grand Cayman's north-west point, which also happens to be the location of some of the best and most accessible dive sites. The scientist, who had worked on a study of the sea bed in the area, claimed that cruise-ship moorings at a depth of 60 to 120 feet would wipe out all the reefs.[13]

All these factors have chipped away at the Caribbean's finest and most prestigious reef, the 150-mile long Belize Barrier Reef, the second largest (to Australia's Great Barrier Reef) in the world. Belize has rapidly expanded its tourist base, from under 100,000 visitors in 1985 to more than a quarter of a million in 1993. The damage to the reef, including rapid depletion of its fauna and well-being, has occurred within the timespan of the tourist boom.

Yet neither the beaches, the reefs, nor the wetlands of the region can be separated from the Caribbean Sea itself. This has become increasingly polluted. Evidence suggests that oil tankers and other ships passing through the Caribbean dump oil and garbage, and there has been anxiety over the possible transshipment of hazardous nuclear substances in ships passing to and from Europe and Japan by way of the Panama Canal.

It is the dumping of cruise ship waste that has been the focus of most concern. Cruises to the region have recorded a phenomenal growth rate (see Chapter 7), and it has been estimated by the International Maritime Organization that up to two kilograms of waste per person per day is generated. While some cruise ships have their own waste-processing facilities, many more do not.

The Marpol Convention, the international treaty on pollution by ships, prohibits the dumping of food waste and sewage in coastal waters and of plastics anywhere at sea. Yet by 1995, only Antigua and Barbuda, Barbados, the Bahamas, Jamaica and St Vincent had ratified Marpol and accepted Annex Five, a key clause prohibiting the dumping of all plastic wastes, including packaging, from all ships at sea. All Caribbean countries must ratify the convention before the 'special area' status of the Caribbean can be enforced.

So the Caribbean remains a dustbin despite the fact that the USA has ratified Annex Five and that most cruise ships are American-owned and based in Florida. 'There can be little doubt that hitherto cruise lines have been somewhat negligent in this area,' wrote a cruise industry analyst,[14] while the Economist Intelligence Unit concluded that despite the denials of cruise lines, 'there is much evidence that dumping of rubbish at sea does take place'.[15]

This was illustrated in 1993 when Princess Cruise Lines was fined US$500,000 after pleading guilty in a US court to violating anti-pollution laws. A passenger had made a video of crew members of the *Regal Princess* dumping plastic bags stuffed with rubbish into the seas off the Florida coast during a Caribbean cruise in 1991. Two years later, another cruise company, Kloster Cruise Lines, was fined US$4,000 by a Cayman Islands court for allowing harmful waste products to be discharged from one of its ships in George Town harbour. The Cayman Islands maximum fine was later raised to US$592,400, in line with US penalties.[16] Other countries have yet to follow suit.

The watchdog body, the Center for Marine Conservation Organization, has noted that some cruise lines have adopted a much 'greener' approach to waste disposal. The Princess Line, for example, has recently been doing 'an excellent job by focussing on waste reduction and recyling', according to Betsy Schrader of the Center. The Princess Line now has a 'zero discharge programme' which has become the industry standard. The larger and newer cruise ships have modern waste-processing facilities, which means that less needs to be disposed of in Caribbean ports. 'We do the compacting and separating of the waste. All plastics are discharged in the US,' says Bob Stenige of the giant Fantasy cruise ship, 'but foods and so on are discharged in the Bahamas.'

The attempt to clean up the ocean has also put extra strain on the land-based disposal facilities of the islands. In fact, the reason why not all countries have signed Marpol is that to sign it would increase the pressure on their own land dumps. By not signing it, countries are not obliged to provide waste-disposal facilities and can refuse to accept garbage from cruise ships. Yet according to the International Maritime Organization, which with the World Bank is organizing a project to deal with ship-generated wastes, this tempts cruise ships to dump at sea, whether legally or illegally.

All over the region, the garbage mounts, usually occupying landfill sites such as wetlands, causing health and environmental hazards to adjacent residential, agricultural and tourist sites. On small islands, space is at a premium. Occasionally residents complain, drawing attention to the problems caused by the dumping of cruise-ship waste. In 1994, residents of St Maarten complained that waste was regularly taken off cruise ships, thereby posing a health risk. 'St Maarten has no proper disposal system. We cannot accommodate our own waste and here we are taking waste from other people,' said one local.[17]

The Caribbean Sea is also the dumping ground for hotel waste. According to a 1994 study commissioned for the Caribbean Tourism Organization at the behest of Caricom governments, the treatment facilities of water waste in many hotels were of 'limited value with regard to the treatment of micro-biological and nutrient removal. It was found that few hotels operated treatment plants that complied with the US Environmental Protection Agency recommendations.' Eighty to ninety per cent of sewage was disposed of in near-shore coastal waters, near hotels, on beaches and around coral reefs and mangroves, without adequate treatment, according to the report, although new sewage plants were on line in Barbados, St Lucia and Jamaica.[18]

One of the major problems was that ministries of health which were mostly responsible for regulating sewage legislation were hampered by lack of trained staff, money and monitoring equipment. According to the Caribbean Tourism Organization study, there was little legislation and little enforcement; regional governments needed to adopt standard criteria for the whole region.

Sometimes tourists become aware of the problem. In Antigua the general dump is The Flashes, a former salt pond on the west coast where wild ducks used to breed. The dump became full of oil, old batteries, dead dogs, dredging material from St John's Harbour (it silts up on occasion), cruise-ship waste and garbage of every kind. In 1993 the Antigua Hotels and Tourist Association wrote to the Minister of Tourism asking him to act to deal with an infestation of flies from the dump. 'The western end of the island which has a large percentage of the hotel rooms in Antigua & Barbuda is now being plagued by flies.' The letter added that guests had checked out of their rooms because of the flies. 'The future of our tourist industry is at stake,' it ended.

Planners and Politicians

All these examples of damage to the Caribbean environment have been caused, either directly or indirectly, by tourism. The protection of the environment, whether the cays of Belize or the wetlands of Jamaica, depends ultimately on political initiative. Yet in many instances, the institutions and mechanisms that are required to best prevent the region from destroying what it needs most are absent. Added to this is a lack of trained people, scientific technology, an educated public and, crucially, adequate financing as well as enforceable legislation.

Many of the reasons for the degradation of the physical environment can be traced to institutional weakness in the public sector, a problem that continues to plague the Caribbean's decision-making processes, and a lack of political will. As Calvin Howell of the Caribbean Conservation Association explains: 'The problem has been exacerbated by an attitude that approves of short-term gain rather than long-term sustainable development.' Or, as Klaus de Albuquerque, an American academic who has written extensively about the Caribbean, concluded (with particular reference to Antigua): 'The hard reality is that the majority of Caribbean governments are the worst regional environmental offenders, and even in the most liberal of democracies, the kinds of participatory planning processes necessary for sustainable utilisation of resources, are often absent.'[19]

A summary of a marine park's management training workshop in 1992 concluded that 'most of the Caribbean's marine protected areas are not being adequately managed'. It also emphasized that management is stymied by a lack of financial, human and infrastructural resources. 'Appropriate institutional and legislative structures, and more vigorous public support are also needed.'[20]

The US Virgin Islands provide a classic example of environmental damage caused by development and inadequate legislation to prevent it. On St John's, home of the Virgin Islands National Park, which was established under the control of the US federal government in 1956, bulldozers have cleared land for smart homes. When the rain comes, mud cascades down the hills to suffocate the coral reefs and sea grass beds. Inches of top soil have been lost as roads remain unpaved and the earth disappears into the sea, ruining the reef.

Similarly, in Antigua, where some of the worst practices obtain, few management structures exist and the cavalier behaviour of politicians has meant that legislation has been rendered almost meaningless. In the case of the Coconut Hall development project of 1992–93, the interests of a developer (backed up by the government) were only thwarted by the efforts of a handful of local people concerned about another attack on the island's coastline. The events illustrate how weak environmental legislation and enforcement, coupled with government collusion and neglect, can allow developers to take control of other people's environment. The story went as follows:

Foster Derrick is a young Antiguan businessman who breeds parrots in his spare time. Outspoken in his criticism of the government, he has watched the way developers have influenced the government, which in turn colludes with the interests of the developer. 'The government has wreaked havoc with the environment,' he says. 'We have allowed this to happen. The developers are inconsiderate and wield influence over the government. Developers buy a tract of land – they get it at a good price because they are seen as facilitators. The quickest way to make money is to build as cheaply as possible and destroy as much as possible. They have no feeling for the place.'

Foster Derrick's home faces an inlet of sea called Mercer's Creek on the north coast of the island in a village called Seatons. On the other side of Mercer's Creek is a peaceful, uninhabited area of low-lying hillside and waterfront. The land is forested with thorn and loblolly trees and, at the water's edge, part of the last stretch of mangrove in Antigua (50 per cent of all Antigua's mangrove has been destroyed since 1980). At one point, however, the green stretches of vegetation end and turn to brown; above this spot, the hillside is greyer and barer. This is the site where the Italian developer, Canzone del Mare, planned to develop a tourist complex. In a one-page proposal submitted to the Antigua Development Control Authority for approval in 1992, Canzone del Mare described the scope of the 86-acre complex: a hotel with swimming pool, housing for some 120 people, shops, casino, open-air theatre, marina, yacht club, roads, tracks for cycles and pedestrians and a parking area for 310 cars.

The Development Control Authority is nominally responsible for planning approval, but its work, according to Foster Derrick, is hampered by staff shortages and governmental pressure. As an environmental profile of Antigua and Barbuda (commissioned by the Caribbean Conservation Association and regional environmental bodies) reported: 'Inadequate development planning and control represent the greatest environmental threats' to Antigua and Barbuda.[21]

In September 1992, the developers started bulldozing, clearing the vegetation from the hillside. It was the first time any local person had been aware of plans to develop Coconut Hall. Furthermore, it was difficult to learn who was behind the project and what was planned. Foster Derrick alerted the local Environment Awareness Group and looked for support from the villagers. This was difficult, he said: 'The majority are afraid to take sides because they are afraid their families could be victimised.' But Foster managed to drum up some publicity and was interviewed on the BBC's *Caribbean Report*.

Then, in November four back-hoe excavators turned up and began to dig up the mangroves. The Development Control Authority issued instructions for this to stop, but three weeks later the excavator arrived again to start destroying more of the mangroves. Foster and some colleagues defied the bulldozer by sitting down in front of it; they did this three more times, putting up a flag saying 'Respect our Laws, Defend our Laws'.

The Development Control Authority wrote to the developers to complain. 'I have found that the state of work currently undertaken is environmentally unfriendly,' wrote Tyrone Peters, the town and country planner. 'Your earth-moving methodology has demonstrated that you care very little about the environment in which you propose to construct your project.' Peters instructed them to stop work immediately until an environmental impact assessment had been carried out. Later, the Minister of Agriculture, Hilroy Humphries, wrote to the developers on Development Control Authority paper giving them permission to go ahead. Peters was subsequently fired.

In April 1994, the bulldozers had not returned. Foster Derrick wondered whether the developers had run out of funds. Yet even if the tourist complex is never built, erosion from the bare hillsides of Coconut Hall will have damaged the inner reefs of the creek, and the mangroves have gone for ever, breaking the 18-mile stretch of Antigua's last stands of mangrove, an important hatchery for the lobsters which tourists crave.

A more controlled example of tourist expansion has been the South-East Peninsula development project on St Kitts. Even so, difficulties emerged. The project was spearheaded by the building of a ten-kilometre road from outside the capital Basseterre to the south-east tip of the uninhabited 4,000-acre peninsula. The peninsula has some of the island's best beaches in an area of dramatic beauty, and the new road twists along the sweeping and still empty vistas of the peninsula with views of beaches and salt ponds at every turn.

The project dates from 1985 when the government of Dr Kennedy Simmonds (the highway bears his name) decided to develop the peninsula, using the expansion of the tourist industry as the rationale. It collected EC$34 million from various sources, with the US Agency for

International Development as a major donor, to develop the peninsula but under stringent controls. A board was established, with representatives of both the public and the private sector, to act as the development control authority and to report to the Minister.

Patrick Williams, manager of the development board, expressed his concerns (and the dilemmas facing Caribbean governments) when in 1994 he said: 'We have attempted not to duplicate the mistakes of other islands. Other destinations have allowed developers to get away with too much. We are being careful; sometimes we wonder whether we are being too strict. But my feeling is that five years on when others have destroyed their beaches, we will still have ours.'

Even so, there has already been fall-out from the development of the peninsula. At the very end of the road, at the tip of the peninsula, a US company, Casablanca, began to build a hotel, only to abandon its work when it went bankrupt. By then it had spent EC$5 million filling in a salt pond to erect a storage structure while its bulldozers had mutilated the landscape.

Apart from the Casablanca project, which was alleged to have the personal support of powerful interests in government, things have moved slowly, although Sandals has expressed interest in land on the peninsula. Despite the best endeavours of the development board, a study commissioned by the Caribbean Conservation Association in 1993 reported concern at the lack of enforcement mechanisms and poor communications between government and public. 'Unless government moves quickly to address some of the outstanding issues relating to land use rationalisation, solid and liquid waste disposal, establishment of protected areas and the enforcement of existing legislation, there are real fears that the utilisation and exploitation of the south-east peninsula will not be sustainable over the long term.' In more optimistic tones, the report said that if the political will to reform its institutional machinery existed, then the plan could be a 'shining example' of sustainable development.[22]

In Belize, management strategies have been under pressure in another direction: keeping up with the enormous expansion in tourist arrivals. Of the thousands of cays that make up Belize's great reef, only two areas are designated as marine reserves and only seven small cays have some protected status.

The Half Moon Caye Natural Monument, for example, is on the site of the first nature reserve in Belize, established to protect a nesting colony of red-footed booby. The reserve was extended from the original atoll to take in the surrounding marine environment known for its 'biological diversity and splendour'.[23] As tourism has expanded, so have the numbers of visitors to Half Moon Caye and in 1989 it was reported that 'sparse supplies of fresh water, inadequate waste disposal facilities and a lack of electricity have led to environmental degradation', while unregulated fishing offshore had diminished the stock of a number of species. The conclusion was that if a management plan was not devised and put into operation soon, it was estimated that both the terrestrial and marine conservation value of the reserve 'will have been extensively and irreversibly diminished'.[24]

Similarly, the Hol Chan Marine Reserve, set up in 1987, is situated close to a rapidly expanding tourist centre on the southern tip of Ambergris Caye, planned to have golf courses, hotels and luxury homes. By 1990, 25,000 tourists a year were visiting the reserve, and despite the area's protected status, its coral reefs had become infected with black band disease, an algae which attacks corals that have been knocked and broken. Experts fear that 'carrying capacity' had been breached, but little data was available to assess this.[25]

Such environmental damage is the result of the public sector's inability to impose careful control over tourism developments. But what has also been working against the 'greening' of the Caribbean is public perception. The region's élite has thrown out the old (associated with backwardness) for modernity and has often been responsible for destroying its own environment, egged on by external financial interests. At the same time, the poor have also damaged the environment in their struggle to survive: they have collected coral to sell, littered the beaches with their own waste and thrown their own garbage into the sea.

With tourism, land has become valued for its economic potential, and landscapes have been changed out of recognition by real estate and tourist facilities. Although land has a specific cultural, economic and religious role in Caribbean societies, it has not traditionally been 'appreciated' in a European sense. This attitude is, of course, changing as societies have become 'modern' and 'tourism awareness' has introduced the idea that natural beauty is to be admired for itself. Thus a perception develops that 'tourists will like that view'. Separately, the Rastafarians have also taken a lead in environmental awareness with their emphasis on the value of what is natural or 'irie', their knowledge of and care for the land, and their rejection of materialism. 'Better a piece of land than a big Cadillac,' according to a St Lucian Rasta elder.[26]

If the Rasta's words are to be heeded, one function of sound environmental management should be the damage-limitation exercise to stop the decline of coasts and reefs, wetlands and rainforest. Another would be to put that understanding to good effect and to see how far tourism can be used to protect the environment rather than to destroy it and so contribute to sustainable development.

Views of Ecotourism

Governments and tourist establishments, locked into their old-fashioned sand-and-sea agenda, have been slow to tune in to this new thinking. However, by the end of the 1980s, interest was beginning to grow in what had become known as ecotourism (otherwise described as responsible, alternative, caring or green tourism).

An early definition of ecotourism was of 'travelling to relatively undisturbed or uncontaminated natural areas with the specific objective of studying, admiring and enjoying the scenery with its wild plants and animals, as well as any existing cultural manifestations (both past and present) found in these areas ....'[27] This demand-led definition, however, omitted anything about the needs of host countries. This prompted modifications, such as this one from the Ecotourism Society: 'Conserving natural environments and the well-being of local people through responsible travel', a definition later amended to include the protection of historical and archaeological resources.

Ecotourism has come to mean usually small-scale, up-market tourism where visitors respect and express interest in local natural history and culture. Compared with mass tourism, ecotourism also supports a larger degree of local involvement, better linkages, a reduction in leakages and increased financial returns leading to sustainable development. Jean Holder of the Caribbean Tourism Organization has also described ecotourism as a tool for learning. Addressing the first Caribbean Ecotourism Conference in Belize in 1991, Holder said that ecotourism could present the last chance for the region:

> to find the formula which does not at one and the same time entice the visitor, while alienating the local residents. All of our tourists may never be ecotourists. But even those, who come primarily to laze on our beaches, can by the provision of creative programmes, be interested to participate in an activity which teaches them a great deal more about us and our country and, ultimately, about themselves.[28]

Alarm at the damage tourism has already inflicted on the environment may have been one reason why the Caribbean began to talk ecotourism. Another was the trend in North America and Europe for 'green' holidays, away from sunbathing and duty-free shopping. Figures showed that by the beginning of the 1990s nature-related travel was the fastest-growing sector in international tourism. According to the World Wildlife Fund, about 15 per cent of the world's 450 million travellers in 1991 were taking hiking shoes and rucksacks on their holidays along with their swimsuits.

Much lip-service is now paid to ecotourism in the Caribbean. It is seen as 'a good thing'; everyone is in favour of it, at least in theory. Even Barbados, a long-time exponent of traditional beach tourism and with few 'undeveloped' wild places left, except its splendid east coast, has expressed an interest in ecotourism. The acting Minister of Tourism was in 1994 all for ecotourism: 'We have trails being developed; we can create things to make the hikes interesting and people don't have to go for miles to get there,' he said. The minister's assumption appeared to embrace the notion that any activity involving a tree rather than a beach was a credible stab at ecotourism.

Many Caribbean countries use the term ecotourism to describe any part of their 'tourist product' that focuses on natural attractions. Responding to demand, they have introduced ecotourism as an extra dimension to standard beachside holidays. Grenada, for instance, opened its 450-acre Levera-Bathway National Park in 1994. Tourism Minister Tillman Thomas said that the park would protect the endangered turtles which nest in the area and simultaneously aid Grenada's economic base. 'Because of the resources here, we have a great potential for developing ecotourism, a product that is in harmony with the environment,'[29] said Thomas.

On a much larger scale, Jamaica's Blue Mountain/John Crow Mountain National Park, the country's first national park, was opened in 1989 to help stop deforestation, which has caused serious soil erosion. The 200,000-acre park has developed a range of recreational and educational activities for tourists and Jamaicans, which will provide employment for local people. The concept behind the park is for Jamaicans to adopt sustainable land-use policies while preserving the area from detrimental development. In 1992, the Blue Mountain/John Crow National Park (and Montego Bay Marine Park) received a US$100,000 'debt for nature' grant from the Puerto Rican Conservation Trust.

At Jack's Hill, a community on the edge of the national park, a special conservation area is being managed by local people to promote ecotourism and sustainable agriculture in the Blue Mountains. Tourists who stay at Maya Lodge, the headquarters of the Jamaican Alternative Tourism, Camping and Hiking Association, use the Blue Mountains for various sporting activities and also spend time with local farmers and residents. Maya Lodge is also a model demonstration site for a community reforestation and environmental education programme and provides support, research and training for other ecotourism operations.

While the Blue Mountain National Park integrates local and tourist needs, the creation of the Virgin Islands National Park on St John's illustrates how conservation can create conflict between local needs and conservationists schooled in North American perceptions about natural wildernesses. Firstly, the landscape of the park, which reverted to 'nature', alienated the local population, who had been used to cultivating the land; secondly, economic benefit to St Johnians was, according to one study, limited. 'The park service has not sought to stimulate local business outside the park, but rather seems to have circumvented it whenever possible,' reported an anthropologist in 1980.[30] Another factor is that ecotourism on St John's is led by American-style and expensive innovations. At Maho Bay Camp, new villas, made from recycled materials, each have a personal computer which tracks and controls energy and water consumption.

Whereas the Virgin Islands National Park is part of the US Park Service, a government agency, the well-being of most national parks in the Caribbean is often dependent on voluntary contributions or funding by outside agencies, such as the World Wildlife Fund. Both the El Yunque Tropical Rain Forest in Puerto Rico, a 28,000-acre bird sanctuary with a rich and rare variety of trees, and the Asa Wright Nature Reserve in Trinidad, which attracts naturalists and ornithologists, depend in part on visitors' receipts. Again, many of the most important protected sites in Belize, such as the Half Moon Caye, the Cockscomb Basin Wildlife Sanctuary and the Community Baboon Sanctuary depend on the voluntary Belize Audubon Society for funding and management. The costs of running sanctuaries and maintaining national parks are high, but introducing entrance fees and merchandizing sales create further management problems.

A distinction, however, must be made between those countries such as Grenada and Jamaica which tie ecotourism in with sustainable environmental projects while at the same time pursuing traditional tourism, and those which claim that ecotourism defines the shape and strategy of their tourist industry. Belize, Dominica and Guyana fall into the latter category.

The attractions of ecotourism as a tourist model for both Belize and Dominica (Guyana, an even later arrival at the tourism table, is discussed separately) was that both countries have stunning landscapes, flora and fauna and marine environments. Both, too, had avoided mass-tourism development by default because of poor communications, both internal and with the outside world, poor infrastructure, and, in the case of Dominica, a lack of white sand beaches. However, both these predominantly agricultural countries have been attracted to ecotourism for the same classic reasons: to diversify the economy (in Dominica's case to offer an alternative to bananas), to generate foreign exchange and to provide jobs.

Belize: Green Dilemmas

In Belize, tourism expanded at a much faster rate than in Dominica. One key reason is that it is a mere two hours' flying time from Miami and some other US cities to Belize City's international airport. Arrivals soared and Belize became fashionably synonymous with ecotourism during the 1980s.

Results have been mixed, with examples of both good and bad ecopractice. The pressure on prime tourist sites such as the reefs, as earlier described, has led to a series of environmental problems, but it is in the structures of ecotourist enterprises that some of the hidden contradictions of ecotourism are best seen.

One of the first effects of the dash to promote Belize as a 'natural attraction' destination was that foreigners arrived to buy land. An estimated 90 per cent of all coastal developments were bought up by foreigners.[31] 'Own your own piece of paradise .... Prices start as low as US$9,950 .... Values are starting to soar,' ran the blurb of an advertisement in the US publication *Belize Currents*, while a two-bedroom villa on the tourist Ambergris Caye cost US$135,000 in 1992. This process was no different to what happened in 'mass' tourism countries where the most attractive, easily accessible land was snapped up by expatriates, being beyond the means of most locals.

Another development in Belize has been the emergence of a powerful expatriate group, which owns and manages many of the ecotourism lodges and small hotels. In the process this group has become a powerful force in the ecotourism business. In 1992, for example, 65 per cent of the membership of the Belize Tourism Industry Association were expatriates.[32] One new ecotourism project is Blancaneaux Lodge, owned by Francis Ford Coppola, the film director. Overlooking rapids and waterfalls and small-scale it may be, but Coppola has taught his Belizean cooks how to make pizza and pasta according to his own recipes (perhaps with sun-dried tomatoes flown in to the lodge's own airstrip). At this point, ecotourism is subverted into surrealism.

There are, however, genuine examples of ecotourism, small-scale, locally managed and with minimum leakages, in Belize. The Community Baboon Sanctuary, for example, is described as a model of sustainable ecotourism: eight villages and many more landowners have adapted their traditional farming methods to protect the black howler monkey. In exchange, they benefit from the tourists who visit the Sanctuary by offering accommodation and so on. Similarly, the Sandy Beach Lodge, south of Dangriga, represents another more genuine face of ecotourism. Built by a women's co-operative and part funded by the Caribbean Conference of Churches, it offers local art, craft and guides.[33]

Ecotourism commentators have noted that Belize's model shows signs of wear and tear, breached by investors, and sometimes threatened by the difficulties of keeping control in local hands given limited funding and skills. One example of such tensions is highlighted by a letter sent in 1993 to the Center for Responsible Tourism in California from the Toledo Ecotourism Association (TEA) in southern Belize. Appealing for advice on how to alert villagers to the dangers of uncontrolled ecotourism, the letter first describes the work of the TEA, which has organized groups in 13 communities and has set up five profitable guesthouses (it is regarded as the largest indigenous ecotourism association in the western hemisphere). 'We have demonstrated that ecotourism based on village visits can be controlled and developed,' wrote TEA chairman, Pablo Ack.

Problems, however, arose with proposals from foreign investors and travel agents to set up other village programmes in competition with the TEA. 'Some of these proposed projects are much better funded than our humble association and we fear that they will use their money and knowledge of business, marketing etc. to weaken the indigenous movement and to control tourism in the villages that we have painstakingly developed,' the letter continued. In another representation, reprinted by the campaigning group Tourism Concern, the TEA explained that before it was formed almost all the tourism in Toledo was controlled either by foreigners or by wealthy Belizeans. The TEA claimed to have changed this situation, working to develop tourism at a manageable pace, training and preparing the people and organizing on 'the traditional Indian community systems of sharing'. The alternative offered by outsiders, said the TEA, would have negative effects:

> Right now there is a foreign travel agent who is trying to promote a big rain forest festival in Toledo this year. He says he thinks we will have hundreds of visitors in three days. He plans to send as many as possible out to stay in the villages in people's homes. We don't feel he has prepared the people to properly take care of these visitors. We have workshops for our food providers to teach them to boil water etc. for visitors. We see a lot of problems from this type of mass tourism without proper preparations.[34]

The TEA feared that what others called ecotourism would destroy their communities. However, despite these concerns, by 1995 the TEA programme appeared to be well established. Grants totalling US$104,000 had been approved to build new guesthouses in 12 villages.[35]

The small-scale, community-controlled ecotourism of the TEA contrasts with the demand-side agenda of ecotour operators, who assembled at the first Caribbean Ecotourism Conference in 1991. (It was, as some commentators observed, somewhat ironic that it was held at the

US-owned, luxury Biltmore Plaza Hotel, built on a mangrove swamp.) One representative from the American Society of Travel Agents declared that there were 'millions of Americans just waiting to come', while investors promised large-scale loans with a 25 per cent US stake attached.[36] In such ways can ecotourism be all things to all people. It is something that Dominica and Guyana have only just begun to confront.

Dominica: Fragile Future

The 'underdevelopment' of Dominica, an even later arrival in the tourism business, has stemmed from a set of classic constraints over and above the absence of white sand beaches. These constraints have, however, acted as a protective mechanism, ensuring that tourist development remained low-key and small-scale. Indeed, until recently the wildness and relative remoteness of Dominica, which has parts of the island marked out as potential World Heritage sites, was considered a disadvantage by the tourist establishment. This changed when it was realized that a landscape of waterfalls, rare indigenous parrots, the second largest boiling lake in the world and the best rainforest in the Caribbean could become assets and were 'marketable'. Calling itself 'the Nature Island of the Caribbean', Dominica steadily began to attract more nature-loving, 'adventure-seeking' tourists during the 1980s.

Since then there has been a steady rise in tourist arrivals, increasing from 24,400 stayovers in 1986 to 56,522 in 1993. This is, however, a fraction of the stayover arrivals recorded in 1993 by neighbouring Martinique (419,007) or Guadeloupe (144,568). Cruise-ship arrivals also rose, and more spectacularly, from 11,500 in 1986 to 124,765 in 1994.[37]

It was not, however, until the early 1990s that the government of Dame Eugenia Charles, faced with the possible collapse of the banana industry, began to push tourism strenuously. This change in direction is reflected in the tourism budget (salaries, promotion, marketing and product development) which rose from EC$433,000 in 1987 to EC$2.1 million in 1993, according to Tourism Director Marie-Jose Edwards.

As a result of the marketing push and Dominica's appearance at trade shows, tour operators began to feature Dominica in their brochures, a move which they considered somewhat pioneering and daring. Unlike tourist accommodation in Belize, almost all of Dominica's 17 hotels and 21 guesthouses in 1994 were owned by Dominicans. Only one of the hotels had more than 50 rooms, and it is usually occupied by students rather than tourists.

These characteristics – local ownership and management, small-scale development and links with the community – are exemplified by Papillote Wilderness Retreat. Its long-term commitment to ecotourism was rewarded in 1994 when it won third prize in the *Islands Magazine* ecotourism award, behind Bonaire National Park and the Turks and Caicos National Museum, 'for combining a small, low-key resort with a programme that highlights local flora and fauna on an island that's already well known for nature tourism', according to the citation.

In a rainforest setting at the head of the Roseau Valley, surrounded by a magnificent garden with natural hot spring baths, Papillote is owned and managed by Dominican Cuthbert Jno-Baptiste and his American-born wife Anne. According to the Jno-Baptistes, Papillote evolved from the raw materials that existed, using what was there: 'We took a very strong position that we would work with the available resources and build up from there. Papillote is an integrated whole with natural features.'

The result of this philosophy is that almost everything is locally made and supplied. Everything in the rooms – the furniture, the cane or calabash lampshades, the ironwork, the bedspreads – except the linen and bathroom fixtures is made in villages, where locals have set up cottage industries to supply Papillote and other outlets. Many of these people had originally learned their skills through a training programme set up by Papillote. A craft shop on the premises sells local sculpture, woodwork and jewellery. The water is tapped from hot and cold springs. All food is locally grown; the only imports are bacon, butter, sugar and flour, all from Caricom.

The young staff at Papillote come from the nearby village of Trafalgar. They are recruited according to their interests and are sent on training courses. 'We try to add to their skills. Whoever learns teaches. We teach them respect for animals and the environment', says Anne Jno-Baptiste. 'We generate US$250,000 a year, of which the rooms are one-third and of that one-third ten per cent goes in commission. Apart from that it all stays in Dominica.'

The customers at Papillote are not paying for smartness. They pay for an environmentally-friendly guesthouse from which to walk, explore, bird-watch, swim and dive. 'It's a select clientele with money. They are more and more focused on global environmental issues. Here it allows them to see the possibilities, to focus on the ideal,' comments Anne Jno-Baptiste.

However, the well-being of this small eco-dominated establishment and other places like it ultimately depends on the 'eco-quality' of the surrounding environment. For it is the island and the immediate environment which attract the guests to Papillote (a recent almost disastrous development was the construction of a hydro-electric power station nearby whose humming generator can be heard on occasion). 'If you take nature away from Dominica, what is there? We have to preserve the rainforest and rivers; otherwise there is nothing more to sell,' says Ken Dill, a Dominican tour operator who specializes in hikes to the interior and nature tours.

As Dominica has boosted its tourism profile, increased its tourist numbers and modernized its infrastructure, the fragile relationship between *any* sort of tourism, the environment and local people has been highlighted.

One of the first results of the increase in tourist numbers was, as in Belize, increased pressure on the sites. The most accessible ones have been most affected. 'Our main concern is about the carrying capacity of the island as a whole and some sites in particular,' stresses Dill. 'At the moment, the physical effect on the sites is still negligible, the effect is on the tourist. No one hates tourism more than a tourist. If you promote ecotourism and then go to a site and find 250 other people there, our sort of ecotourist gets annoyed.'

Felix Gregoire, Permanent Secretary in the Ministry of Agriculture and a former head of the Forestry Division, agrees that the environmental damage remains minimal. But there is another problem. 'There are no facilities on the sites and that puts pressure on manage-ment,' says Gregoire. 'It is important to open more trails to take the pressure off the well-established sites.'

The increase in tourist numbers has also increased the costs of managing the environment. One possible solution is to introduce fees for access to some of the key sites as a way of generating funds for management and conservation and, importantly, as a way of bringing about optimum use without degradation. Three sites in Dominica were due to introduce entry fees in 1995. This decision was not without its critics who asked why locals should have to pay for access to their own national parks.

Another side-effect of the tourist boom has been a change in the relationship between Dominicans and tourists. 'The trouble with tourism is that it spoils the people,' comments the blunt-speaking former Prime Minister Eugenia Charles. Ken Dill has noticed that local people have become more aggressive towards tourists who want, for example, to take their photograph. There has also been an increase in the 'harassment' of tourists at sites such as the popular Trafalgar Falls, where unofficial guides tout for business (see Chapter 3). At the same time, those in villages not yet visited by tourists express their delight at the prospect of tourists and openly welcome outsiders.

While most stayover visitors to Dominica fall into some kind of ecotourist category, its cruise-ship tourists have a very different agenda.

They are the closest thing to mass tourism that Dominica has experienced. With a brand-new cruise-ship berth at the Cabrits National Park, in the north of the island, and an improved deep-water facility near the capital, Roseau, up to 1,000 people per day pour off the cruise ships. Most of them take a whirlwind tour by minibus of a few of the island's best-known and most accessible sites. 'If cruise ships develop to four or five a day and four or five times a week, it will be a turn-off for the ecotourists,' warns Dill, who has to make sure his own customers do not bump into the cruise tourists when they visit the Emerald Pool, a short nature trail in the Morne Trois Pitons National Park leading to a small waterfall. The carrying capacity of three sites, including the Emerald Pool, is being studied but there are some forestry experts who consider that places like the Emerald Pool will have to be 'sacrificed'.

And it is the cruise-ship tourists (and their highly visible profile) who some critics believe have compromised the government's commitment to ecotourism. 'The concept of nature tourism has not been translated into reality,' claims Atherton Martin, president of the Dominica Conservation Association. 'The contradictions are in developments like cruise tourism, high-input agriculture, plans to build in the botanic gardens, voting with Japan against the whale sanctuary and promoting Dominica at conventional travel fairs. The goal must be the whole country as a destination.'

The government, however, rejects the accusation that it has abandoned ecotourism. 'I don't see a conflict between cruise and nature tourism,' says Charles Savarin, general manager of the National Development Council, which embraces the Division of Tourism. 'Our perception is that the Nature Island of the Caribbean is not a national park in which we live. It has got to provide for the people to enjoy a quality of life. Tourism has to be a tool for development.' Similarly, Charles Maynard, the Minister of Tourism, argues: 'Cruise tourism is compatible with ecotourism. It helps to get our island talked about. The maintenance of our sites and dispersal of the cruise passengers will ease up the pressure.'

Yet there are other aspects of government policy which have also worried the conservationists. The new hydro-electric power project has reduced the flow of water into the Trafalgar Falls, while a road has been extended to give more convenient access to the Falls themselves. Building roads for tourists' convenience concerns those who want to protect the forests and rivers.

Former Prime Minister Charles had at one time favoured building a road to within one mile of the remote Boiling Lake so that non-hikers could reach it. Such a development 'to provide motorable access to tourist sites' was, in fact, part of an action plan prepared by the National Consultative Committee in 1991. Such moves have been put on the agenda, even though the Boiling Lake is within the Morne Trois Pitons National Park (established in 1975), and despite the views of those, like Ken Dill, whose customers come to Dominica especially to experience the arduous hike to the Boiling Lake with not a T-shirt stand in sight.

In contrast to the small-scale hotels that have long characterized Dominica's tourism, a large hotel with foreign backing was on the drawing-board in the early 1990s. The hotel emerged out of the introduction of the controversial 'economic citizenship policy', a government-initiated programme in which business people from the Pacific Rim were invited to invest in tourist and other approved projects in return for a passport. The Caribbean Shangri-La Hotel, to be built in the dramatic valley of the Layou River, was originally planned to have 250 rooms, 400 time-share units, a convention hall and a shopping centre. This project, described as a misplaced folly by many, was defended by Charles Savarin as the means to help with Dominica's marketing. 'You need to create a hotel that will help with promotion,' he says. 'We don't benefit from airlines, hotels chains or tour operators, so it places strain on public finances to market Dominica.'

While some have expressed alarm about the trends that the focus on tourism has brought, Dominicans in general welcome the new emphasis. Irvin Knight is the mayor of Portsmouth, Dominica's second town: 'We have no choice except for the development of tourism. There is a wave of consciousness about it. I think Dominica could be used as a model; our underdevelopment could become an asset. Here, in Portsmouth, most of the people welcome tourism although they have little awareness of it.'

Expectations are high, with villages far from the usual tourist track hoping for business. There is, however, concern about who will be able to take advantage of increased tourism: 'How would the tourist dollar come to the grassroots?' asked one man at a meeting in a remote northern village. Adeleine Detouche, of the Scotts Head Improvement Committee, says: 'We are concerned we have nothing to offer – only the beauty. We can't take advantage of tourism. Nothing is left behind with us.' Her village is sometimes visited by cruise-ship passengers who admire the jutting headland attached to the mainland by a narrow isthmus that separates the Caribbean Sea from the Atlantic. The Improvement Committee hopes to provide a snack bar and a beach changing-room with long-awaited funds from USAID.

By 1995, an ECU250,000 project was attempting to assess all the competing interests and plan a managed strategy for ecotourism. The two-year project, 'Integrating Conservation with Ecotourism', was headed by Peter Evans, an English environmentalist, who has been working with staff from Dominica's Forestry Division and from the Ministries of Tourism and Community Development. The project's aim, funded by the European Union, is to look at ways to alleviate the problems caused by the cruise-ship tourists. In practice this means taking the pressure off the most popular sites, such as the Trafalgar Falls and the Emerald Pool, by selecting 20 new ecotourist sites and drawing up management plans. At the same time, the project will provide for eco-tourists by opening up more trails, developing interpretation sites and publishing guides and booklets. Evans was also looking at the best way to involve the community, such as providing guidelines for guesthouses and bed-and-breakfast accommodation, while analysing exactly who benefits from both ecotourism and cruise-ship tourism and how.

The task for Dominica is to make ecotourism work for itself on its own terms, and to have the political will not to be deflected by short-term gain or superficially attractive schemes which deliver little. The entry of the wild card, cruise-ship tourism, could, however, jeopardize Dominica's reputation as Nature Island of the Caribbean.

Guyana: Promise and Threat

As tourist numbers increased, the delicate fine-tuning required to control ecotourism threw up new issues in both Dominica and Belize. In Guyana, the last Caribbean territory to join the tourist game, the pressure of numbers is not yet a problem. But Guyana's infant ecotourist industry raises yet more interesting questions about the viability of 'green' tourism.

Guyana is a vast country of forest and savannah on the north-west shoulder of South America with some of the tallest waterfalls in the world, and an interior of great beauty and mystery populated largely by Amerindians. Before 1991 it had no minister of tourism, no tourism association, no tourist literature, few hotels, even fewer tourist facilities and, of course, no tourists. By 1993 the first stirrings of a brand-new tourist industry were attracting possibly 500 genuine tourists to Guyana (the unreliable figures given by the Caribbean Tourism Organization include business arrivals and returning Guyanese).

Behind the Forte Crest Hotel of Guyana's capital, Georgetown, is the Atlantic Ocean, its grey-brown waters lapping at a sea wall that stretches into the distance in both directions. Those waters carry the sediment from Guyana's great river basins which flow into the Atlantic from the Brazilian border. And it is the still largely inaccessible interior which has become the focus of Guyana's new ecotourist industry.

The absence of white beaches is one explanation for Guyana's lack of tourists; the other is political. President Forbes Burnham, who died in office in 1985, promoted a 'no dependency syndrome'. So tourism, with its alien influences and foreign money, was considered inconsistent with Burnham's vision of 'co-operative socialism' and was actively discouraged. Burnham's successor, President Desmond Hoyte, however, reversed the anti-tourism policy, announcing that tourism was to be part of a new thrust to revitalize the sagging economy through the private sector and foreign investment.

By 1987, a National Tourism and Development Policy of the Co-operative Republic of Guyana had been drawn up. This stated that the new government believed tourism could 'offer significant contributions to national revenue and foreign exchange earnings indefinitely'.[38] The Ministry of Trade became the Ministry of Trade and Tourism, and a tourism department within the Ministry was set up to promote Guyana's natural attractions (staffed by two people, it was once described as 'about the smallest tourism organization in the world'.) The government of Cheddi Jagan, elected in 1992, also continued to back ecotourism.

In a sense, Guyana has had no choice in the matter. The only sort of tourism that could be developed, at least in the immediate future, is ecotourism. Guyana's recent politics, its economic crises and its extra-ordinary topography make for a country with a poorly developed infra-structure: few roads, poor air links, erratic electricity and water and telephone supplies and restricted financial facilities. A 1989 consultancy report was blunt: tourism was impossible to develop if transport was not improved and if Timehri Airport (Guyana's only airport of international standard and size) could not improve its capacity. Its suggestions for upgrading the infrastructure ranged from licensing boat services ('transport by steamer or ferry is uncomfortable, dirty and dangerous') to erecting road signs and establishing a casino.[39]

However, for Paul Stevenson, manager of the Forte Crest, the lack of infrastructure is a protection against too fast a development. It minimizes the impact on the environment and maximizes the opportunities for ecotourists. 'Our tourism is unique. We're developing a tourism in a low-volume, high-spend market that doesn't require a sophisticated infrastructure. We're cautioning the government that over-development will crucify us. Our lack of infrastructure will continue to protect. For example, it would be difficult to put a Club Med in place here.'

Yet even without a sophisticated infrastructure there has been a surge of interest in tourism. 'Everyone is now jumping into the tourist industry,' says Stevenson. Some people have even suggested that the site of the infamous Jonestown cult massacre should be 'restored' as a tourist attraction. The acceleration of tourist initiatives has alarmed some critics. Patrick Williams, head of the geography department at the University of Guyana, believes that it is too early to start bringing tourists to the country. He argues that while tourism might look lucrative in a national context, it could at this stage be damaging.

At the first national conference on tourism, organized by the University of Guyana in 1993, Williams said that the government needed to establish codes and laws, especially in relation to the Amerindians, and to ensure proper monitoring of tourism operations. No environmental assessment studies had been carried out, he said, and there was insufficient manpower and finance. The government, however, appeared to be taking a back seat. 'The government doesn't want any involvement. In any case, it doesn't know how to handle the industry,' says Paul Stevenson. In 1994, 11 out of the 13 members of the Tourism Advisory Board, whose role is to advise the Minister of Tourism, were not even involved in the industry, complained the private sector.

The Tourism Association of Guyana (TAG), formed in 1991 to represent the private sector, also wants proper regulations. Tony Thorne, its Australian-born vice-president who runs Tropical Adventures, one of Guyana's tour operators, says he wants the government to produce a five-year plan for tourism 'but we can't get them to do it'. He insists that there needs to be proper licensing, standards and safety regulations. Without them, the tourist industry is unaccountable and there are all sorts of opportunities for abuse. However, according to Richard Humphrey of Georgetown's Tower Hotel, TAG is not very well supported. One of the reasons, he says, is that 'It's perceived as a white people's organization with the big hotels running it.'

Indeed, Guyana's new-born tourist industry has been dominated by those with investment money, the knowledge to put together attractive 'eco-packages' and the contacts to market them. In 1994, TAG's guide listed ten resorts or interior camps on rivers and in the savannah and eight Guyana-based tour operators offering trips. Tour operators also had plans for week-long overland treks to Kaieteur Falls and explorations of the Rupunini Savannahs by truck.

Timberhead, the closest resort to Georgetown, is one of three lodges run by Tropical Adventures, which is backed by Forte Crest Hotel. A three-hour journey from Georgetown by road and river, Timberhead is 'a collection of three native jungle lodges', overlooking the extraordinary black waters of the Pokerero Creek. 'At night you can lie on crisp white linen sheets under mosquito nets and look out across the savannah,' says the brochure. It is beautiful, simple but comfortable. Visitors go jungle walking, swim, canoe, fish and bird-watch. In 1994, it cost US$120 per person for a one-night, two-day trip including transport, all meals and an Amerindian guide.

The Amerindians have been at the sharp end of the ecotourist boom. They have been promoted as one of the main 'attractions' of Guyana's tourist package. One of the internal airways, Trans Guyana Aviation, for example, advertises its services thus: 'We will take you to the wonders of our hinterland – numerous waterfalls and waterways, countless species of birds, animals and plant life, unspoiled Amerindian settlements.'

In the past, visits to the interior were closed to foreigners or required special permission; this is still true in some areas. However, the recent opening up of the interior to foreign loggers and mining companies has already exposed the vulnerable Amerindians. 'Tourism is an added pressure,' says Desrey Fox of the Amerindian Research Unit at the University of Guyana, who is concerned that in the talk about ecotourism the Amerindians once again have not been consulted. Janette Forte, also of the Research Unit, believes that Amerindians should become involved in the tourist industry, 'not just as the guides and camp hands – and certainly not as the destination for curious sight-seers – but with training and support, as entrepreneurs who also provide ecotours'. It might, she adds, even help to reverse their present powerlessness and be a tool for sustainable development in preserving natural areas. By providing alternative employment, tourism could be a buffer against unregulated logging and mining, against the illegal hunting of animals and birds and against the drug trade.

Meanwhile, at Timberhead, part of the tour incorporates a short stop at the Santa Mission, the Amerindian community on whose land the resort was built. 'We try to minimize the effect on the village; we only spend half an hour there,' says Tony Thorne. The Mission is the most 'exposed' of all Indian communities and its people travel regularly to Georgetown to shop. Even so, tourists have caused some disruption to the community. The young woman teacher at Santa Mission says: 'We don't want to be seen as "antique things". It's OK to have visitors twice a week but when they come and swim in the river here, changing their clothes, we are not happy about that. We try to teach our children a moral way.'

Timberhead, however, has given some employment to the people of the Mission; it also provides community support and has helped to train women to resurrect their craft-making skills to supply the Mission's craft shop. Timberhead's land was originally a 'gift' from the Mission in exchange for financial help; later a 25-year lease was renegotiated.

While the Amerindians have begun to learn about the benefits and perils of tourism, the grandees of the private sector have begun to market their new 'product'. This seems closer to Belize's ecotourism than to Dominica's, moulded by a wealthy élite into an up-market product.

Meanwhile, the Minister of Trade, Tourism and Industry, Shree Chan, draws attention to the financial constraints of a country in which 90 per cent of each dollar earned goes on debt repayment. Mr Chan wants to control the 'negative side of tourism because the average tourist wouldn't want to come'. However, he also says that there are people interested in building golf courses and conference facilities in Guyana. 'There's enough land,' he points out. A private-sector-led economy means that Guyana's vastness is now vulnerable to the loggers (a Malaysian company has offered to build a large hotel in Georgetown's botanic gardens in exchange for logging rights), the miners *and* the tourists. And Tony Thorne of TAG is already concerned about the future, calling for the government 'to investigate the saturation point of tourism in Guyana and set a ceiling on both the numbers of operators and tourists'.

Conclusion

Ecotourism has become a central platform of tourist development in Belize, Dominica and Guyana, as well as being incorporated as an alternative 'niche' within the more conventional markets of other destinations. It has provided a sort of lifeline, but, as we have seen, it is not without its difficulties. While it can conserve the environment, it also makes demands on it, and while it can offer sustainable development and integrate local people, it can also alienate them almost as easily as mass tourism.

As Erlet Cater, a British geographer and commentator on Third-World ecotourism has written: 'There is a real danger that ecotourism may merely replicate the economic, social and physical problems already associated with conventional tourism. The only difference ... is that often previously undeveloped areas, with delicately balanced physical and cultural environments, are being brought into the locus of international tourism.'[40] At that point, ecotourism in the Caribbean, or indeed anywhere else, no longer has any specific meaning.

Yet the environment of the Caribbean needs to remain the centre-piece of the region's enchantment. Firstly, it must do so to provide a sustainable future for its people, and secondly it must do so to fulfil the fantasies of those millions of visitors who, on leaving their plane, take their first sniff of that still sweet Caribbean air.

Notes

1. Christopher Columbus, *Journal of the First Voyage*, California, 1990, p. 51.

2. E.A. Hastings Jay, *A Glimpse of the Tropics*, London, 1900, p. 38.

3. Martha Gellhorn, *Travels with Myself and Another*, London, 1983, p. 70.

4. *Ibid.*, p. 107.

5. Peter Bacon, 'Use of Wetlands for Tourism in the Insular Caribbean', *Annals of Tourism Research*, vol. 14, 1987, pp.104–17.

6. Jean Holder, 'Tourism and Environmental Planning: An Irrevocable Commitment', *Caribiana*, Caribbean Conservation Association, 1988.

7. West Indian Commission, *Time for Action: Overview of the Report of the West Indian Commission*, Barbados, 1992, p. 107.

8. Antigua and Barbuda Tourist Office, press release, 1994.

9. Klaus de Albuquerque, 'Conflicting Claims on Antigua Coastal Resources: the Case of the McKinnons and Jolly Hill Salt Ponds' in Norman Girvan and David Simmons (eds), *Caribbean Ecology and Economics*, Barbados, 1991.

10. *Caribbean Insight*, London, December 1993.

11. *Caribbean Week*, Barbados, 16–29 April 1994.

12. Roger Hamilton, 'Joining the Coastal Erosion Battle', *The IDB*, Washington DC, September/October 1992.

13. Caribbean News Agency (CANA), 13 July 1994.

14. *Lloyd's Ship Manager, Cruise and Ferry Supplement*, London, August/September 1994.

15. Economist Intelligence Unit, *Tourism in the Caribbean*, London, 1993.

16. *Lloyd's Ship Manager, op. cit.*

17. CANA, 20 June 1994.

18. CANA, 2 October 1994.

19. De Albuquerque, *op. cit.*

20. *Caribbean Conservation News*, Barbados, vol. 6, no. 1, March 1993.

21. Caribbean Conservation Council and Islands Resources Foundation, *Antigua-Barbuda Environmental Profile*, Barbados, 1991.

22. David Simmons and Janice Cumberbatch, *South-East Peninsular Development Project in St Kitts*, Caribbean Conservation Association, Barbados, 1993.

23. Peter Furley (ed.), *Advances in Biogeographical Research in Belize*, Biogeographical Monographs, no. 3, 1989, p. 75.

24. *Ibid.*, p. 76.

25. Erlet Cater, 'Profits from Paradise', *Geographical Magazine*, London, March 1992.

26. Yves Renard, 'Perceptions of the Environment', Caribbean Conservation Association, Barbados, 1979, p. 53.

27. Vera Ann Brereton, *Eco-Tourism in the Caribbean*, Caribbean Hotel Association Handbook, 1993.

28. Jean Holder, paper delivered at first Caribbean Ecotourism Conference, Belize, 1991, mimeo.

29. CANA, 16 May 1994.

30. Karen Fog Olwig, 'National Parks, Tourism and Local Development: A West Indian Case', *Human Organisation*, vol. 39, no. 1, 1980.

31. Cater, *op. cit.*

32. Egbert Higinio and Ian Munt, 'Belize: Eco-tourism Gone Awry', NACLA *Report on the Americas*, New York, vol. 26, 1993, p. 10.

33. Cater, *op. cit.*

34. Toledo Ecotourism Association, 'Rainforest SOS', cited in *Tourism in Focus*, London, no. 13, 1994.

35. *Caribbean Week*, 27 May–9 June 1995.

36. Higinio and Munt, *op. cit.*, p. 10.

37. Caribbean Tourism Organisation, *Caribbean Tourism Statistical News*, Barbados, 1995. Figures for Guadeloupe are for hotel registration only and those for Martinique are estimates.

38. Festus Brotherton Jr, 'The Politics of Tourism in a Caribbean Authoritarian State', *Caribbean Affairs*, Trinidad, vol. 3, no. 2, 1990, p. 51.

39. CHC Consulting Group, 'Developing Tourism for Guyana', Dublin, 1989.

40. Cater, *op. cit.*

CHAPTER 6

The Holiday and Its Makers:

The Tourists

Late afternoon, Grantley Adams International Airport, Barbados. The American Airlines flight to New York has left, the very rich have departed by Concorde for London, and long queues form at the British Airways check-in desk for the overnight flight to Gatwick. Almost all the passengers are white tourists, with skins rosied and bronzed by sunshine; some of the women and children have had their hair braided, a souvenir of 'native' style; the men carry outsize straw hats and are still wearing brightly patterned shorts and T-shirts with slogans such as 'Life is a Beach' or 'Jammin' Barbados'. Some hold duty-free Cockspur rum or gift-wrapped packs of flying fish, the Barbadian speciality. The final holiday jokes and goodbyes have been said to taxi-drivers, couriers and the representatives from the large tour operators such as Kuoni, Thomson and Airtours.

The departing tourists are mainly middle-aged, some are young honeymoon couples, there is a sprinkling of friends and family groups; only a few look seriously wealthy, older perhaps with deeper tans, linen suits, golf clubs or tennis racquets. But for the most part the tourists, like most visitors these days to the Caribbean, are ordinary folk on a two-week package holiday. They have had, for the most part, a great time.

Barbados, one of the earliest Caribbean holiday destinations, now attracts a broad tourist base: from south-coast cheap and cheerful, £399 each for 14 nights, flight and room (three sharing) at the Firholme Hotel and Studios, Maxwell, to west-coast super-luxury snobbery at Sandy Lane Hotel (£3,252 for seven nights, flight and half board), probably the most exclusive 'property' on the island.

Opened in 1961, Sandy Lane was built on a former sugar estate (another example of how history links the old plantocracy with the new), a two-storey Palladian creation built in local stone, recently refurbished in a style where Italianate meets Laura Ashley. Both old and new money hole up at Sandy Lane: European aristocracy, American financiers, sports stars and a predictable showbiz line-up of names like Julie Andrews, Michael Winner, Oliver Reed and Frank Sinatra.

Luciano Pavarotti and his family stayed at Sandy Lane in February 1994. The Pavarottis had a suite (or two) on the ground floor which looks out between mahogany trees to the beach. While the tenor frolicked in the sea – his face as pink as bougainvillaea, his beard bobbing above the swell – his gourmet private lunch on the terrace beyond the splendour of his rooms was prepared: a white tent-like structure rose protectively like a giant parasol over a table set with linen and crystal. Two chefs from Sardinia cooked his pasta.

On the small gently curving beach, an elderly blonde woman in a black beach frock settles in to face the sun. She lies on a lounger tended by friendly elderly attendants in white hats like Spanish matadors. The sunbathers are given a towel, asked whether they wish to lie in sun or shade and told to display the yellow flag when they require service. Security guards with walkie-talkies hover discreetly. The long, hot morning ends at the ocean-fronted restaurant where a 'sumptuous lunch buffet' is served. The days drift by amidst attentive service and courtesy.

The west-coast tourists like luxury in bucketfuls. They stay in places such as Sandy Lane, tucked away from normal life behind heavily guarded perimeter gates, with private drives of royal palms sweeping down to marbled reception halls, swimming pools and fountains – and always beyond there is the Caribbean Sea. (Some of these hotels, although not Sandy Lane, are called 'clubs', a legacy of the days when you did not have to be a member but just the right colour to be admitted.) Even more exclusive are the private homes. An example is Heron Bay, the US$20 million holiday home of Sir Anthony Bamford, whose family made money out of steel beam supports. Guests such as Joan Collins drop in to stay in a cottage in the grounds for New Year and to party with the likes of Rocco Forte (whose family owns Sandy Lane), David Frost and Robert Sangster at the Carambola Restaurant. For those who care, 'winter' in the Caribbean retains its snobbish ring.

They do it differently on the south coast at places like the Firholme Hotel, whose clientele is about as likely to tuck into a Sandy Lane buffet as a Barbadian cane-cutter is. The south coasters pour off the charter flights on the cheaper package tours. They tend to stay in modest self-catering hotels and condos (not all on the beach), nip across to the supermarkets for tins of spaghetti hoops, have a day out on the wild east coast in their hired mini-moke, eat at Chefette's takeaway facing a turquoise sea, sunbathe at Rockley Beach, drink rum punch at a pirate party aboard the Jolly Roger, dine on ribs and pasta, burgers and garlic bread, and have cocktails called Thousand Flushes or Bajan Silk Panty. At night, they disco and karaoke at the Reggae Lounge, the Ship Inn with 'the feel of an old English pub' or Harbour Lights ('exclusive open air beachfront club with top live entertainment').

Between these extremes of holiday style are middle-class families with children or older people escaping the northern winter. At Worthing, a Canadian widow sunbathes by the pool of an 'apartment hotel', overlooking Dover Beach. 'This is my eighteenth visit. I come for four weeks every year and have already put my deposit down for next year.' She finds Barbados congenial and 'very British'; the sandwiches are made of nice thin bread and the tea is good. Over the years, things have changed, she says. 'The beaches are emptier but the supermarkets are better stocked and the roads and pavements have improved.' A British couple with two children who stayed on the west and south coasts ('They assume you're richer on the west coast') in self-catering accommodation had found the island friendly and safe. 'We were never made to feel uncomfortable. We hired a car, shopped locally and felt very much at home. Everyone was very helpful.'

Tourists to Barbados, representing around 5 per cent of all stayover visitors to the whole region, come from all over the world. In 1993, there were 395,979 of them (compared to 50,000 in 1963, 222,080 in 1973 and 328,338 in 1983). More than 40 per cent came from Europe, predominantly the UK; 29 per cent from the USA; 12 per cent from Canada; and less than 20 per cent from the rest of the world, including the Caribbean itself and Latin America. There were even a few Japanese and South Africans.[1]

For the Caribbean as a whole, a slightly different pattern emerges. The USA provides the majority of stayover visitors (52.4 per cent in 1993); Europe (17 per cent); and Canada (5.8 per cent). Some 8 per cent of visitors that year came from within the Caribbean, with 16.5 per cent being either 'other' or unspecified.[2]

While the USA remains the most important market, its share has shrunk. In contrast, the European market has expanded. In 1993 more than two and a quarter million Europeans visited the region; three times more than in 1985. The growth rate averaged 10 per cent per year between 1989 and 1993. The largest group (522,000) were the French although this included large numbers of French West Indians travelling back from metropolitan France. The second largest concentration was the British (also with more than half a million arrivals, representing 22.6 per cent of the European market). The Germans (404,000), Dutch (145,000) and Italians (148,000) were other growing markets, with both Germany and Italy doubling their arrival figures in just a few years.

Different nationalities favour different islands. Americans, the majority of whom come from the Atlantic seaboard states and the mid-West, like Puerto Rico (29 per cent of all US stayovers) and the Bahamas (17 per cent), with 9 per cent going to Jamaica and 8 per cent to the Dominican Republic.

Europeans spread themselves more widely. In 1993, the British liked Jamaica (114,000) best, while Barbados (100,000), long the favourite destination, fell to second place. The next most popular destinations were Antigua and Barbuda (50,300), St Lucia (49,000), both of which had grown considerably in popularity, and the Bahamas (40,000). These five destinations, all former British colonies, accounted for 69.2 per cent of all tourists visiting the region from the UK. The least known for the British were the Dutch Antilles and the French Caribbean.

Germans tend to favour the Dominican Republic (143,404 through Puerta Plata alone) and Cuba (63,003). Three English-speaking islands came next in popularity: Jamaica (36,140), the Bahamas (36,015) and Barbados (28,920). These five accounted for 76.1 per cent of all German tourists to the Caribbean in 1993. For the French, the most popular destinations were Martinique, Guadeloupe and Cuba, while the Dominican Republic also gained ground.[3]

Traditionally, most visitors arrived during the long northern winters. This was the pattern set by the super-rich before the arrival of long-haul jets. Now, the Bahamas can be reached from Florida in under an hour while New York is only four hours from Jamaica. Even for Europeans, travelling times are manageable, with the Eastern Caribbean only nine hours' flying time away. This has changed the profile of the Caribbean holiday-maker; now, even those with short holidays and average incomes can afford it. Americans average around one week in the region and Europeans nearly two weeks.

The other change that accessibility has brought is that the Caribbean is no longer an exclusively winter destination. The busy 'high season' from December to March remains the fashionable time to be in the Caribbean, but arrivals are now much more evenly spread over the year. The summer, with its lower rates, is also popular, especially with first-timers and honeymooners, with July and August in particular doing well.

Up-market, Down-market

These changes have broken the élitist mould of the Caribbean tourist. As in Barbados, the region now receives a cross-section of visitors. The rich, however, remain loyal to the Caribbean as part of the winter calendar. Barbados' west coast and some hotels in Antigua pick up this clientele who now also spread out to chic resorts on smaller islands like Anguilla and Virgin Gorda or to private islands such as Mustique, where they have created their own white ghettos. Once artists, writers and drop-outs visited the Caribbean. There are no longer Hemingways in Cuba or Graham Greenes in Haiti although for a few years the radical chic of Europe and North America made the trip to Grenada to express their solidarity with the regime of Maurice Bishop. Cuba, too, became attractive for 'study tours' and those interested in Castro's Revolution until its tourism policy widened the profile of its visitors.

The Caribbean does not feature much in up-market advertisements for specialist tours to 'adventurous' places. More typically, tourists to the Caribbean are like mass tourists anywhere, conservative rather than radical, seeking suburban security in the sun.

North American tourists to the Caribbean are likely to have an average age of 40 and a household income of around US$60,000 (compared to US$70,000 for the average US visitor to Europe). They are no longer particularly rich nor particularly well-educated, although some specialist tour operators still attract a more moneyed clientele. British tourists remain somewhat more up-market. More than 85 per cent of the customers of the London-based company Caribbean Connection, for instance, are between 45 and 65, are company directors and pro-fessionals, and more than 60 per cent of them have an income of £50,000 or more. Patrick Leigh Fermor's lament in *The Traveller's Tree* that Barbados (or more precisely white Barbados) reflected 'the social and intellectual values and prejudices of a Golf Club in Outer London'[4] would probably still suffice today as the intellectual snob's verdict on Caribbean tourists.

Whatever their tastes, however, it is the wealthier tourists who find favour with the region's tourism establishment. Islands remain anxious 'not to go down-market' or 'not to get like Barbados and the Bahamas', now identified as overdeveloped and catering for the masses. The up-market visitor makes the best tourist, according to local wisdom.

Tour operators, hoteliers and tourism officials all agree that they prefer up-market visitors. This is partly because they spend more, but it is also to do with lifestyles and attitudes. 'The exclusive tourist fits in better,' says Drew Foster, Chairman of Caribbean Connection. 'They cause fewer problems, they don't ask for drugs, they aren't rude and they don't force locals to change their ways.' The older, quieter, wealthier (if paternalist) guest is in a traditional mould. Another UK tour operator, Frank Bellamy of TransAtlantic Wings, stresses that clients must have respect and understand that the environment and culture belong to the host communities. 'My type of client wants to meet Caribbean people and eat Caribbean food. That works very well in some places; but others such as St Thomas and Puerto Rico have just been overwhelmed.' The best relationship, says Bellamy, is in a place like Anguilla where 'tourists speak to staff politely, go back again and again and there's no ill-feeling. It's a few people spending a lot of money.'

The down-market tourists, who are seen as graduates from the Costa Brava, have had a mixed reception. They tend to come on a charter with a 'room only' booking and, whether true or not, they are seen as penny-pinching, young and more likely to create social problems: 'the tattoo-bearing biscuit and cheese brigade', as one Minister of Tourism said. The influx of what was perceived as 'yobbo' English to Barbados, for example, when the charters first started to arrive, caused concern over reports of racist behaviour.

Young backpackers, of whatever class, have also traditionally been identified as down-market. The Caribbean establishment has a certain suspicion of scruffy visitors who travel on local buses, buy food from the market and probably stay in humbler guesthouses. Without couriers, reps and tour agents to supervise them, they are free agents and sometimes viewed as potentially troublesome, as liable to wander off the beaten track, or become involved in drugs and caught up with locals. As a result, non-package tour visitors sometimes receive a less than friendly welcome from customs and immigration officials.

Heaven on Earth

Europeans and North Americans search out the Caribbean for all the classic reasons: climate, beaches and landscape. It is also safe from disease and, for the most part, from dangerous beasts, and someone somewhere speaks the language (English, French, Dutch or Spanish). For European first-timers, it is the next stop after the Mediterranean for those who want to go further afield. They also visit the Caribbean for 'a holiday in a lifetime', to 'make a dream come true', to turn a fantasy into reality.

The visitors' book at Bluff House, Green Turtle Cay, on the Bahamian island of Abaco is filled with passionate thanks-yous from guests, penned as they leave their holiday haven for the journey back home. The messages read: 'This surely must be paradise. Can't wait to come back.' And 'Another day in paradise for two weeks. Glorious holiday. Kind and friendly people.' And, simply, 'Heaven On Earth.'

It is the fortune, and the misfortune, of the Caribbean to conjure up the idea of 'heaven on earth' or 'a little bit of paradise' in the collective European imagination. Although in pre-Columbian Europe it was the east with its wonders and riches which originally enshrined images of paradise, the west evoked the mythical 'blessed islands', symbolic and timeless places of gentle fruitfulness and harmony. That utopia was to some extent reinforced by Columbus who speculated that he had encountered a terrestrial paradise. In his footsteps were countless travellers bringing back news of its natural beauty. Thus the region, whatever the brutality of its history, kept its reputation as a Garden of Eden before the Fall. The idea of a tropical island was a further seductive image: small, a 'jewel' in a necklace chain, far from centres of industry and pollution, a simple place, straight out of *Robinson Crusoe*.

Not only the place, but the people, too, are required to conform to this stereotype. The Caribbean person, from the Amerindians whom Columbus met in that initial encounter to the twentieth-century taxi-driver whom tourists meet at the airport, is expected to satisfy those images associated with paradise and Eden. The images are crude: of happy, carefree, fun-loving men and women, colourful in behaviour, whose life is one of daytime indolence beneath the palms and a night-time of pleasure through music, dance and sex.

In the Caribbean, the mythology of blackness reinforces this focus on play and partying. Those still powerful representations stretch down the years from the plantocracy, through the racism of the nineteenth-century English historian J.A. Froude's observations on the black peoples of the Caribbean ('they are naked and not ashamed ... they are perfectly happy'⁵) to the more careless clichés of the modern travel brochure. The two aspects of place and people come together in a riot of exotic fun and sun-soaked escapism where tourists can 'go native'. A 1978 *New Yorker* cartoon of a middle-aged couple talking over drinks bears the caption: 'Let's go to the Caribbean or someplace and give our brains a rest.'

The fantasy is reinforced by two factors. Ordinary people are transported to luxury, to live 'like royalty' in a style they never experience at home (alternatively there are the rich who 'slum it' on holiday) while everyone, whoever they are, leaves behind everyday life, 'adult' duties and professional labels, when they don their shorts and T-shirts, bikinis and sarongs, cameras and beachbags. They are far away from home, in an unfamiliar environment where no one knows them and where, so the brochures keep on telling them, hedonism is the key quality of the place.

The brochures concentrate on the hotels, beaches, landscape and fun. The introduction to the Caribbean section of Thomson's Faraway Shores brochure for winter 1994 states, for instance: 'Our Opinion: A Carib-bean holiday is what Thomson Faraway Shores is all about – clear blue seas, golden sands and gently swaying coconut palms. Whichever island you choose you are sure to receive a warm welcome.' Or, the verdict of Kuoni: 'offering everything from lush landscapes to golden coral beaches, from calm turquoise waters and above all a tropical climate to entice you to swim, sunbathe, dive and relax'. Tradewinds enthuses that:

'Big, lush and beautiful, Jamaica has a vibrancy all of its own. The good beaches and beautiful interior are accompanied by a pulsating reggae beat.' And that Antigua is: 'An outstanding vision of 365 golden sandy beaches capped by a turquoise green sea – you will be spoilt for choice.'

The other ingredient to complete this picture of an alluring paradise is the link between the Caribbean and sex and romance. As the sun sets in a thousand photographs, couples embrace, and as waters lap the sand, they walk barefoot hand in hand. The Caribbean market is mainly couples; some all-inclusives are even for couples only. Sandals, for example, has as its slogan 'Where Love Comes to Stay'. Its brochure boasts:

> *Couples in love always stay at Sandals, because they always fall in love with the resorts as much as they do with each other. All nine resorts are tropical hideaways exclusively created for couples, designed for romance and completely all-inclusive… At Sandals, couples can do it all or nothing at all. But most of all, they'll experience the most romantic and exciting vacation ever.*

The Issa group even has an all-inclusive called Couples. Its blurb says: 'Enter Couples, a world bounded by romance. A white sand beach skirted on one side by clear blue Caribbean water, on the other by a lush, flowering tropical jungle. This is your hideaway, a perfect latitude to do nothing but satisfy your desires for food and play and love …'

Weddings and honeymoons are now big business for Caribbean hotels. Sandals in Jamaica organizes 2,000 weddings a year. As the Kuoni brochure says: 'More and more people are choosing to marry in idyllic tropical locations and many hotels are now making an amazing offer.' For 'Your Wedding in Paradise' (at a cost of from £210 extra per couple), the bride and groom receive the services of a minister or registrar, a wedding cake, a bottle of sparkling wine, a decorated gazebo, a bouquet and buttonhole, a best man and maid of honour (if required), a professional video, photographs and a fruit basket. Wedding extras on hand include a calypso band, classical harpist, helicopter transfer and a lace-covered wedding photo album. For a nurse from Devon, her wedding was on the beach in St Lucia. 'My husband had said, if you want to marry me, it'll be on a beach in the Caribbean. We've got photos of my husband dropping me in the sea in my wedding dress. It was our day and an hour after the wedding I was back in the pool with a glass of champagne and my husband was off waterskiing.'

The Caribbean can delight Europeans and North Americans for its sand, sea and its laid-back reputation alone. 'It was a holiday promise we had made to ourselves,' say an elderly English couple enjoying Grande

Anse beach in Grenada. 'The classic Caribbean holiday. We stay on the beach, we're not adventurers. We just want to sleep and get used to the sun.' 'When you think of the Caribbean, you think of Jamaica', says a 30-year-old naval serviceman who spent two weeks in Montego Bay. He went to have a beach holiday, to see the island and meet the people in a 'very relaxed atmosphere'.

Besides the brochures, another source of information about the Caribbean are the travel pages of newspapers and magazines. Much of this coverage is worthy, respectful if uninteresting, and merely reinforces the stereotypes. This may be as much the fault of the tourist boards which offer journalists free trips as the writers themselves; not only do tourist boards encourage journalists to experience only the conventional and the predictable, but many of them still push the sun-and-sand image of the Caribbean. When writers discover somewhere different, such as Guyana or Dominica or the mountains of Jamaica, the results are more interesting.

Fantasy and Reality

Meanwhile, those romantic 'desert island' images of the brochures and the magazines triumph over the real and painful complexities and paradoxes of Caribbean life and culture. Those fantasies mock the history of the Caribbean: from the almost complete annihilation of the Amerindians, through slavery and the plantation system, to migration, the difficulties of nationhood and the forging of new identities and economic strategies.

Most tourists know little of all this. Until recently, the fantasies projected by brochures and travel agents also failed to distinguish between one island and the next, building on the impression of nothing but sand, sea and sun from the Bahamas to Bonaire. 'Most of them don't know anything about the island,' admits a Kuoni tour rep in Antigua. 'Nowadays they've heard about Antigua because of the TV programme *Blind Date*. They might know of a famous person who has stayed here, and the unifying factor is Viv Richards – everyone knows about him.' Or, as the Airtours manager in Barbados says: 'They have high expectations, they have an image that the Caribbean is all white beaches and green waters like the Bacardi ad. They expect it to be like the Grenadines and the ones that don't like it complain about the pavements and buildings, that it's dirty.'

A Yorkshire secretary and her builder boyfriend have been to Barbados four times: 'It's like our second home now.' However, her first impressions made her feel uncomfortable. 'All I could see in the brochures were golden beaches, but on the way from the airport it looked so different. The sheep and cows looked so thin; everything looked brown and bleak and all those wooden shacks .... But then we got to the hotel and everyone was very friendly.'

Tourists want locals, whether working in tourism or not, to be friendly. This 'friendly' requirement is a problem for many Third-World countries grappling with tourism (see Chapter 3). The Caribbean, in particular, defined largely by outside forces and with the shape of its tourist industry laid down by external demands, has to conform to its warm-hearted image. It is, after all, this image which sells holidays.

Many tourists to the Caribbean are aware at some level of the discrepancies between their own holiday accommodation standards and the world outside the resorts. One response acknowledges, but shrugs off, local poverty. 'They live in shacks like hen houses. It makes you feel guilty but we were told there was no starvation,' says a woman to a fellow tourist on her way home from St Lucia. At a somewhat deeper level, some tourists make the connection between the differences in standards of living. 'Sometimes it made me uncomfortable,' admits the Devonshire nurse. 'Compared to them we were millionaires. Sometimes I would take off my jewellery, not wear my engagement ring because people would look at it and I would feel guilty', she said. 'We felt this particularly in Jamaica. In St Lucia people were better off and the women looked so elegant.'

A tourist to Jamaica had tried to explain to people that he and his friends were not well off. 'We said that we are not rich. When our holiday money is gone, it's gone. We said we had to work fifty weeks out of the year to save up for this holiday. It was an expensive holiday for us, but it was hard to explain this to people and we spent a fortune on tips to get anything done because it was assumed that we were rich.'

Tourists want to believe that the hosts are 'friendly' because 'meeting' other people is seen as a good thing. In the 1960s, when the least known corners of the globe (for the most part the Third World) were being 'discovered' by tourists, travel was seen as desirable, not just for the old cliché about 'broadening the mind'. The theory was that travel could be an equal encounter between locals and visitors. It was even pompously described by an international body of travel organizations as 'a most desirable human activity deserving the praise and encouragement of all peoples and all governments'. Since then, much of this thinking has been discredited, for the evidence suggests that such interactions are plagued by complexities that anthropologists are yet to understand.

Most tourists have a limited view of the Caribbean: the airport, the hotel, the beach and the sights. Their encounters with local people and their everyday life are limited. This is particularly true if the tourists stay in an all-inclusive where the resort becomes the centre of the holiday. There is little incentive for tourists to move out of the commercial environment of hotel, duty-free shops, gift shops and restaurants. The more developed the tourism, the less possibility there is for a social rather than an economic exchange.

In many instances, the only locals whom the tourists meet are the hotel staff and the tour operator rep (who is sometimes an expatriate), the taxi-driver, the beach vendor and the hustler. Thus the tourist's impression of 'local' is defined. This narrow definition tends to reinforce stereotypical images.

Tourists who want to 'meet the locals' express the greatest of pleasure at encounters which do not involve money: to be invited to a private party; to be given fruit from a yard or help with directions; to be shown round a school or join in a game of dominoes. Tourists praise holidays where 'the people just seemed delighted to see us and to show us around. They were so proud of their country and wanted us to have a great time.' Crime and the fear of it limit those encounters. One man who had hoped that he would have a chance to 'meet the locals' on holiday in Montego Bay recalls: 'On the first morning we decided to go for a stroll but near the craft market we were told to empty our pockets and lost J$400. The courier later told us that it was best to go out in a group and then only in the day. The holiday was worth it but we did have problems that I hadn't expected.'

'They like the beaches and the sunshine and think the locals are generally friendly,' was the verdict of a British Airways Holidays representative in Antigua. A 1991 visitor satisfaction survey of tourists leaving Barbados, carried out by System Caribbean, found that 'what they most enjoyed' were: beaches and climate (60 per cent); friendly people (27 per cent); and scenery (10 per cent). A similar judgment emerged from 300 Americans on their way home from Montego Bay, Jamaica. Their list of positive factors was as follows: scenery (60.4 per cent); people (20.8 per cent); hotels (9.4 per cent); culture (7.5 per cent); everything (1.9 per cent). And would they recommend Jamaica? 'Yes,' said 85.1 per cent. And would they return? 'Yes,' said 83 per cent.[6]

What tourists dislike are the vendors who harass them. Although almost one-quarter of visitors said that nothing displeased them about their visit to Jamaica, others complained about vendors, poverty and begging, drug dealers, crime and feeling unsafe. The less commercial the tourism, the less the harassment. The problem most often mentioned by the respondents in the 1991 Barbados survey, for example, was harassment. 'Beach harassment seems to be the most outstanding of the negative features of the Barbados tourist product. It is the aspect with the largest potential for having adverse repercussions on the tourist industry among those things over which local control can be effected.'[7]

Selling Sunshine

Tourist satisfaction depends on the 'product'. What is called 'product development' is the responsibility of tourist boards throughout the region, usually in partnership with the private sector. Selling the region to potential tourists is seen as a key function of the industry, and marketing campaigns are where more of the money, training and expertise of the industry is now focused.

One of the Caribbean's problems has been, as we have seen, the narrow image of the region and the inability of potential visitors to differentiate between different islands. As John Bell, executive vice-president of the Caribbean Hotel Association, wrote: 'For the last 30 years, the Caribbean has been fragmented in the market, an unrelated patchwork quilt of mini-destinations, mostly with limited budgets. The average North American or European can no more tell them apart, or in some cases whether they are in the Caribbean or Micronesia, than fly to the moon.'[8]

Holiday choices are made on very random information, based on hearsay rather than knowledge. 'We had heard Antigua was very expensive, that Jamaica had a "wild fun" image, but that Grenada was quiet,' says an elderly Englishwoman. A social worker from Sheffield says, 'Barbados sounded like it had the most to do, was the cleanest and the safest.' A midwife from Lancashire recalls, 'As a once in a lifetime holiday I thought Jamaica was like the heart of the Caribbean – beautiful scenery, relaxed, easy-going, good music.' And according to a young Scot, 'We expected the Dominican Republic to be a paradise island, all sand, with no industry and no proper roads.'

In the past, each Caribbean country was responsible for its own marketing programme (echoing the Caribbean's overall difficulties in moulding a regional dynamic, whether economic or political). The marketing and advertising have been piecemeal and unfocused. 'No one is thinking big enough,' claims Drew Foster, chairman of Caribbean Connection, who would like to see a Caribbean Centre, showcasing the region's assets, set up in a major Western capital.

However, in the early 1990s things began to change when dependency on the US market and wavering arrival figures prompted the region to get together and launch its first ever co-ordinated print and television advertising campaign. The US$12 million cost was financed by the private sector (hotels, airlines, cruise lines, tour operators and so on) and the member states of the Caribbean Tourism Organization (CTO).

Twenty-eight member countries participated (only three countries of the CTO's membership were absent: Haiti, too poor; Cuba, forbidden by the US trade sanctions; and St Vincent and the Grenadines which curiously chose not to be involved). The campaign was launched in 1993 with a 60-second TV commercial to the sound of the Beach Boys' song 'Kokomo'. Its aim was to promote 'image awareness' and, most importantly, to show variety, according to Michael Youngman, director of marketing for the CTO. 'The Caribbean has always had a problem because except for a few places it is not well known – and the truth is that it's more than just a few places,' he says.

The commercial was followed up with a 260-page glossy book, *Caribbean Vacation Planner*, 'the only guide put together by the peoples of the Caribbean', designed both for the trade and for the consumer. Inquiries, according to Youngman, were far higher than had been anticipated. Half a million copies were distributed.

The *Caribbean Vacation Planner* reflects a fundamental shift in the promotion of the Caribbean. Country by country, from Anguilla to Venezuela, it is its people and architecture, mountains and rivers that are highlighted rather than merely beaches. And where beaches are featured, it is the sporting dimension which is dominant. As Youngman points out, 'The beach will always be the number one attraction but what has changed is that more and more people are looking for alternatives.'

American travel agents were also targeted in the attempt to regenerate the US market. In 1994, some 3,000 agents signed up for individual city training programmes to become Caribbean specialists and so more effectively advise their customers.

The result of this Caribbean assault on the US market had already begun to take effect in 1993 when a 10.4 per cent growth rate over 1992 was reported. 'The advertisment worked. There's nothing else to explain it. The US market had been stagnant for 10 years,' concludes Mr Youngman.

The Caribbean meanwhile was also concentrating its marketing efforts in Europe. In 1993, a three-year US$10 million 'tourism development programme' for the Caribbean began, funded by the European Development Fund. Two-thirds of its budget was aimed at European market development, with the rest going in 'product' development. Its aim was to attract up to 90,000 more European tourists a year to the Caribbean. New markets such as Italy, Spain and Germany were particularly targeted. Promotion was improved in the more established countries. European marketing committees were formed to bring together tour operators, national tourism organizations, airlines and other travel industry groups. The other aspect of the programme was to raise the awareness of Caribbean nationals working in the tourist industry. Traineeships were set up with airlines and tour operators in Europe for marketing and language skills. Travel agents were also a priority, with a correspondence course launched in 1993 aimed at up to 10,000 agents from the European Union and Switzerland.

While the whole of the Caribbean is a beneficiary of the tourism development programme, a second European-funded programme concentrated on the seven-nation Organization of Eastern Caribbean States (OECS). It, too, looked at the Caribbean 'product' end, while the marketing component involved the training of three OECS nationals based in London, Paris and Frankfurt. Its task was to develop new programmes with tour operators, participate in promotional activities and maintain effective links with the travel press. High-quality glossy brochures were produced to inform the travel trade of the specific attractions of each OECS country and other promotional material was geared to potential hotel investors.

Most Caribbean countries have national tourism organization offices overseas in the same way as they have their own embassies. However, there is little co-ordination and co-operation, even where amalgamation would be a more efficient use of limited resources. Meanwhile, tourism offices of the smaller islands continue to be run in places like New York, Toronto and London, staffed by well-meaning but undertrained personnel. Sometimes their staff are composed of nationals who have lived overseas for many years and do not know much about the country they represent. As a result, some of these smaller tourism offices function as little more than brochure envelope-stuffers.

While new European markets are being explored, the Caribbean also has its eye on its neighbour, Latin America. Political and economic links, especially with Central America, are being slowly consolidated and Latin America's middle class is seen as a potential customer. But the hopes of ministers of tourism for Colombians and Argentinians to visit Barbados, for example, cannot materialize without appropriate scheduled air links. For the most part, these do not exist. Inter-regional tourism also has some potential, especially with a growing middle class. Other south–south tourism connections are yet to be developed, although Grenada under the PRG was once interested in looking at such markets.

One other market has been largely ignored by much of the Caribbean. According to Lebron Morgan, regional advertising sales director for the Afro-American magazine *Essence*, the Caribbean chases every other market, including Latin America and Asia, but ignores his 5.2 million readership. 'When I think about vacations, about exposing my family, my children, my wife to a situation, I'm very sensitive about where I take them.' He believes that the marketing people need to realize that 'I don't think like the general market in America. They think they know black America but they really don't.'[9] It is not enough to have images of black tourists in promotional literature, argues Morgan, 'we need to get the invitation ... to come on down'. A similar point was made by the president of the US Black Travel and Tourist Association, Lloyd Williams, in a 1995 press report: 'It's unfortunate that while Caribbean destinations are failing to tap into the estimated US$43 billion black travel market in the United States, European nations and places like the Pacific rim are promoting themselves among blacks.'[10]

Non-resident returning nationals are also a category ignored by tourist boards. They go to the Caribbean for weddings, family gatherings and also for holidays, as do growing numbers of black British. Among the conclusions of the Organization of American States 1994 analysis of Jamaica's tourism economy was that 'non-resident Jamaicans, whom the Jamaica Tourist Board does not even consider tourists, represented nine per cent of total visitors and contributed 7.4 per cent of total expenditure'.[11] This represents a considerable amount, given that returning nationals usually stay in private homes.

To attract tourists, industry officials involved in marketing are constantly on the move, to trade shows, seminars for travel agents and travel business conferences. To have a presence is the thing. At the annual World Travel Market in London, for example, a whole area is turned into a 'Caribbean Village', part funded by the European Community. The largest tourist destinations, such as the Bahamas, Jamaica, Barbados and Cuba, build gingerbread-fashioned enclosures, decorated with armfuls of anthuriums, tables and parasols, and generously dish out rum punches. There, the minister of tourism, scores of blazered tourist board officials, hoteliers, public relations officials, marketing managers, hotel owners, diving operators and time-share reps do business in an endless round of meetings with tour operators and travel agents.

For the smaller hotels or tour companies with less muscle and marketing financing, it is hardly worth it. 'The tourist board pay part of the package, but you have to sell your hotel in the five minutes you have with a tour operator and travel agent. They can't even remember you or your hotel at the end of the day,' says one Barbadian hotelier from the south coast. Other hotels approach it differently by paying for travel agents to make their own 'familiarization' trips.

Trade shows reveal how far marketing is a mixture (and not always an easy one) between the public and private sectors of the tourist business. Indeed, the private sector gained considerable influence in the political climate of the 1980s and is now more readily accepted within the institutions of the tourist industry. Where once the private sector would go out and sell for itself, there are now many more opportunities for partnerships. Yet tensions remain between the two sectors, and the private sector claims that governments neither understand marketing (a claim that the professionals would endorse) nor spend enough money on it.

The Dominican Republic, a major tourism destination, is unique in leaving the private sector to shoulder all the promotional side of the industry. In 1993, it spent less than US$100,000 on promotion, compared to US$15 million in Jamaica and US$25 million in the Bahamas. St Maarten had a rather similar attitude, which its hoteliers noted with some regret. It was only in late 1994 that St Maarten readmitted itself to the CTO, having refused to pay its membership fees for many years.

Jamaica has the Caribbean's largest individual advertising budget. The Jamaica campaign is extensive and sophisticated, with slogans such as 'Heavenly Jamaica, Hell for the Indecisive' and '500 years ago, Columbus logged Jamaica. Now It's Your Turn'. Its print advertisements use high-class colour photography to appear in up-market newspapers and magazines.

Like the rest of the Caribbean, but very much a pioneer, the Jamaican tourist industry has attempted to get away from the idea of the island-as-beach. The slogan, introduced during Michael Manley's first administration of the late 1970s, was 'We're More Than A Beach, We're A Country'. This was both a nationalist appeal to Jamaicans to have pride in their own identity and also a way of introducing tourists to the island's rich culture and hinterland. It was an affirmation of Jamaica and Jamaicans.

Jamaica's advertising had also fundamentally shifted from the 1960s' message which portrayed white tourists 'being served' by blacks as an intrinsic attribute of the holiday. In 1968 the Jamaica Tourist Board had advertised its villas for rent as 'The Life You Wish You Led'. The villas, said the advertisement, come 'equipped with gentle people named Ivy or Maud or Malcolm who will cook, tend, mend, diaper, and launder for you. Who will "Mister Peter, please" you all day long, pamper you with homemade coconut pie, admire you when you look "soft" [handsome], giggle at your jokes and weep when you leave.' In the 1990s advertising mode, tourists do things for themselves: explore, hike, ride, raft, windsurf, golf and so on. 'I don't think we've had images of waiters in our advertising material for a very long time,' says David Winter, account director of FCB Advertising in London, which has looked after the Jamaican Tourist Board's account since 1990. 'We want to show variety, that Jamaica is more than beach and palm trees. No other Caribbean island has such a contrast. Hence the shots of people. We have to identify the product in its most viable form for our market.'

The agency's 1995 campaign for television (some of which was a joint public/private sector promotion with Sandals) uses images in which Jamaicans feature more often than tourists. There are reggae musicians, dancers, artists, children, country people; the faces range over age, gender and colour. The strong representation of Jamaicans is almost incidentally intercut with tourists riding horses, rafting on rivers, ending with romance and a sunset. The music is Bob Marley's 'One Love', which provides the main message of the advertisement. 'Some of the more conservative elements in Jamaica didn't want us to use reggae because they didn't think the connotations were suitable,' says Winter.

Other Caribbean countries have also been seeking to modernize their image in a similar direction. The Bahamas Ministry of Tourism, examining its marketing situation in 1993, declared that it would 'expand the product to include those features of the destination that are outside the hotels and resorts in order to capture the full flavour of the destinations and the points of differentiation that make them unique'.[12]

Both the new umbrella approach and a more diversified image for the region were helping to sell the Caribbean by the early 1990s. Luring the tourists to its shores and sending them home happy was also the region's response to another challenge: the floating hotels on every Caribbean horizon.

Notes

1. Caribbean Tourism Organization, *Caribbean Tourism Statistical Yearbook 1993*, Barbados, 1994.

2. *Ibid.*

3. *Ibid.*

4. Patrick Leigh Fermor, *The Traveller's Tree*, London, 1984, p. 132.

5. J.A. Froude, *The English in the West Indies*, London, 1888, p. 43.

6. Dennis Gayle, 'The Jamaican Tourist Industry' in Dennis Gayle and Jonathan Goodrich (eds), *Tourism, Marketing and Management in the Caribbean*, London, 1993, p. 53.

7. System Caribbean Ltd, 'Visitor Satisfaction Survey', Barbados, 1991.

8. John Bell, 'Caribbean Tourism in the Year 2000', in Gayle and Goodrich, *op. cit.*, p. 233.

9. *Caribbean Week*, Barbados, 25 June–8 July 1994.

10. *The Gleaner*, Jamaica, 15 April 1995.

11. Organization of American States, *Economic Analysis of Tourism in Jamaica*, Washington DC, 1994.

12. Bahamas Ministry of Tourism, Tourism Review Task Force, 1993.

CHAPTER 7

Sailing into the Sunset:

The Cruise-ship Industry

The first journeys across the Caribbean Sea were made by Amerindian canoeists who settled the island chains, paddling north from the river systems of the Orinoco and the Amazon. Hundreds of years later the Spanish explorers arrived, and when other European powers joined the fight for control of the Caribbean it was the sea, not the land, which saw their greatest battles. Then the sea became an economic highway: for slavers, traders, buccaneers and fishermen; or it became a passageway for escaped slaves, indentured labourers and settlers, and later still a watery flight path for emigrants and boat people.

These shipping channels (except for those traditionally used by Caribs and fishermen) were linked with the economic and political power blocs of Europe and North America rather than with each other, for each harbour was a juncture of imperial arrival and departure. Caribbean ports are still working places. Container ships arrive with imports from tableware to tractors, most from the USA, and they depart with bananas from Martinique or St Vincent for Europe. Now, however, by far the biggest vessels in port are cruise ships, also from the USA, on pleasure journeys that no longer pay attention to those old colonial lines.

Criss-crossing the Caribbean Sea, largely out of Miami, these great white whales come and go quicker than the banana boats loading up alongside them. There is time though for seven hours or so on land, from the morning arrival to departure in late afternoon.

Down the gangway come the cruise-ship passengers, straight into a purpose-built, duty-free shopping mall, or into streets strung out with tourist shops. Just like the last port of call, most terminals have pizza houses, ice cream parlours, souvenir shops, perhaps a casino or two and hoardings with familiar transnational names: Dollar Rent a Car, Colombia Diamonds, Benetton, Gucci and Little Switzerland. There is time to fit in shopping, an island tour or either a trip to a beach or to the cruise line's private island. Ranks of minibuses line up to whisk them off on their pre-booked, pre-paid tours arranged by the cruise lines with a few chosen ground operators. Those who have failed to book can take their chances and get a cheaper deal with taxi-drivers.

The most popular ports of call are the ones with the best duty-free shopping and casinos. The shops are ice-cold and could be on Fifth Avenue: the gifts, under glass, are much the same whether in Ocho Rios or Antigua – jewellery, perfumes, china figurines of pastel-coloured cottages, milk maids or puppies. Each destination, however, is in competition with the next to provide a shoppers' paradise. St Kitts, for example, with its modest duty-free mall in Basseterre, must try to compete with St Maarten, its flashy Americanized neighbour, stiff with shops and casinos. 'We would like to see a greater turnover so we are upgrading our duty-free outlets,' says Hilary Wattley, the marketing manager for St Kitts Division of Tourism. Or Grenada, where there is little to buy and only the charm of St George's to attract the tourists. 'We need more and fancier shopping. There are not enough attractions and shops for the cruise people,' says Andrew Bierzynski, a charter boat operator.

Armed with leaflets on shops recommended by the cruise ships, cruisers know which are the best and cheapest destinations. Not St Kitts or Grenada, for sure, and even Antigua is not a star attraction. A young couple in Antigua's duty-free Heritage Quay are not planning to spend much money there. They are saving it for St Thomas, in the US Virgin Islands. 'We might as well go back on board and get some breakfast.' They have heard that shopping is better in St Thomas.

By afternoon, the passengers with their purchases drift back to the ship to eat (food is included in the cruise price) or to join those who have never left (preferring to glimpse the island from the rails). The last somewhat drunken stragglers, with T-shirts reading 'Drink Till You Sink', are scooped up the gangway. Soon, the quayside will be almost empty, as shopkeepers count their takings and taxi-drivers give up for the day. Only beggars and scavenging dogs remain. The ship disappears, lights twinkling, on its way to another sunset at sea.

The Cruise Boom

The Caribbean cruise business is enormous, and still getting bigger. 'The untapped potential in the Caribbean – where we're putting more tonnage over the next several years – is vast,' claims Julie Benson of Princess Lines, a subsidiary of P&O Cruises.[1] The Caribbean already has more than half of the world capacity of cruise 'bed days', and its share is growing. In the Caribbean itself, where there were more than six million 'bed days' in 1993, it is expanding faster than land-based tourism. Cruising has grown from an estimated 900,850 passengers in 1983 to 2.3

million in 1993 (these figures include the Mexican east coast and are based on the number of bed days divided by 6.9, the average number of days in a cruise).[2] It is expected to almost double again by the year 2000. In ten selected Caribbean ports, cruise-ship arrivals trebled between 1982 and 1992, while land-based arrivals for the same destinations doubled.[3]

The industry runs at a remarkable capacity of more than 90 per cent, far higher than land-based tourism, and both the number of ships and their overall size are increasing. At least 28 new ships are due to be delivered to the cruise companies by 1998; most are destined for the Caribbean. The biggest companies, Royal Caribbean Cruise Line (RCCL), Carnival Cruise, Holland America and Princess, are leading the way. RCCL has three ships on order, all for more than 1,800 passengers; Princess is to spend almost US$1 billion on three ships; while the biggest line, Carnival, was due to add 11 ships to its fleet by 1996. Disney Corporation is also entering the cruise market, with its first ship due to sail in 1999. Even the smaller companies are increasing their fleets, building vessels for 300 or so passengers for the luxury market or for the even more select sail-ship market.[4]

Both Carnival and Princess have on order the two biggest liners ever, *Tiffany* at 100,000 tonnes and *Grand Princess* at 105,000 tonnes respectively. Carnival is spending US$400 million on *Tiffany* which is being built in Italy and is due for delivery in late 1996. Like the new Princess Line ship, it will be too large to go through the Panama Canal and is thus confined to the Caribbean.[5]

Seventy-seven cruise ships with passenger capacities averaging more than 1,000 each were working the Caribbean routes in 1993. Nearly one-third (496) of the cruises sailed out of Miami; 463 began from the important airline hub of San Juan, Puerto Rico, while 178 cruises originated in Port Everglades, Florida. Of non-American bases, 97 cruises began in Aruba, 37 in Antigua, 21 in Playa de Ponce, Puerto Rico, and 17 in Fort de France, Martinique. Other ports, such as those of Barbados and Belize, notched up a mere handful.[6]

The ships steam on a variety of routes, depending on the point of departure or the length of the cruise. The Bahamas, a traditional cruise destination close to Florida, was the busiest port of call, with 1.8 million cruise-ship arrivals in 1994. Next most popular was the US Virgin Islands (1.2 million), followed by St Maarten (718,553), Puerto Rico (680,195), the Cayman Islands (599,387) and Jamaica (595,036).[7]

Many destinations have recorded spectacular growth. St Lucia, for example, had 58,000 cruise-ship arrivals in 1986 but 173,538 in 1994, while Dominica recorded 124,765 in 1994, up from 11,500 in 1986. In the early 1990s, other islands with an expanding cruise-ship market were

St Kitts and Nevis, Aruba and Curaçao.[8] Even Haiti, abandoned by the cruise-ship industry in 1993 when sanctions against its military regime were announced, was back on the itinerary by 1995.

Rocking the Boat

Yet while the cruise lines steam ahead, unloading more and more passengers off bigger and more luxurious ships on to the docksides of small Caribbean states, fundamental questions have begun to be asked about the benefits of the cruise-ship industry to the Caribbean and its people, and its long-term effect on the region's own land-based tourism.

This became painfully clear in a dispute between the Caribbean Community (Caricom) and the Florida-Caribbean Cruise Association (FCCA), which represents the 14 major cruise lines. The row, over cruise passenger head tax, came to a head in 1993 when the FCCA resigned, albeit briefly, from the Caribbean Tourism Organization (CTO). The story went as follows:

Departure taxes for both airline and cruise passengers have traditionally been set by individual governments. The tax is one way in which the tourist industry contributes to the expenses involved in providing appropriate port or airport facilities. In the case of the cruise tax, this has varied from nothing (St Maarten) to US$2 (Dominica) to US$15 (Bahamas). Inter-country rivalry and what are considered to be differences in the quality of facilities offered to cruise ships by each destination were said to explain the discrepancy.

However, in January 1992 the Organization of Eastern Caribbean States (OECS) agreed to adopt a standard head tax of US$10 to take effect in October of that year. However, this decision was superseded when Caricom, the wider regional organization, came up with another plan to adopt a unified tax. It was to be set at US$5 in April 1994, to be raised to US$7.5 in October that year and to US$10 by 1995.[9]

For the Caribbean this was a major step forward, since earlier discussions about increasing the head tax had taken place only bilaterally, giving the cruise operators an in-built advantage. They could play one country off against another by threatening to skip one destination for another with a lower tax. This time the region as a whole seemed to be flexing its muscles. As Jean Holder, Secretary-General of the CTO, said: 'The concept of the minimum tax, set at a reasonable level, was intended to enable the weak destinations to earn a little much needed revenue, to create some Caribbean solidarity and thus effect an adjustment to the strategic advantage which is held largely by the cruise lines. Its success is dependent entirely on each country keeping the agreement.'[10]

Caricom's move raised the possibility of a regional approach, not just about the head tax but about other important issues surrounding the cruise industry. John Compton, the St Lucian Prime Minister, expressed the opinion that the region would 'no longer accept mirrors and baubles for the use of its patrimony'.[11]

The decision did not please the cruise lines. 'To solve the hotel problem by raising taxes on cruise ships is stupid and punitive,' said Bob Dickinson, president of Carnival Cruise Lines.[12] Retaliation was not long in coming. The RCCL announced that it would drop St Lucia, one of the seven OECS states, from its itinerary. The *Nordic Prince*, which had made 18 calls to St Lucia in 1991, also decided to go elsewhere. The boycott of St Lucia resulted in calls of solidarity from other CTO members, but in the event they were empty promises. Dominica even took up the *Nordic Prince*'s offer to call there.

Meanwhile, the tax issue was becoming symptomatic of the tensions between the cruise ships and the region's land-based tourist industry. The Caribbean Hotel Association, with its own concerns about what it saw as the expansionist behaviour of the cruise industry, had asked the former Jamaican Prime Minister, Michael Manley, to head a Caribbean Tourism Development Task Force. When Manley was thought to be taking an anti-cruise line and when the Jamaican Butch Stewart, head of the Sandals chain, compared the cruise lines to a 'giant sea serpent which is gobbling up the region's plant, personnel and profits', the row became even more intense.[13] As the CTO seemed to remain silent about it all, the FCCA resigned.

Those on the side of the cruise ships expressed their barely disguised contempt for the Caribbean's hotel industry. Without the cruise industry, said Joel Abed in *Travel Trade News*, 'to both promote and present its attractions and facilities to potential vacationers, the Caribbean resort industry, as we know it today, would all-too-quickly become a virtual tourist desert'.[14] Bob Dickinson of Carnival expressed his position only marginally less aggressively. 'They're not only biting the hand that feeds them, they're yanking off the whole arm,' he said.[15]

The tax row provoked outbursts of passionate rhetoric from the region. There was a general distrust of what was considered to be imperious behaviour by the cruise lines. Yet despite this, and the agreement made at the highest level in Caricom, the unified passenger head tax was not achieved within the agreed time span.

This failure dismayed many sections of the Caribbean tourist industry. It demonstrated the inability of the region to take a unified stand and it also showed just how powerful the cruise industry's grip was. Royston Hopkin, the Grenadian president of the Caribbean Hotel Association in 1994, concedes: 'The cruise ship lobby is very strong and the governments have been very weak. The cruise lines sweetened the governments who were not united. We gave our best shot but by the time the heads of government got to it the three-tier system was introduced and this weakened our position.'

Peter Odle, president of the Barbados Hotel Association, is another aggrieved hotelier. 'I was against cruise ships from the beginning,' he says:

> The Caribbean will not realize the cruise business is a disservice until it's nearly too late. The cruise ships are using our most precious asset – the sea – polluting it like hell and not making any significant contribution to our economy. And instead of taking a firm stand, the governments are all over the place; there is a lack of political will.

Similar sentiments were expressed by Allen Chastenet, a former director of the St Lucia Tourist Board: 'If anyone is sucking the Caribbean dry it is the cruise ships.'

Jean Holder also took the position that Caribbean governments have the right to take action to make the competition between land and sea tourism more equitable.[16] From the shore, it seems that foreign cruise lines have built-in advantages over land-based tourism which they use, at the expense of the Caribbean, in a particularly rapacious manner.

Firstly, cruise ships are seen not to pay as many taxes as the land-based industry. For hotels, taxation either doubles the price of many purchases or restricts the hotelier to buying from Caricom producers only. Hotels must also pay corporation tax and casino tax profits. In contrast, cruise ships are movable feasts which sail away into the sunset, their bars and casinos untaxed. Secondly, raising money to build hotels is problematic even though construction work employs local labour and supports local financial institutions. Far from being built in the Caribbean, cruise-ship contracts go to subsidized shipyards (at least until 1996) in Europe, where long-term, low-interest loans are also available.

Caribbean hotels provide jobs for locals, with work permits required for the employment of non-nationals. Cruise ships operating in the Caribbean, on the other hand, are free to employ whom they wish. According to the FCCA, its member cruise lines employed more than 6,500 Caribbean nationals on board cruise ships in 1994.[17] This represented 26 per cent of on-board workers, and was an increase of 1,500 over 1992 figures. However, in 1994, the only Caribbean nationals on board the Carnival Line's *Fantasy*, the second biggest cruise ship in the world, were some Bahamians working in the casino and the calypso band. In what was judged by some to be a curiously vague piece of economics, the FCCA estimated in 1994 that 'cruise-related expenditures' were 'associated with 82,071 full-time equivalent jobs in the Caribbean region'.[18]

Many lines employ European officers and a Third-World crew. The officers on the Carnival's *Fantasy*, for instance, are Italian, while what is called its 'international' crew is from Latin America, India and the Philippines. Those from the poorest parts of the Third World are paid low wages. In contrast, employees in the land-based industry are mostly paid union rates. Caribbean employees also contribute to their country's revenue by paying income tax; cruise employees do not pay tax to Caribbean governments.

While the numbers of Caribbean nationals employed on the ships may have increased, the amount of Caribbean products purchased by cruise lines remains small. Caribbean supplies to the cruise industry as a percentage of total requirements are estimated at between 1 and 5 per cent. According to the FCCA, member cruise lines spent US$51.2 million on Caribbean supplies in 1993. Technical inputs such as petroleum products, parts and chemicals represent US$30 million (59 per cent of total expenditure), while handling services such as warehousing and stevedoring at ports account for US$7.1 million or 14 per cent of total expenditure. Just over a quarter of the cruise lines' expenditure in the Caribbean was on food and drink (US$13.8 million), of which half was on beer and liquor. Foods included fruit and vegetables, dairy products, bread, water, spices, seafood, coffee and sugar.[19] If this figure is at all accurate, only US$6 per passenger is spent on food and drink grown and produced within the Caribbean.

The list of significant Caribbean suppliers is short: Bico Ice Cream and Pine Hill Dairy, both of Barbados; Dominica Coconut Products; Commonwealth Brewery of the Bahamas; Tropical Beverages of Trinidad; and Red Stripe Beer of Jamaica.[20] The result is that not only are most cruise ships supplied by US companies, but that fresh products from outside the region are also flown or shipped in to the Caribbean during a cruise. Thus, in one ludicrous example, a barge from Venezuela filled with bananas supplies the cruise ships in St Lucia, one of the Caribbean's major banana producers.

Since the tax row, the FCCA has made an effort to play a more sensitive role; most of these sourcing companies participated in a cruise trade fair in San Francisco in 1994 at which the FCCA provided booth space for Caribbean producers. It was an opportunity, said the FCCA, for these companies 'to strengthen their contacts within individual cruise lines, make new contacts and learn from other successful suppliers of cruise lines'.[21]

The difficulties (quantity, quality, regularity of supply, delivering on time) faced by Caribbean suppliers are similar, but greater, to those they face in supplying the land-based industry (see Chapter 2). In a commitment to high standards, the cruise lines make tough demands on their suppliers. Part of the RCCL's mission statement, for example, pledges 'to locate, buy and deliver the highest quality of specified goods and services at the fairest overall cost possible in a timely manner'.[22] The supplies must be competitive with products from Hong Kong and Taiwan; they must be on time; and they must be delivered under appropriate conditions. They must also fit US tastes. American cruise passengers expect, according to RCCL's head of purchasing, steak from grain-fed cattle and brand-familiar products, such as yogurt and cereal. Such demands are beyond most Caribbean producers.

From this low base, selling Caribbean goods to the cruise lines has proceeded in a painfully slow manner. It really began in the early 1990s with a CTO initiative which, according to Jean Holder, brought together the Caricom Export Development programme and cruise lines to discuss sourcing needs. Even the successful and efficient Dominica Coconut Products took three years to sign a contract with the RCCL to supply 3 million bars of soap a year.[23] Most producers and tourist boards have been only vaguely aware of the needs of the cruise lines and even less able to deal in the quantity and the quality required. The small scale of many producers and the lack of developed regional exporting and marketing groupings have further limited the opportunities.

Yet despite what appears to be an uneven match between sea and land tourism in the Caribbean, regional governments have continued to give the cruise ships their blessing, boasting of the increase in cruise-ship passenger arrivals over the years. Responding to the needs of bigger ships, for example, they expanded and upgraded port facilities throughout the late 1980s and early 1990s. The ships tie up at deep-water ports, especially deepened, widened and modernized by local governments. The potential to offer a homeporting facility (using a cruise destination as an arrival and departure point, as successfully developed by San Juan) has been another reason behind the port improvements.

Both old and new cruise destinations have been investing millions of dollars on new facilities. In the Eastern Caribbean, all the islands have been paying attention to their cruise-ship facilities. Dominica has spent US$28 million on a dock extension at its Roseau port and a wharf and terminal building at the Cabrits, a national park on the north of the island, to boost its cruise-ship arrival figures. The terminal opened in 1991, and in that year cruise arrivals increased from 6,800 to 65,000. St Kitts, too, was looking to expand its cruise business. In 1994, a US$16.25 million loan agreement was signed with the Bank of Nova Scotia to construct a new cruise-ship berth separate from the dust and cargo of the old port.[24] In 1995, St Vincent also announced a cruise-ship berth development at its capital, Kingstown, to be funded by the Kuwaiti Fund and the European Investment Bank.[25]

Big Spenders?

St Vincent is anxious that cruise ships call at Kingstown and spend money there rather than drop anchor off some remote Grenadine island. The cruise lines, however, can reduce the number of days in port by buying or leasing their own island or by anchoring off a deserted stretch of beach. As *Caribbean Travel News Europe* noted: 'Increasingly, the trend is for cruise lines to go one step further from taking their passengers around the Caribbean islands – and to give them one – all to themselves.'[26] This policy was begun in the early 1980s by Norwegian Cruise Line, which owns Great Stirrup Cay in the Bahamas, now 'remodelled' with a wider beach, a barbecue area and water sports.

Other lines also have their own private beaches, where what is called 'cruise-style service' is on hand with barbecue and bar provided by cruise staff. Princess Cruises own Princess Cay on Eleuthera, Bahamas ('For total tropical tranquillity, it's hard to beat this land of lotus-eaters'), and Saline Bay, Mayreau, in the Grenadines ('every castaway's first choice'). The RCCL owns Coco Cay, also on the Bahamas, and leases Labadee in Haiti, an isolated promontory on the north coast. It is claimed that at one time the cruisers were not even told that they were visiting Haiti.

When cruise lines create their own version of paradise, they avoid port fees and passenger head taxes while protecting their customers from the less-than-paradisiacal reality of much Caribbean life. Desert-island days, days at sea, island tours booked through the cruise ship: all are ways in which cruise lines can persuade customers to buy their services and in which they can control the quality and quantity of the holiday experience. Another way is to attract customers to spend money on board in the shops, boutiques and bars, available at all times (except when the ships are in port) and often at competitive prices compared to goods sold on land. The Princess Line brochure states: 'There's no need for you to be in port to go shopping. Both *Canberra* and *Sea Princess* carry a remarkably comprehensive selection of goods ... ' As the Economist Intelligence Unit's 1993 report on the Caribbean points out: 'On board shopping, which by definition is duty-free, is being promoted increasingly aggressively as a means of maximising their share of a passenger's overall holiday expenditure.'[27]

The *Fantasy* of Carnival Cruise Lines is a typical giant cruise ship which provides its customers with just about everything they could desire. Sailing out of Cape Canaveral bound for Nassau and Freeport, its 2,634 passengers have paid as little as US$195 for a three-day cruise. It has two dining rooms, nine bars and lounges, including Cleopatra's Bar decorated with hieroglyphics and Egyptian statuary and the Cat's Lounge (maximum 118 people) with its consumer graphics, tables in the shape of bottle tops and cats' eyes glinting from the ceiling. There is a casino and concert hall for 'Las Vegas style revues', and 1,022 'accommodation units', most of which convert to 'king size beds', while 28 have bathtub whirlpools. There are three outdoor swimming pools, a 500-feet banked and padded jogging track and a nautical spa and health club. The belly of this gleaming ship boasts two glass elevators that surround The Spectrum, a twirling lump of coloured, geometric kitsch.

'This is a tremendously dynamic industry. It's great value for money; everyone can afford a cruise. Everything is done for you and the marketing is tremendous. The passengers see the ship as the destination,' claims Robert Stegina of the *Fantasy*. If this is so, what then is left for the ports of call? How much do customers spend on land if the ship becomes the centrepiece of the holiday?

Cruise lines argue that they make a major contribution to the economic well-being of the region. Their reasoning was most recently affirmed in a 1994 FCCA report which was carried out by accountants Price Waterhouse and was entitled 'The Economic Impact of the Passenger Cruise Industry on the Caribbean'. The survey claimed that the cruise industry pumps US$3.9 billion annually into the Caribbean region. Of this, US$845 million was contributed by the cruise lines; US$207 million by the crews; and US$2.9 billion by the passengers themselves.[28]

The survey was based on interviews with 500 passengers in February 1994 in six Caribbean ports (Nassau, Barbados, San Juan, St Thomas, Ocho Rios and Montego Bay) and one US port, Key West, Florida. The average expenditure per person per cruise was estimated at US$539, which worked out at an average of US$154 per person per port, based on a seven-day cruise and 3.5 destination calls per cruise.[29] Of the six Caribbean ports, the US Virgin Islands headed the list with a per person expenditure of US$372; next came Montego Bay, Jamaica (US$191); the Bahamas (US$155); Ocho Rios, Jamaica (US$138); Barbados (US$95); and San Juan, Puerto Rico (US$72). Key West, a curious choice, given that it is more a hub port than a port of call, averaged US$53.[30]

These figures were first presented at the FCCA's cruise conference in Barbados in October 1994, a timely occasion for the cruise industry to rebuild its relationship with the Caribbean after the difficulties arising out of the head tax row. The problem was that not everyone accepted these statistics.

A scathing attack came from sociologist Klaus de Albuquerque of the College of Charleston, South Carolina. Professor de Albuquerque questioned both Price Waterhouse's methodology and its conclusions. He made specific criticisms of the figures used in assessing the multiplier effect (the extent to which tourism spending filters through an economy); these, according to Professor de Albuquerque, inflated the indirect contribution made by the cruise industry to the region's economies. The FCCA had suggested that a cruise passenger's initial expenditure of US$100 produces, through successive rounds of spending, an 'expenditure induced impact' of US$250, or '2.5 times the initial expenditure'. This is far higher than is usually computed (see Chapter 2).[31]

Professor de Albuquerque also pointed out that the Price Waterhouse figures for passenger expenditure were 55 per cent higher than the figures it prepared in 1992 in an earlier report, and, indeed, far higher than other estimates made by tourist boards and the Economist Intelligence Unit at around the same time.[32] For example, in the 1994 report the US Virgin Islands figure of US$372 is 80 per cent higher than the 1992 report figure of US$209.13. That again was way above the Economist Intelligence Unit's figure, which stood at US$139. Similarly, passenger spend for Ocho Rios and Montego Bay stood at US$138 and US$191 respectively in the 1994 report. This, the report noted, was a 41 per cent and a 95 per cent increase respectively over the 1992 report figure, which totalled US$98, for an unspecified Jamaican port or ports.[33] In any case, the US$98 figure in the 1992 report was far higher than that given in a detailed Organization of American States report on the Jamaican tourist industry, which estimated an average US$51.55 cruise passenger expenditure figure in 1992.[34]

Professor de Albuquerque concluded that either 'something extraordinary' had been happening to cruise-passenger spending patterns, or the 1994 survey (which in any case had not used the same ports as in 1992) was based on a number of errors 'including a bias toward surveying higher spending passengers in high expenditure ports'. It was like comparing apples with oranges, he remarked.[35]

A further breakdown of expenditure in the survey showed that 45 per cent of passenger onshore expenditure went on duty-free shopping, 17 per cent on tours and attractions and 8 per cent on food. This showed a similar pattern to earlier studies which showed that duty-free shopping captured much of the cruise passengers' budget. In the US Virgin Islands, for example, 80 per cent of the total spent by cruise passengers ashore went on shopping, while according to a survey in Martinique, a medium-sized cruise destination, more than half of the US$42 per capita expenditure went on shopping, much of that being on duty-free items such as perfume, clothes, jewellery and alcohol.

Moreover, another FCCA survey, by Market Facts Inc., proffered the information that every cruise passenger spent US$363 on duty-free shopping, based on 1993 passenger figures. If this survey can be compared to the 1994 Price Waterhouse report, which revealed total onshore expenditure of US$539 per passenger per cruise, then it could be estimated that some 67 per cent of all cruise-passenger expenditure is on duty-free goods. What the survey does not point out, however, is one crucial point: duty-free goods have, according to the Economist Intelligence Unit, 'relatively low local value-added' power. This in itself would significantly decrease the multiplier effect.

Another reason why the Caribbean is sometimes suspicious of the cruise industry is that, compared to land-based tourism, its financial contribution to the regional tourism industry is low. Jean Holder of the CTO calculated its share at 10 per cent in 1993,[36] while the Economist Intelligence Unit plumped for 6 per cent in 1990.[37] Even in the Bahamas, the largest of the cruise destinations, where cruise arrivals (more than 2 million) outstrip stayover tourists, Director of Tourism Vincent Vanderpool-Wallace puts the cruise industry's contribution at only 10 per cent of the total. Martinique, with 429,000 cruise visitors in 1993, estimated the figure at 6.2 per cent.[38] Jamaica's 1994 Organization of American States report concluded that cruise-ship passengers contributed only 3.6 per cent of tourist expenditure, 'more than a quarter of which was for goods at in-bond stores which contribute little to the economy'.[39]

Big Business

Conflicting statistics, major leakages of spending, especially of duty-free goods, and a generally low contribution to the overall income generated by tourism in the Caribbean are themselves indicators of the economic limitations of the cruise industry. But even more fundamentally, who earns the money spent by the cruise industry? Who benefits from the government's expenditure on port and shopping facilities and such expenses as extra police security?

The cruise-ship disembarkation points, with their car rentals, taxi services, helicopters and tour-operator booths all under one roof, are largely controlled either by transnational chains, by local élites or by established expatriates. These groups make private contracts with the cruise lines to act as their agents; they also own many of the retail outlets.

In Barbados, for example, the new Bridgetown Cruise Terminal opened in January 1994. A joint venture between the port authority, three local companies (Cave Shepherd, Harrison's and Beer & Beverage Ltd) and the public (25 per cent of the shares), its financial structure was criticized by, among others, Professor Hilary Beckles of the University of the West Indies at Cave Hill. 'Those three companies have used their position to franchise to the duty-free outlets. They have restructured the white corporate structure of Broad Street [the capital's main shopping area] and duplicated it at the cruise terminal.' While chairman of the port authority, Edmund Harrison, has denied any such monopolization of the terminal, opportunities for the smaller entrepreneur appear to be limited. At the same time, the older Pelican Village, built in the 1970s as a centre for craft and other small-business initiatives, was acknowledged to be losing business to the smart new terminal, and its restaurant went into receivership in 1995.

The extent of the interlocking of interests between cruise ships and local big business at the expense of local small business is at the heart of the debate about the cruise industry's economic contribution to the region.

Complaints by small businesses in the Cayman Islands, for instance, illustrate this particular issue. In 1994, taxi-drivers, watersports businesses and tour operators threatened to hold anti-cruise-ship demonstrations if their grievances were not addressed. The main complaint of the Committee against Cruise Ship Abuse of Local Watersports/Taxi Owners was that cruise lines pre-booked passengers on island and watersports tours with a few, foreign-controlled companies. 'Small operators like us do not have the financial resources, marketing infrastructure or contacts to approach the cruise lines in Miami,' said chairman Ron Ebanks. Cruise passengers were charged US$30 by the cruise ships for a snorkelling trip that was minutes from the cruise dock and where equipment could be rented at the site from local suppliers for US$8. Ebanks also charged that cruise ships told passengers not to use local taxis but to take a tour sold on board.[40]

There have been similar complaints from small retailers in Nassau and Freeport in the Bahamas, where T-shirt sellers claim that cruise-ship staff accompany cruisers on shopping trips, recommending certain stores which have paid for advertising space or which are big enough to offer concessions. The retailers allege that shopping is controlled by the few large outlets which have made financial deals with the cruise lines.

Such difficulties and the occasional insults and patronizing manner of some cruise officials have further confirmed suspicions that the cruise industry is a foreign-controlled body which seeks to make deals to its own advantage rather than in partnership with the Caribbean. While the immediate bitterness sparked off by the tax row had simmered down by the end of 1994, even the CTO's diplomatic Jean Holder remarked that while some cruise lines seek a partnership in co-operation, others 'seem to see the Caribbean simply as an area of exploitation for profit'.[41]

Whatever the temperature of the relationship, cruise companies remain fierce and powerful competitors. They also spend large sums in promoting themselves. In 1993 alone, the two giant companies, Carnival and Royal Caribbean, spent almost US$82 million on advertising. (Compare this to the US$12 million spent on the CTO's first regional US campaign in 1993.) Behind the campaigns is the 'concept', which was spelled out by Bob Dickinson of Carnival Cruise Lines when he listed six aspects of the cruise 'product' which, he said, were superior to a land-based holiday: value for money; a 'trouble-free' environment; excellent food; the 'romance of the sea'; superior activities and entertainment; and 'an atmosphere of pampering service'.[42]

These factors are emphasized in cruise advertising, a constant presence on North American television and in the print media. And cruise-ship brochures dazzle with descriptions of a life of luxury on board. 'Sail with us in 1994, and you'll discover a world of attentive service and courtesy you simply cannot find ashore,' boasts a P&O brochure. As FCCA executive director Michelle Paige told *Caribbean Week*, the passengers require excellent service on land because they are accustomed to the high standards on board. The Caribbean, she said, 'could do a better job of providing a better service'.[43]

The Princess brochure, for instance, exudes self-congratulation: pampering includes a 'fluffy white bathrobe' and 'delicious *petits fours* to welcome you to your cabin and a foil-wrapped chocolate left on your pillow each night'. Then there is the gala buffet, which, according to the same brochure, is an 'ingenious display of gastronomic artistry that's a tribute to the skills of ice-carving and sugar-sculpture .... But for sheer flamboyance, nothing can match the Champagne Waterfall, a glittering pyramid of 600 glasses with bubbly cascading from top to bottom. Magnifique! And the perfect introduction to the night ahead ...'

Petits fours, ice-carvings and champagne waterfalls have little to do with the Caribbean but if the ship is the destination, the Caribbean itself loses relevance except as a vague and shimmering backdrop. Or, as Carnival's Bob Dickinson puts it: 'The limited number of countries and ports offered is not a deterrent to Carnival customers; after all the ship is the attraction, not the port of call.'[44]

Both the covert message of the cruise industry and its upfront promotional material compare cruise tourism favourably to land-based tourism. 'Should anyone be in doubt that the cruise ships are in competition with us, the attached photocopy of a Royal Caribbean advertisement should set their mind at rest,' was the curt memorandum sent by John Bell, executive vice-president of the Caribbean Hotel Association, to his board of directors and member hotel associations in 1994. The advertisement was headed 'Why A Hotel Should Be Your Last Resort', and the introductory blurb began:

> There's not a lobby on earth that can stack up to the Centrum on a Royal Caribbean ship. Now compare all that a Royal Caribbean cruise offers versus a typical resort and you'll stop pretty quickly. There just is no comparison .... A Royal Caribbean cruise ship is a resort of the very first order. Choosing anything less should be your last resort.

The cruise lines combine that sort of aggressive promotion with a hard-sell system to retailers. Nearly all cruises in the US market are sold through travel agents who are visited by armies of sales representatives. The commission on sales paid to the agents tends to be higher than that paid for hotel-based holidays. At the same time, the cruise business has been discounting, anxious to fill the berths and so maintain its high occupancy rates. Carnival's pricing strategy is budgeted for an amazing 100 per cent occupancy, which means that for the moment prices can be kept down. Caribbean hotels are unable to respond.

While some cruise analysts have pondered the wisdom of the rampant expansion in ships and berths, the big cruise lines continue to report healthy figures. Increasingly the giant lines are becoming an oligarchy as economies of scale push out the smaller operators. P&O, for example, announced an increase in half-year profits of 52 per cent in 1994, with profits from its cruise division rising from US$51 million in 1993 to US$63.75 million in 1994. Similarly, Carnival had record revenues and net income in the first quarter of 1994, attributed to additional capacity and improvement in passenger yields.[45]

And the passengers, mainly American, keep on coming, and no longer are they just the old and the rich. The market is changing: the young are being targeted by advertising and are responding. Before 1989, 29 per cent of first-time cruisers were between 25 and 40 years of age; that age group now represents nearly half of first-time cruisers, and it is that sector which is expected to grow, to take longer vacations and to spend more. The average age of the passengers surveyed by the FCCA in 1994 was 41.9 years. Cruises now attract honeymooners and families. Other 'niche' markets such as conference cruises and theme cruises around sports, music and education are on the increase.

The cruise lines argue that they market the Caribbean as well as the ship. A cruise, they say, provides an introduction to the region, a floating showcase for the charms of the Caribbean. One study suggested that up to 25 per cent of stayover tourists had first sampled their holiday choice from the rails of a cruise ship. Another survey indicated that 40 per cent of cruise passengers would like to return to the Caribbean for a land-based holiday.

The Caribbean often misses opportunities to entice cruisers back on to dry-land holidays, say the cruise lines. According to the FCCA's Michelle Paige, only one Caribbean destination, the Cayman Islands, responded to an FCCA request to provide a promotional video to be shown to cruisers before they arrived at port. Destinations, she says, do not package themselves as well as they could or advertise their attractions. 'If we don't make the passengers feel comfortable, they are going to get right back on the ship.'[46]

Possibilities of partnership, stressed by both the CTO and the FCCA in their more conciliatory moods, have begun to be explored in marketing, employment strategies, sourcing and so on. There is also much talk within the region of a more concerted approach towards the unresolved problems presented by the cruise industry. A regional cruise tourism committee, as suggested by the CTO, could increase overall benefits as well as presenting a united front to the mighty cruise lines. Yet the introduction of some sort of licensing system for cruise ships in which contracts and guidelines would be observed on both sides seems far away. In the meantime, the cruise lines are often perceived as using the Caribbean islands as a chain of low-charge 'parking lots', coming and going as they see fit.

Of course, the cruise lines are not the only users of the Caribbean Sea. There is a growing group of tourists who also use the sea as the focus of their holiday for waterskiing, surfing, windsurfing, fishing, sailing, diving or snorkelling. Fishing and sailing, chartered and bareboat, remain the up-market pursuits. Fishing, in particular, has been a sport for tourists from the early days, and it remains particularly popular in the Bahamas where record catches are made in deep-sea game fishing, while in the shallows fishing for barracuda and bonefish is popular.

The British Virgin Islands, one of the region's largest watersport destinations, stresses the attractions of its unspoilt islands and cays. 'One can imagine no better holiday for a fisherman than cruising in a motor-boat among the islands ... with food and conversation enriched from the day's catch,' enthused a circular from the West India Committee in 1921. Then, there was no mention of sailing, but by 1958, *McKay's Guide* mentioned that the islands had 'wonderful sailing in the waters off their coasts' and advised that: 'With time on your hands in St Thomas and a liking for the sea, you couldn't do better than to charter one of the many boats available for the purpose, and cruise among these islands for as many days as you can spare.' Ten years later, another guide book commented that 'this part of the Caribbean is becoming known as a yachtsman's paradise'.

The British Virgin Islands has forbidden obtrusive development, but encourages marinas and luxury secluded resorts. The main focus of development has been the yacht charter business, which began in 1967. There are now more than 300 yachts-for-hire out of the British Virgin Islands which makes it the largest, bareback charter fleet in the world. Charter yacht tourists outnumber hotel tourists and spend more money than them.[47]

Modern-style marinas now dot the Caribbean, hang-outs for a largely young, American clientele, who pay handsomely for a week's charter. For the yachties, the Caribbean is the fashionable place to be in the winter months when the sailing élite of the world converges on Martinique after the Route Du Rhum transatlantic run or St Lucia for Christmas following the Atlantic Rally for Cruisers. The regatta season then moves on to St Maarten, Puerto Rico and the Virgin Islands before ending in April, with Antigua's Sailing Week at English Harbour, where Nicholson's Yachtyard, an expatriate stronghold, was one of the first charter bases in the Caribbean in the 1940s.

The fishing, sailing and windsurfing tourists are different from the beach-based tourists. They tend to be more up-market, and traditionally, socially and racially select (in an island like Barbados this is still the case). However, at another level, they are more informal than other tourists. On Bequia, for example, the yachties, who cultivate a lotus-eating manner, hang around St Elizabeth Bay and its bars, which are owned by bare-footed expatriates. Whereas the tourist establishment eyes the boat people with some suspicion (they may be rich but they are scruffy), the yachties themselves appear less affronted by authentic Caribbean life than the nervous package tourists. In any case, they make a significant, and direct, contribution to island economies, depending on local people for provisions and information. In many cases, farmers supply direct to sailors at the marinas. In Grenada, for example, a small farming co-operative relies on business with sailors for its success and expansion (see Chapter 3).

However, much of the ownership of watersports business is in expatriate hands. This is partly because of the capital expenditure involved and partly because of the ambivalent nature of the relationship of Caribbean peoples to the sea. While the sea is all around them, and while as fishermen and boatbuilders they are linked to it, they have not traditionally seen it as a place to be exploited for sport. Hence, watersport tourism has been run by and for white foreigners; with some exceptions this remains largely the case, along with such subsidiary businesses as ships' chandlers and marine supermarkets.

Outsiders dominate both as employers and employees in the watersports business. The yacht charter owners tend to give jobs to other expatriates, often well-connected young men who spend the winter seeking work around Caribbean marinas. According to Jeremy Wright, who owns Boardsailing BVI and is chairman of the Caribbean Windsurfing Association: 'My business employs outsiders due to the skills required in looking after the tourists who arrive with differing abilities. I occasionally employ locals yet find that they generally do not get that excited in the teaching and the beach operation side of things. This is the opposite to the outsider who, of course, loves the chance to work in this environment.'

Diving and snorkelling have also emerged as an important niche market, for the Caribbean has some of the best diving in the world. Islands like Bonaire and the Cayman Islands, for instance, are long established and have promoted themselves almost exclusively as dive destinations. New destinations, like Dominica, are also beginning to build up their reputations.

Divers, like yachties, are adventurous, relatively wealthy and, most importantly, conscious of the environment. In the Bahamas, the Exuma National Park, administered by the Bahamas National Trust, has developed a 'support fleet' of yachties, who each contribute US$30 a year to its upkeep. Nick Wardle, of the National Trust, says that the well-being of the Park, the first in the Bahamas, relies on goodwill and that the scheme is a strong replenishment exercise. 'The Park is remote; we want to keep it like that. No one is allowed to take anything from it.'

The Caribbean Sea is the resource of all who use it. Yet it is under threat from a range of environmental problems, from dumping to sewage disposal and the destruction of reefs (see Chapter 5), and all its users, whether cruise ships or jetskiers, are to some extent to blame.

The only way to regulate the operations of cruise ships and to protect the marine environment would be to create regional regulatory bodies embracing every state on or bordering the Caribbean Sea. The Caribbean Tourist Organisation has, on many occasions, appealed to the region 'as a matter of urgency' to put together a joint environmental plan to regulate behaviour, enforce regulations and punish offenders. Other groupings, such as the Caribbean ecotourism conferences, have also called on the region to establish a body to safeguard the marine environment.

Meanwhile, the threat of the Caribbean Sea being used to transport nuclear waste has made the region even more aware that its waters are a vital component of its patrimony. As Jean Holder points out, the Caribbean has 'few resources left which give us any real bargaining power'.[48] One of those is the Caribbean Sea.

Notes

1. Associated Press, London, 25 December 1994.

2. Figures provided by Peter Wild of G.P. Wild (International) Ltd. The Caribbean Tourism Organization statistics show cruise-ship arrivals totalling more than 9 million: this represents the total number of disembarkations and not the total number of passengers.

3. *Lloyd's Ship Manager, Cruise and Ferry Review*, London, August/September 1994.

4. *New York Times*, New York, 15 June 1994.

5. *International Cruise Market Monitor*, G.P. Wild (International) Ltd, London, 1994.

6. *Lloyd's Ship Manager, op. cit.*

7. Caribbean Tourism Organization, *Caribbean Statistical News*, Barbados, 1995.

8. *Ibid.*

9. Jean Holder, 'Getting the Most from Cruise Tourism for the Caribbean', address to conference at Coopers Lybrand International, Barbados, 1993.

10. *Ibid.*

11. *Caribbean Week*, Barbados, 26 June 1993.

12. *Travel Trade News Edition*, 7 June 1993.

13. *Ibid.*

14. *Ibid.*

15. Holder, *op. cit.*

16. *Ibid.*

17. Price Waterhouse, 'The Economic Impact of the Passenger Cruise Industry on the Caribbean' FCCA, Florida, 1994.

18. *Ibid.*

19. FCCA, Newsletter, July 1994.

20. *Ibid.*

21. *Ibid.*

22. Edward G. Bollinger, vice-president of purchasing, properties and logistics, RCCL, address given to the CTO, San Juan, Puerto Rico, 9 July 1992.

23. *Caribbean Week*, 12–25 November 1994.

24. *The Democrat for St Kitts*, St Kitts, 26 March 1994.

25. *Caribbean Insight*, London, January 1995.

26. *Caribbean Travel News Europe*, Summer 1993.

27. Economist Intelligence Unit, *Tourism in the Caribbean*, London, 1993.

28. Price Waterhouse, 1994, *op. cit.*

29. *Ibid.*

30. *Ibid.*

31. *Caribbean Week*, 21 January-3 February 1995.

32. Economist Intelligence Unit, *op. cit.*

33. *Caribbean Week, op. cit.*

34. Organization of American States, *Economic Analysis of Tourism in Jamaica*, Washington DC, 1994.

35. *Caribbean Week, op. cit.*

36. Holder, *op. cit.*

37. Economist Intelligence Unit, *op. cit.*

38. Agence Régionale de Développement Touristique de la Martinique, *Principales données sur le tourisme à la Martinique*, Martinique, 1993.

39. Organization of American States, *op. cit.*

40. Caribbean News Agency, 5 November 1994.

41. Holder, *op. cit.*

42. Robert Dickinson, 'Cruise Industry Outlook in the Caribbean' in Dennis Gayle and Jonathan Goodrich (eds), *Tourism, Marketing and Management in the Caribbean*, London, 1993, p. 118.

43. *Caribbean Week*, 12–25 November 1994.

44. Dickinson, *op. cit.*

45. *International Cruise Market Monitor, op. cit.*

46. CANA, 26 May 1994.

47. James W. Lett, 'Ludic and Liminoid Aspects of Charter Yacht Tourism in the Caribbean', *Annals of Tourism Research*, vol. 10, 1983, pp. 35–56.

48. Jean Holder, 'Regional Integration, Tourism and Caribbean Sovereignty', mimeo, 1993.

CHAPTER 8

Reclaiming the Heritage Trail:

Culture and Identity

'Island in the Sun' was the first number featured in the finale of Jubilation, the nightly show at the Crystal Palace Resort and Casino at Nassau's 'fabled' Cable Beach where white America is urged to 'sway to Caribbean rhythms as our Las Vegas-style revue takes on a tropical twist'. The backdrop, which had been changed for the finale, was a stretch of blue sea with a cruise ship on the horizon.

On came the male dancers in striped trousers, one on roller-skates, the prelude to the arrival of a topless female dancer, who was wheeled on to the stage lounging on a large plastic banana, waving merrily. After the gentle melody of 'Island in the Sun', the music changed to the soca number 'Dollar', and finally to 'Don't Worry, Be Happy', with the dancers in jaunty holiday hats and flowing chiffon scarves. A 'pantomime dame' waddled across the stage dressed as a large-breasted, big-bottomed black woman in a faded cotton frock, sneakers and wig.

The last number was announced by a blonde-haired singer as an expression of 'our Bahamian culture'. Musicians paraded, drumming and blowing cowbells, horns and whistles, while dancers appeared in costume in a stage recreation of the Bahamas' great post-Christmas festival, Junkanoo. Meanwhile, because it was December and Junkanoo fever was at its height, a group of waiters came down the aisle, also dancing, blowing on whistles, sounding cowbells and beating drums, to great applause.

Like the Crystal Palace Resort itself, Jubilation may be in the Caribbean but it is not of the Caribbean. It was two hours of high-class American kitsch, its gesture to the Bahamas taking place in those final minutes.

The icons of the Caribbean were the songs, which were labelled 'a medley of island songs'. There was 'Island in the Sun', written by the Jamaican singer Harry Belafonte as the title song of the film of the same name in 1957. It is now an instantly recognizable anthem played to tourists all over the Anglophone Caribbean. The other two songs have different origins: the soca 'Dollar' became a commercial success for the Trinidadian singer Taxi and, in the early 1990s was a dance favourite all over the region and beyond, while 'Don't Worry, Be Happy' with its calypso rhythms comes, in fact, from the 1988 film *Cocktail*, and was written by Bobby McFerrin, the black American singer, and sung with a 'Caribbean accent'.

The finale, with its holiday atmosphere and references to beaches, nudity and fun, used the banana (no joke in the region) and the cruise ship as the emblems of the Caribbean as well as the music. Of the dancers, more than half were local, including the dancer who introduced 'our Bahamian culture' number and the Junkanoo musicians. One of the male dancers played the 'mammy', the market woman, a comforting black figure of unthreatening fun, with a feeling more of white folk memories of the American south than of the Caribbean.

Into that culturally deracinated programme came the Junkanoo waiters in their working uniforms (appropriately enough because to dress up before Junkanoo violates tradition). As if 'rushing' on the streets of Nassau, their performance was rooted in their own experience and history. They even managed to upstage the main performance.

Jubilation illustrated the two polarities of cultural expression as 'shown' to tourists in the Caribbean. The first was the formal, expensive, foreign-driven performance which is put on to please visitors, to reinforce the tourists' perceptions of the Caribbean and to give them what the Caribbean thinks they want. The second was the informal (if not spontaneous) display of local creativity by the waiters which in form represents the fusion of cultural influences (in this case from Africa and Europe) and in content remains a function of rebellion, of resistance against authority.

Jubilation (and similar representations) threaten, at many levels, to overwhelm the Caribbean with its slick otherness and metropolitan tastes. In many instances, tourism has bred cultural decline despite the efforts of those who are attempting to reclaim control. 'We are busy fighting the mentality that says that if it's not required by tourists or liked by them then it's not needed. Because if we don't stop it, we don't have anything left to give our children,' says Kim Outten of the Pompey Museum, Nassau. The most recent struggle for the Caribbean has been both to nurture its indigenous art forms, to create and perform for its own peoples, amid the demands of tourism, while at the same time finding imaginative ways of 'using' tourists as patrons rather than being used by them. Indeed, there are now significant points at which the interaction between tourism and Caribbean culture has created a new dynamic.

The Intangible Heritage

The genesis and expression of Caribbean culture throughout the region have been shaped by a shared experience of history: of European colonization, indigenous destruction, slavery, indentureship, the struggles for freedom, migration and independence. Those experiences have made for societies where everything and everyone which reached Caribbean shores has been creolized, that is, transformed into being part of a Caribbean identity. That force represents part of the region's creative genius and its strength.

However, most of the Caribbean (with the notable exception of post-revolutionary Cuba) has also suffered from a sense of inferiority. As William Demas, then president of the Caribbean Development Bank, said in a 1973 address to students in Jamaica: 'The deep and disturbing identity problem remains. The problem is ... one of not recognising that we as a people have many features of uniqueness – that is to say, a basis upon which a sense of identity can be built. It is fundamentally a typical West Indian problem of lack of self-confidence.'[1]

In the 1970s, awareness of such problems was sharpened by the recent or imminent independence of most Anglophone countries and a subsequent birth of nationhood, by the civil rights and Black Power movements in the USA and by the tensions generated by the Cold War. And as the growing tourist industry made increasing claims on the region, there was alarm about cultural dependency, the way in which the region's beliefs and values appeared to be determined by North America. This process followed the long-time cultural conditioning by Europe through colonization. The Caribbean, it was argued, was not defined by its own peoples, but by tourists and others according to their own needs and perceptions of sun-baked islands. This cultural standard-setting by metropolitan interests was linked to the Caribbean's political and economic dependence. As Demas said in an address to the University of Guyana in 1970, the 'New Caribbean Man' must 'devise ways and means of reducing the negative aspects of the metropolitan impact on the New Caribbean Society'; this society must be 'selective in its contacts with the metropolis – no less in economics, than in ideology, culture and values'.[2]

The Caribbean was in danger of becoming in thrall to North America and Europe in a recreation of colonialism and the plantation system by other means. This imitation of the metropole (as described by the Trinidadian V.S. Naipaul in his novel *The Mimic Men*) was what the Bahamian-born actor Sidney Poitier experienced when he returned home one year after the Bahamas gained its independence in 1973. He wrote in his 1980 autobiography, *This Life*:

*It disturbed me deeply that there was no cultural life expressing the his-
tory of the people — absolutely none. I did see wood carvings, but they
were imported from Haiti to sell to tourists in The Bahamas... It was
tourism, so enormously successful over the years, that had contaminated —
diluted — debased — the shape of all things cultural in those islands, until
there was no longer any real semblance of a Bahamian cultural identity.
People even danced to Bahamian musicians playing other people's music —
Jamaican music or American artificial calypso music; tunes from the
American hit parade or the American 'soul' top ten.*[3]

Nearly a quarter of a century on from Demas' warnings and Poitier's
lament, much nation-building has been done and achievements in all art
forms have been recognized, not just regionally but internationally.
There are the visual arts of Jamaica, Haiti, Cuba, Guyana; the great
cultural festivals, now known as the festival arts, of Carnival and Junkanoo; the internationally acclaimed music of reggae, calypso, salsa, mer-
engue and zouk; a fine body of literature (including St Lucia's Derek
Walcott, the Nobel Prize winner); and a vibrant folk culture and customs
that are recognized and encouraged. The expression of all this cultural
activity has, since 1971, found an outlet in the regional festival, Carifesta,
pioneered by Guyana's former President, Forbes Burnham, and held, at
intervals, in different countries of the Caribbean. Yet, despite such
achievement, the shadow of dependency remains.

Much of what is admired within the Caribbean and is seen to be
'better' remains foreign (usually North American), whether in design,
technology, food or the visual arts. And while the tourists continue to
flock in, the leaders of the tourist industry, whether local or foreign, have
seemed generally unconcerned to protect the authenticity of Caribbean
dance forms, carvings or architectural detail.

A fundamental reason for such neglect is that the Caribbean tourist
industry does not depend on castles, ancient buildings, art galleries and
museums. The Caribbean's cultural forms are not on display as they are
in Venice or Prague, Delhi or Cairo. Such formal, urban environments
are not the common currency of the Caribbean tourist industry. The
heritage business has been a late arrival and only recently a tool for
tourism.

Meanwhile the 'people's culture', more vulnerable and diffuse, has
been at risk, sometimes appearing to be flattened into the all-purpose
caricature: a smiling guitarist in a Hawaiian shirt crooning 'Jamaica
Farewell', with its chorus line 'I Left My Little Girl in Kingston Town'
(to be adapted to Nassau town or Castries town or whatever town is
relevant). As Professor Elliott Parris, of Howard University, noted in

1983: 'If we ignore our history and the cultural legacy that it has left us, we run the risk of developing tourism as an industry which puts the dollar first and our people last. We are saying to ourselves, perhaps unconsciously: we are the field labourers on the modern plantation of the tourist industry.'[4]

A decade later the 'modern plantation' continues. Reg Samuel is the research officer in Antigua's Ministry of Culture. His is one of the voices raised against the impact of the tourist industry on his island, blaming it for the loss and degradation of what is unique to Antigua and its history. 'Tourism has impacted on us very seriously,' he says. 'Our total lifestyle – art, food, music, dress, architecture, celebrations – has been altered. We have lost our character.' He argues that Antigua tries to please tourists by giving them what they know. 'We try to imitate Americans and their ways. We give the impression that what tourists want is what they have and not what we have. Let the tourist know what we have'.

In music, for example, Samuel points out that the steel band, which arrived in Antigua early on with returning oil workers from Trinidad, has been neglected or lost its way, while other musical forms have virtually disappeared. 'We have distinctive forms such as the iron band, which emerged in the 1940s, played with hub caps. The tourist should be hearing this particular music that's unique to Antigua.'

Instead, tourists are offered Heritage Quay, a modern duty-free complex of boutiques and souvenir shops, which promotes itself with a poster for 'a night of Antiguan culture' with 'steel band, limbo dancers, gambling, children performing, late evening shopping.' Such entertainment is common in Antigua where, according to Tim Hector, Opposition Senator and editor of *Outlet* newspaper, young people have been 'ripped from any rootedness in a folk culture'. Instead, wrote Hector, 'Folk culture has become a marketable commodity, readily and monotonously packaged as Yellow Bird, limbo without meaning, except as tourist entertainment, steelbands which now draw no response from the people for whom the music is produced, and a national dish which is really Kentucky and Fries. A culture has been turned on its head.'[5]

Antigua's disregard for its own identity is perhaps more acute than anywhere else in the Caribbean. This is partly the result of its small size, the nature of its tourist industry (largely foreign-controlled, dominated by expatriates and investors and linked to organized crime) and the debased character of its government. Antigua demonstrates the ease with which cultural patrimony becomes threatened.

Antigua is not alone. Other countries, in particular in the Anglophone Caribbean and the Dutch territories, have also failed to define themselves clearly to tourists. As a result, tourists have retained the power to create their own (often uninformed) images of the Caribbean. The whole region thus becomes a homogenized whole, its contrasts and distinctive heritages either neglected or lost.

The successful export of calypso, salsa and reggae to the USA and Europe has meant that those musical forms have become standard-bearers of Caribbean culture. The negative effect of this achievement has been to put at risk the lesser known and more fragile forms of regional music, such as Antigua's iron band and the big drums of Carriacou. On Grenada's tiny sister island Carriacou, Big Drum, three *lapeau cabrit* (goat skin) drums, is the traditional musical form. Yet when the cruise ships call, it is a steel band which goes on board to entertain: the steel band rather than the unique Big Drum has become the sound of Carriacou.

Using 'culture' as an ingredient of a tourist industry means work for performers and artists. Much of the entertainment is in hotels which put on musical evenings and floor shows and sometimes buy local paintings and carvings. Once on cruise ships or in hotels, music, dance and art tend to become part of a safe suburban environment. Like the licensed street vendors, the performers who work the hotels have to respond to the requirements of the hoteliers: they shape the tourist experience by deciding who should perform what. 'The people who run the industry are from a different culture and totally disregard our culture,' says one prominent St Lucian. 'They do not breathe down our neck, but there is a reluctance to perform anything that might raise difficulties.'

Hotel entertainment may well be the only expression of Caribbean culture offered to tourists. Along with 'saloon' reggae, steel band, and sometimes jazz, what the tourist brochures call 'native' floor shows are the most common form of hotel entertainment. These sometimes consist of a fashion show interspersed with 'exotic' dancing which may include fire-eating, limbo dancing and glass-breaking. While there is some evidence that limbo dancing is a legacy of the Middle Passage (the journey from Africa to the Caribbean), the 'native' show versions have long lost any validity, while fire-eating is usually dismissed as degrading nonsense. A lack of authenticity plagues most tourist shows all over the Third World, and the Caribbean is no exception.

In Barbados, a twice-weekly show called '1627 and All That' ('a spectacular cultural feast') takes place in the courtyard of the Museum. In a package which includes a free tour of the Museum, a 'sumptuous Barbadian buffet dinner' and a complimentary bar, the show is a private-sector initiative employing local dance groups. Alissandra Cummins, the Museum's director, has some reservations about the production. It is, she says, 'better than some shows which have no relevance at all to Barbadian culture. However, I'm not totally comfortable with what they produce.' There are elements which may come from other Caribbean cultures but are not Barbadian, she adds, and while there is 'a generous attribution to Africa', it is non-specific.

The sort of compromises imposed (or allowed) by tourism in the representation of a culture is of concern to those who seek to protect and develop it. Raymond Lawrence, Dominica's Chief Cultural Officer, has observed what has happened to other countries who have lost many of their indigenous forms through pandering to the tourist. Dominica needs to 'learn from the experience of others', he says. 'We need to strengthen Dominica's folk traditions so that authenticity can be kept when tourism hits us in a big way.' What concerns Lawrence is to continue to 'present ourselves authentically to ourselves'. He hopes that financial rewards will not tempt groups to 'dilute their presentations with dances shortened to become something without value'. *Belé*, for example, a dance in which the dancer performs to the drummer, cannot, explains Lawrence, be turned in to a 'hello' entertainment in which performers play to an audience. 'We want to keep it that way.'

Even more remote from the typical 'floor show' than the intimacy of Dominica's *belé* are, of course, Haiti's voodoo ceremonies. Before Haiti's tourist industry collapsed in the early 1980s, voodoo performances were put on for visitors. At one voodoo centre outside Port-au-Prince, for example, two-hour-long shows were put on six nights a week. Although voodoo tourism contained all the elements of a staged performance, with an entrance fee, stage and waiters serving drinks, the nature of Haitian culture blurs the edges between 'real' and 'false' and between theatre and religion. The shows were described by an anthropologist, Alan Goldberg:

> *The ceremony begins with songs for the particular spirits being called that night. The first episode of spirit possession behaviour occurs about 10.40, usually featuring the sacrifice of a pigeon which is dispatched when the possessed person bites its head off. After the first spirit is sent away another possession may occur or an intermission may mark the end of the first part of the show.*

Although performed for tourists (albeit far removed from the typical package tourists), the performers allowed the event to 'become converted into a situation of staged authenticity', according to Goldberg. The existence of a tourist audience did not in itself invalidate the experience.[6]

Street Culture

If voodoo tourism can fill that grey area between the staged and the authentic, so, in many ways, can the other great cultural set-pieces of the

Caribbean, its public street festivals – Carnival, Junkanoo (Bahamas), Crop-Over (Barbados), Christmas Sports (St Kitts) and Mashramani (Guyana). These annual flowerings of music, dance, theatre, language and costume have long histories; most are rooted in the Caribbean's experience of slavery and liberation. To what extent, however, have they flourished or withered at the hands of the marketing departments of tourist boards? Or, indeed, do they and can they ignore tourism?

The best-known, biggest and most visually extravagant of all is the Trinidad Carnival, which takes place on the Monday and Tuesday before Ash Wednesday. The two days of street bacchanal date from emancipation and represent a great outpouring of black dissent and resistance through mockery, satire and display as well as commentary on contemporary life. As Gordon Lewis described it: 'From its opening moment of *jour ouvert* and the "ole mas" costume bands to its finale, forty-eight hours later, in the dusk of Mardi Carnival, the Trinidadian populace gives itself up to the "jump up", the tempestuous abandon of Carnival.'[7]

Richer, more naturally endowed and diversified than other economies, Trinidad has never bothered much with tourism. So Carnival in Trinidad was neither created for tourists nor has it been recreated for them like Crop-Over in Barbados, or become a distant shadow, as in St Thomas. Trinidad's Carnival has robustly retained its own identity.

Yet it has changed over the years, and it has been influenced by tourism. Even before the Second World War, Carnival organizers had an eye on the tourist market. In 1939, the Carnival Improvement Committee was established, an offshoot of what was called the new Tourist and Exhibitions Board. Its aim was to 'lift Carnival', to make it 'one of the star attractions of the tourist season'. Some calypsonians composed on this theme: Attila, for example, wrote that tourists 'get happy and gay', finding Trinidad 'a paradise on earth/that is what the tourists say'.[8]

Beneath the welcoming patter, however, there was another issue on the Carnival Improvement Committee's agenda. Its aim was to censor Carnival, to clean it up, to make it more decorous and less wild. In 1951, to the list of annual Carnival don'ts (such as don't dress in an immodest or scanty costume and don't sing any immoral or suggestive tunes) was added: 'Don't forget that visitors are in your midst. Give them the best impression of the festival.'[9] This development, according to Trinidadian writer Lawrence Scott, was 'about how organisers wanted Carnival to be presented to the outside world – it was an awareness of what others think of us'.

Middle-class tastes were also behind commercializing trends in the 1950s when company sponsorship first became a significant element of

Carnival. The merchants (as in most Caribbean countries, the white and light-skinned élite) sought to take control of Carnival by putting it on Port of Spain's central open space, the Savannah, with expensive seating and big prizes, at the expense of the street calypsonians and road-marchers. The calypsonians retaliated. Sparrow's 'Carnival Boycott' pointed out that it was calypso that was the 'root' of Carnival and steelband the 'foot'.[10]

Forty years on, Carnival in the 1990s has competitions for calypso, pan and thousand-strong costume bands, all sharing in the glory, and all required set-pieces. Television rights, sponsorship from big business, recording opportunities, big prizes, expensive seats, pricey costumes and overseas marketing have contributed to a certain reduction in spontaneity. Yet Carnival remains at the centre of the nation's psyche, an expression of Trinidad's nationhood. It is a lure for Trinidadians from overseas and other Caribbean nationals more than it is for tourists.

There are other smaller, less spectacular, Lenten carnivals around the region, mainly in predominantly Catholic islands, such as Martinique and Dominica. As in Trinidad's Port of Spain, these carnivals are urban experiences and as such now have a commercial input. Yet although there are those who lament the passing of the 'good old days', regional carnivals retain their roots and many of their rituals. They are local celebrations where tourists are welcome to observe or even join in. But, as in Trinidad, tourists are peripheral. The village festivals commemorating saints' days, celebrated in Dominica, for example, are entirely local affairs as are the rural festivals of La Rose and La Marguerite in St Lucia.

In the Bahamas, the equivalent to Carnival is Junkanoo, a Christmas festival. Junkanoo (also known in Jamaica as John Canoe) reaches back to Africa, probably linked to the legendary John Konny, an eighteenth-century tribal leader from the Gold Coast; and like Carnival it remains an expression of freedom, associated with acts of rebellion and challenge. Its history is also dotted with instances of threats by colonial authorities to ban the 'rush' down Nassau's business centre, Bay Street. Yet the parade of costumes, once made of sacking and sponges and now of cardboard and coloured crepe paper, and the hundreds-strong bands with goat-skin drums, cowbells and trumpets, have flourished and have become a magnificent, home-grown attraction created for and performed by groups of Bahamians for themselves. The groups represent communities with a strong sense of belonging and collective identity; in this way, tourists are almost entirely excluded from participation, their role being to observe, enjoy and spend money among the crowds of Nassau and Freeport, the two main Junkanoo locations.

Yet this spectator role of the tourist has been crucial to the survival of Junkanoo. Gail Saunders, director of the Bahamas archives, believes that without tourism Junkanoo might have died out. She dates the first impact of tourism on Junkanoo from the late 1940s when Sir Stafford Sands, the first head of the Bahamas Development Board, put some money into the festival. The white colonial élite recognized the attractions to tourists of the African Junkanoo festival and provided it with an economic framework which enabled the bands to become organized and more ambitious. In 1958, an American guide book wrote: 'costumed and masked natives dance ancient rhythms and parade .... A real experience – don't miss it.'[11]

In the 1960s, Junkanoo was also given an extra impetus by the involvement of young middle-class Bahamian artists inspired by Black Power and the anti-colonial movement. Jackson Burnside, a Bahamian architect and artist who designs for the Saxons Superstars band, recalled, 'In Junkanoo I found how it had grown from Africa, but beyond Africa – into something that is ours, only ours. In the process, it happens to be the best show on earth.'[12] Through the nexus of community, business and tourism, Junkanoo in the Bahamas has reasserted itself. While it has changed through tourism, it is seen to have done so without compromising its integrity.

On the other side of the Caribbean, the festival of Crop-Over in Barbados is another example of how tourism realigns traditional festivals. Crop-Over evolved from the celebration of the end of the sugar-cane harvest by both planters and slaves. By the end of the nineteenth century it had developed into a procession of carts, decorated with flowers and coloured material, bearing the last of the canes into the plantation yard. After the labourers had paraded with an effigy of Mr Harding, a figure whom they sometimes burnt, there was dancing and music. However, with the decline in sugar and the arrival of more modern forms of entertainment, Crop-Over was all but dead by the 1940s, only to be revived in 1964 by the Board of Tourism.

According to the authoritative *A–Z of Barbadian Heritage*, 'the present-day festival is very different from the old-time Crop Over'.[13] What has happened is that it has become a four-week summer festival (traditionally the low tourist season), transformed by business sponsorship and the marketing machinations of tourism officials into a sequence of organized events such as calypso, king and queen of the crop competitions and a carnival-style parade called Kadooment. The ghosts of Crop-Over past are witnessed in the parade of decorated carts. But the parade has become 'commoditized'. 'Corporate Barbados benefits enormously from Crop Over; it is something that is mutually beneficial,' says the chief cultural officer of the National Cultural Foundation, the organizer of Crop-Over. 'We would like to see corporate Barbados advertising, using, for example, the decorated cart parade as a medium for advertising.'[14]

Other devices are used to maximize the tourist potential of indigenous local festivals, sometimes with damaging consequences. One is to move traditional celebrations from Christmas to summer. Antigua's carnival, for example, was deliberately conceived in 1957 to boost tourist arrivals during the slack season (May to July); now it has been moved to July/August (also a slow tourist period) to coincide with the anniversary of Emancipation. Without the Christmas celebrations and parades, the traditional figures, such as John Bull, the clowns and mocojumbies also disappeared.

Festivals are also invented to boost the range of tourist attractions and, by definition, tourist numbers. In the Cayman Islands, Pirates Week was coined at the end of the 1970s to take place at the end of October, again a slow tourist period. This carnival-style entertainment has become a national event, an excuse for costumes, parades and partying. In the Bahamas, Goombay (probably from a Malian word for festival) was invented by the Tourist Board as a Friday night street dance and then became limited to the summer (again an attraction for the low tourist season), an occasion for performances, food and craft.

Whatever their derivation and history, however deep or shallow their cultural roots, Caribbean festivals have remained, for the most part, a celebration that depends on the participation of local people. As much as anything, this may be a function of their location on the streets. The jump-up in Gros Islet, St Lucia, is an interesting example. Started as a local, small-business initiative, it has become a successful institution in which locals and tourists mix every Friday night on the streets of the village for music, food and drink.

Other 'cultural events' have been launched in response to tourism. When they are rooted in the community like Jamaica's Sunsplash, they tend to succeed; where they depend on tourist patronage and thus reflect tourist tastes, as with St Lucia's Jazz Festival, their success is less assured.

Sunsplash, the great annual celebration of reggae, began with a group of Jamaican businessmen who created a company called Synergy to promote reggae. Since the first Sunsplash in 1976, each year up to 100,000 people, both tourists and Jamaican, have attended the week-long event. Its achievement has been to keep the faith of its original function, to be a showcase for reggae, both homegrown and from overseas. 'The Jamaicans are proud that other countries are interested in playing reggae,' says David Roddigan, the British DJ, who has followed the fortunes of Sunsplash for many years. 'It has never compromised itself. The organisers have played it from their hearts – they are committed to the concept of Sunsplash.'

Threats to its future have come not from tourism, but from a forced change of venue and Jamaican business politics. Its first home was Montego Bay, a perfect location for tourists, for Jamaicans who would take their own holiday there and for the reggae industry. Yet in 1993, Sunsplash was forced to move from Montego Bay to Jamworld, outside Kingston. There it has not fared so well, with lower attendances and lower takings. Not being a tourist centre, Kingston does not provide a 'tap' audience, nor is it so attractive to Jamaicans themselves. In 1995 attempts were being made to move it back to the north coast, possibly to Ocho Rios.

The Heritage Trail

Jamaica's successful promotion of reggae nationally, regionally and internationally reflects Jamaica's mature attitude towards its own rich cultural life, looking outwards but staying grounded in local experience. The example of Sunsplash has been noted and acted on elsewhere in the region. Slowly, the idea of using more than beaches to attract tourists to the region has been generating interest.

This move to widen the tourist base to include 'cultural' or 'heritage' tourism has partly been caused by increased awareness and pride in Caribbean history within the region. It has also been nudged by the global fashion for recreating history. More pragmatically, it has been prompted by concern about falling arrival rates in 'older' tourism destinations. Examples of conservation and restoration for the tourist market come from all over the region, from the Dominican Republic to Bonaire.

One interesting example of official attempts to harness heritage to tourism is the Seville Great House and Heritage Park in St Ann's Bay on the north coast of Jamaica. Seville, now owned and operated by the Jamaica National Heritage Trust, a government agency, was opened in 1994. It was an Arawak settlement before becoming the first Spanish capital of Jamaica and then, under British occupation and slavery, a sugar plantation with a great house and African village. St Ann's Bay was also where Columbus was shipwrecked in 1493, while the town of St Ann's was the birthplace of Marcus Garvey. Speaking at its opening, the Minister of Education and Culture pointed to the value to Jamaicans (as well as to tourists) of such sites. The importance of Seville, he said, lay with its potential to provide 'an interpretation of what is basically a microcosm of Jamaica's history at one location. This is what will empower us to speak with understanding, honesty and truth about who we are as a people.'[15]

Jamaica's Tourism Action plan (TAP) has also been working on plans to restore and improve not just the great houses, but also towns and villages, recognizing the heritage of Jamaica's masons, carpenters and wood-workers in the creation of Jamaica-Georgian architecture. A book, *Jamaica's Heritage – An Untapped Resource*, by three English architects and conservationists, published in 1991 in co-operation with TAP, not only illustrated Jamaica's rich architectural history, but also made a proposal for a Jamaica Heritage Trail that would link the different parts of the island (the Emancipation Trail, the Gingerbread House Trail and the Plantation Trail). This would make it possible for tourists to explore Jamaica's towns and villages thematically through its architectural history. From great house to railway station and vernacular cabin, the book is enthusiastic about the potential for visitors to see the other 'remarkable' Jamaica, to enable rural Jamaica to generate its own tourist income.[16]

In Barbados, history has been dusted down, cleaned up and put on display. But it has been more selective than the Jamaica Heritage Trail proposals. The bit of history that Barbados has chosen to market is its plantation houses, the economic epicentres of the sugar industry and slavery. Yet the reconstruction has been partial. Sunbury Plantation House, for example, is described in the 1994 tourist handout, *The Ins and Outs of Barbados*, as 'creating a vivid impression of the life of a sugar plantation in the 18th and 19th century'. Yet its blurb mentions only the house's magnificent antiques and paintings, while ignoring the slave contribution to the estate.

A similar thing has happened at the Dows Hill Interpretation Centre in Antigua. Perched on a hillside with a magnificent view of English Harbour, Nelson's old dockyard and once the base of English naval power in the West Indies, the Centre provides in light and sound a Euro-centred version of Antigua's history as narrated by a small boy. Funded and developed by the Canadian government agency, CIDA, in conjunction with the National Parks Authority, it alienates Antiguans like cultural officer Reg Samuel. 'We don't relate to it at all,' he says.

English Harbour itself has been the subject of similar criticism. Since 1955, the dockyard and its surrounding buildings have been carefully restored. Now the whole area is a marina with a ship's chandlery, marine serices and yacht club. It also has a museum, restaurants, art gallery, picture framing, boutique, bakery and craft shops, all created for the tourists on a day out from their hotels. It is attractive, tasteful, expensive and very European. Most of the businesses are owned and run by whites. For Samuels, 'It is an English colony run by expatriates.'

Slavery and the story of resistance to it usually remain untold in heritage tourism (museums have become the pioneers in promoting that part of Caribbean history). This is partly because most slave accommodation, built of wood or wattle and daub, has disappeared or has been destroyed. Perhaps a more fundamental reason is that, until comparatively recently, black history has been ignored. Before independence, this was because history was 'organized' by colonial officials; after independence, Caribbean tourist officials were ignorant of their own history, or unskilled in presenting it or controlled by metropolitan tour operators. One result, in contrast to Jamaica's Seville project, is that heritage tourism has become 'for tourists only' – at best being ignored by local people, at worst alienating them.

Bonaire, in the Netherlands Antilles, however, has restored an example of its slave huts. These tiny stone houses, whose entrances are only waist-high, were built by and for the slaves who worked on the nearby salt ponds. Dating from 1850, they were restored by the National Parks Foundation of the Netherlands Antilles in a rare commemoration of slavery and vernacular architecture.[17]

Alissandra Cummins of the Barbados Museum drew attention to the process in her description of the impact of Acworth's 1951 colonial survey of the historic buildings of the West Indies; this concentrated on the European-influenced estate houses and ignored the vernacular. She wrote: 'The lack of popular support for these conservation efforts was hardly surprising and historic preservation remained on the periphery of local cultural consciousness for decades.'[18] Jamaica and Guyana, Cuba and Haiti were the only exceptions.

The development of museums in the Caribbean in many ways paralleled that of heritage tourism with its concentration on colonial achievement. Museums were the traditional storehouses of knowledge and bearers of the cultural chalice, but their white curators had a largely Euro-centric view of the world. For tourists, a visit to the museum, if there was one, had meant exhibits of Amerindian and colonial relics mixed with natural history. As the Barbados Minister of Culture said in 1980, the Barbados Museum told the visitor about Barbadian merchants and planters but 'little or nothing about slaves, plantation labourers or peasant farmers'.[19]

Only in the last decade has this changed. As Ms Cummins explains: 'How Caribbean history is presented is largely the result of its institutions – the older the institution is, the greater the rigidity of interpretation, which reflects the interests largely of colonials. The new institutions have a totally different perspective.' In these there is less glass and porcelain, fewer portraits of stern white patriarchs and a new emphasis on social history and the Caribbean masses. Under Ms Cummins, the focus of the Barbados Museum has changed, showing black culture and legitimizing

'Caribbean culture, making visible what was once a hidden past'. Other Caribbean countries are making similar changes; in the Bahamas, the Pompey Museum in Nassau, the region's first museum on slavery and emancipation (named after the leader of a slave uprising against an absentee landlord in Exuma), opened in 1992, while in Tobago, the museum noticeboard contains an appeal for contributions representing Tobago's African past.

While the focus has shifted, the role of museums and historic sites ('the outside child of tourism') has yet to be, according to Ms Cummins, fully recognized or defined: 'For while each country in the region has sought to incorporate a cultural development policy in its overall national development strategy, all too often the policy option has been that of "cultural tourism", as a justification for any activity in this section and certainly as a priority before integration within the Caribbean cultural context.'[20]

There is, however, enormous potential for linking tourism with museums, says Alissandra Cummins. Yet Caribbean governments have largely underestimated the interests of tourists. 'The tourist comes to the museum to get a clear picture of who Barbadians are,' she says, drawing attention to the comments in the visitors' book. 'The tourist wants a lot more in terms of slavery and the slave trade, particularly the black tourist. Tourists are also intrigued by sports. We need to get out and tell the stories about cricket and racing in Barbados.'

It is not only the Anglophone Caribbean which has experienced the difficulties surrounding some heritage tourism. In Cuba, the interests of tourism have threatened to marginalize the poor of colonial Old Havana (population 100,000). This part of the city was declared a UN World Heritage site in 1982. Since then churches, hotels and colonial mansions in the crumbling heart of the city, which dates from the sixteenth century, have been restored (part funded by UNESCO) while local housing conditions remain poor.

When the government realized that there was little for tourists to buy in Old Havana, a state agency, Habaguanex SA, was set up in 1994 to provide food and drink, entertainment and souvenirs for tourists and to earn dollars to be ploughed back into the restoration work. Yet tourism and a dollar economy sit uneasily with the peso-earning Cubans crammed into their crumbling and insanitary accommodation and struggling to eat. The potential for unrest (and so-called 'anti-social' behaviour like begging) forced a compromise, according to the magazine *Cuba Business*, which reported in June 1994 that 10 per cent of the services would be available in pesos. Where this was difficult to implement, 10 per cent of the produce would be distributed to local schools and old people's homes. Other profits from Habaguanex would go to improve housing and infrastructure for Cubans.[21]

The idea that tourists could be interested in a built environment beyond a beach is not restricted to Cuba. Slowly the rest of the region has awakened to the attractions of its own architecture. Yet for decades, with a disregard for its own architectural traditions, the Caribbean tore down its old buildings to promote other people's. Both foreign chains and local developers built (and continue to do so) hotels inappropriate to place and purpose: foreigners because they did not care, locals because they associated old buildings with backwardness and assumed that foreigners required (and liked) the paraphernalia of modern, urban societies. Philistine and desperate-for-investment Caribbean governments sanctioned such developments. As a result, Caribbean resorts often look like somewhere else, usually Florida but perhaps Spain, Mexico or Italy. Hotel brochures boast that their charmless complexes have villas with 'Spanish roofs' and reception halls of 'Italian marble'.

The rush to build for tourism resulted in many pieces of vandalism. Among the worst was the destruction of the Amerindian caves in St Maarten, discovered during the construction of the Concord Hotel (now the Maho Beach Hotel). Amerindians used caves as places of worship, and petroglyphs and other images have been found there. On the discovery of the caves, the site supervisor told the government which expressed no interest, and when building began again, parts of the caves were destroyed and one was used as a septic tank. During the months that the caves were exposed, at least three limestone statues were found, one white, one red, painted with dyes, and one black. The red and white statues are thought to date from around AD1300 and to have been carved by the Tainos. Only very few such carvings have ever been found and it is not known what petroglyphs and other statues might have been in the caves now smothered by rubble and sewage.

The new trends in heritage tourism have not only turned plantation houses into museums, but have also transformed them into hotels (such as the up-market examples on Nevis), while parts of the capital of Aruba, Oranjestad, have even been rebuilt in colonial style. There is also more attention paid to vernacular architecture (paralleling the developments in museums), if sometimes only in a post-modernist mode. Sandals resort in Antigua, for instance, is painted in 'Caribbean colours'; Chris Blackwell's new hotel outside Nassau has cottages, vernacular in colours and style; and even parts of downtown Philipsburg, capital of St Maarten, have been restored in 'Caribbean style'. All such appropriations draw attention to a tradition which echoes the homes of ordinary people, outside the tourist zones.

However, this trend has been criticized for encouraging an all-purpose Caribbean architectural 'heritage', which only loosely belongs in time and place. The restored tourist shopping district in Charlotte Amalie, St Thomas, for example, has architectural details which are not specific to St Thomas but rather reproduce general perceptions of gingerbread work, verandahs and hipped roofs. The result, according to the architectural historian William Chapman, is the creation of 'something that is more fantasy than homage and erodes the value of remaining authentic design and fabric'.[22]

Art for Art's Sake?

Art in the Caribbean, once largely shaped by and for colonials (although both Cuba and Haiti had art schools by the beginning of the nineteenth century), has been indigenized, with both trained artists and intuitives drawing their inspiration from their own traditions and influences. For those countries, such as Jamaica, with a longer history of artistic achievement, artists have forged new directions sustained by their peers, teachers and a local market. Where there has been state patronage, such as in Guyana, there has also been a flourishing art movement.

Where there has been less of a tradition, little local support and an established tourist industry, metropolitan tastes have tended to provide a barometer. As Alissandra Cummins comments: 'Painters used to paint what the tourist wanted – the hibiscus was everywhere.' Sunsets and coconut palms were other favourite subjects for artists, who exploited the tourist interest in the naive, the primitive and the 'exotic'.

Yet patronage from tourism has also created a breadth of demand which has encouraged every sort of artist, from street vendors to painters patronized by overseas dealers. In Barbados, a sizeable community of expatriates with discerning eyes have bought local art, employed local craftsmen and kept works of art in the country. Sales have nourished talent despite the cryptic comment of one commentator on Jamaican art, who observed some time ago that 'Gaston Tabois once charmed with his fresh, naive, gaily primitive vignettes of country and city life, but he found it hard to recover after Elizabeth Taylor had bought some of his work. Similarly, David Palmer at Falmouth had a rude strength and truthfulness but has produced disappointing work since Sir Winston Churchill dropped by.'[23]

Whatever the truth of that view, the success of Jamaica's art community has spawned hundreds of local carvers and artists who work on the beach or in shacks along the roadside selling their paintings and sculptures like other street vendors. Official Tourist Board publications, too, endorse artists and sculptures, urging tourists to buy a local piece of art as a souvenir. Jamaica's *Travel News*, for example, pictures Rastafarian wood carvers; underneath a carving, the caption reads: 'Pick up a carving at the Falls'. The 'airport art' of the Caribbean is dominated by the Haitians who hang out their wares, copied a thousand times, on pavements and parking lots from the Dominican Republic to Antigua.

For Roland Richardson, an artist from St Martin, international recognition (through tourism) can raise standards and provide new directions. Richardson belives that tourism can forge links whereby he and other artists can find international expression for their work. He lives in a pretty house with a view down to a jagged coastline outside the village of French Quarters, away from St Martin's chic tourist centres where restaurants serve 'snowpeas in citrus sauce'. In his studio, open to all-comers once a week, he shows his canvases and talks with passion about his island and its tourists.

Another of Richardson's achievements is a publication called *Discover*, a scholarly and beautifully produced full-colour magazine with a print run of 100,000 copies. Richardson is its editor-in-chief. Sustained by ample advertising and distributed free to every hotel room, *Discover*, which was launched in 1987, celebrates every aspect of the island's culture. Without tourism *Discover* would not have existed. As Richardson argues: 'It's late but we need to deal with tourism creatively and intelligently. It offers "constructive" possibilities.' Dismissing the negative influences of tourism as 'too common, too stupid to list', he believes that tourism can be turned around and be used to 'maintain the health of our culture'.

Richardson also sees tourism as a vehicle to heighten the profile of the Caribbean and offers as an example the Dutch airline KLM, which has sponsored art exhibitions in Europe featuring Caribbean work. 'As an artist I am aware that our Caribbean identity is becoming known on an international scale.' The whole tourist package has encouraged the use of art, dance and music, with hotels providing sponsorship and exhibition space, he says. 'Promotion needs to nourish the arts and this will increase the richness of the resource.'

Similarly, a mixture of local patronage and international links nourished Haiti's artists. Inspired by the world of the spirits, they have long been singled out for the quality of their work. Many became rich and famous, embraced by the American art establishment. Taking their cue from the critics, tourists also became consumers of Haitian art, their artistic interests motivating trips to Port-au-Prince.

This process, unsurprisingly, again spawned a multitude of artists of all kinds: painters with their surreal and voodoo images, sculptors in wood and metal-work, the 'airport artists' and the small boys who fashion delicate miniature cathedrals out of paper. All suffered when tourism virtually ended during the 1980s. Yet for one metalworker, at least, sanctions inspired new creations; the sculptor Gabriel Bien-Aimé turned to using car spare parts when steel drums became scarce.[24]

In contrast, in Cuba it has been argued that the crisis for art has been brought about by the arrival, not the departure, of tourists. The Cuban art critic Gerardo Mosquera has described the impact of tourism on Cuban culture as 'unique and troublesome', in particular pointing to the new-wave cottage industry of craft souvenirs made exclusively for tourists and 'usually devoid of any charm or inventive power'. There, Fidel Castro and Che Guevara have been turned from revolutionary heroes into tourist icons; wooden plaques bear slogans such as 'Always Forward to Victory' (available in five languages) and baseball hats with Che's signature, while the symbols of Afro-Cuban religions have become tourist-friendly.[25]

Yet what Mosquera sees as the trivialization of a culture has become a theme for contemporary Cuban artists who, for the first time since the Revolution, have to deal with the concept of a commercial market. Exhibiting their work at Havana's Plaza de la Catedral, a street market for independent craft workers, they show copies of known artists' work and the popular images demanded by tourists. (One artist, however, found that his works of social criticism were popular, at US$25 a picture, and he was subsequently offered an exhibition in the USA.)

This complex new relationship – art commentating on the tourist industry but at the same time working through it and with it – has been explored by a young Cuban artist, Tania Bruguera. Her work, called 'Postwar Memory', is made up of souvenir paraphernalia of T-shirts, posters, key-holders, ashtrays and so on. 'I wanted to show that what we are selling are pieces of our own misery, of our own failure.'[26]

The representation of a nation through souvenir knick-knacks is endemic to much of the Caribbean where shops overflow with rubbishy imported souvenirs. In one major tourist shop in Da Costa mall, Bridgetown, Barbados, there are baseball caps from China, coasters from Hong Kong, spoons from the USA, wooden fruit from Venezuela and straw-hats from Mexico. In Antigua, you can buy drinking glasses from Korea, carved turtles from Taiwan and even glass snowstorms with palm trees from China. The island features only because its name is printed, stamped or woven on to the souvenir.

This lumpen invasion of other people's artefacts is partly the result of a tourist demand for souvenirs and crafts that is far greater than local supplies can satisfy. A study by the Caribbean Community, Caricom, indicated that with the exception of Jamaica and Barbados, the craft industry was in stagnation or decline. The problem was caused by a lack of training, government support, financial aid and knowledge about marketing and promotion. Handicrafts was another example of the failure to capitalize on the key issue of linkages (see Chapter 2).

The Bahamas, for instance, has long been famous for its straw-work, a tradition that evolved from domestic need into more decorative (with raffia weave) styles. As demand increased and insufficient supplies of plaited straw arrived from the Out Islands of the Bahamas, many of the craft workers gave up weaving to become importers. Although the Out Islands still produce fine straw-work in the style of West Africa, many of the 500 vendors at Nassau's Straw Market now club together to buy Asian straw-goods out of Florida.

The popularity of straw-work with tourists has, however, had one positive effect. Bahamians who had earlier rejected straw-work, identifying it with poverty and thinking it 'unrefined', have now started to buy and enjoy it as a representation of their own culture.

The straw-work of the Bahamas is not the only example of this curious interaction between tourism and culture in which traditional craft becomes locally recognized only after its 'approval' by tourists. The pottery of Nevis has had a similar history and transformation. Nevis pottery, which dates back to the eighteenth century and African traditions, went into decline with migration, the attraction of other work and its low status. Money earned from pottery was known as 'dirty money' and associated, like Bahamian straw-work, with dispossession and poverty.

Yet in the early 1980s attempts to 'upgrade' pottery-making techniques were introduced by a development project. At the same time, the old-style pottery was becoming sought after by hotels and visitors (Nevis tends to attract somewhat up-market tourists). Together these processes changed the perceptions of Nevisians towards their own pottery; it had now become desirable and 'modern'. According to anthropologist Karen Olwig, recognition by tourists for the pottery has helped Nevisians 'to accept an important part of their cultural heritage, which has not otherwise won much recognition in the island society'.[27]

There is inevitably a limit to the extent to which the Caribbean wishes to be exposed to the tourist gaze, whether or not the encounter generates money, encourages authenticity and promotes self-awareness. At a deeper level, there is a reluctance to make public all its traditions and to turn its myths into T-shirts. The thinking is that the most vulnerable and private aspects of Caribbean expression must remain so. In Barbados, Alissandra Cummins takes up this point of view. 'I would hesitate, for example, to get the Barbadian Landship movement involved in tourism because of the risk of exploitation and the negation of our culture.' (The Landship movement, which never features in guide books or Tourist Board brochures, is a friendly society dating from the nineteenth century whose members parade in naval uniform imitating the manoeuvres of a ship at sea; typically it fuses European and African elements into something more than the original.)

A similar point is made by Kim Outten of the Pompey Museum, Nassau, who is worried about the new enthusiasm for official endorsement of local festivals, created for tourists by the Tourist Board. 'I'm concerned that it's just as dangerous to shift from an emphasis on sun, sea and sand tourism to putting on local festivals every few months. It implies that that is all Bahamians do all the time. The bottom line is how much of our culture do we want to sell?'

The Caribbean consciousness, in its many shapes and forms, remains in the rural hinterlands, on urban streets and along the 'trace' or 'gap' where the tourist minibuses never go. Traditions, of religious rites, storytelling, fishing festivals, Carnival, bush medicine, pantomime, the oral language and so on, flourish and evolve despite the prescriptions of the tourist industry.

Yet somehow a compatible future must be found for tourism and the Caribbean's cultural identity. Both need each other, rather as tourism and the environment need each other (see Chapter 5). Otherwise, as Professor Parris warned at a Caribbean seminar on cultural patrimony in 1983: 'If we ignore our culture ... one morning we will wake up and there will be no more visitors. Visitors will simply have ceased to find us interesting, since we would have become just like them and they will opt to get their suntans somewhere closer to home where the airfares and the meals are cheaper.'[28]

Notes

1. William Demas, 'Change and Renewal in the Caribbean', *Challenges in the New Caribbean*, no. 2, Caribbean Conference of Churches, Barbados, 1975, p. 55.

2. *Ibid.*, p. 3.

3. Cited in Philip Cash, Shirley Gordon and Gail Saunders, *Sources of Bahamian History*, London, 1991, p. 337.

4. Elliott Parris, 'Cultural Patrimony and the Tourism Product: Towards a Mutually Beneficial Relationship', OAS regional seminar, 1983.

5. *Outlet*, Antigua and Barbuda, 11 March 1994.

6. Alan Goldberg, 'Identity and Experience in Haitian Voodoo Shows', *Annals of Tourism Research*, vol. 10, 1983, pp. 479–95.

7. Gordon K. Lewis, *The Growth of the Modern West Indies*, New York, 1968, p. 30.

8. Gordon Roehler, *Calypso and Society in Pre-Independence Trinidad*, Port of Spain, 1990, p. 328.

9. *Ibid.*, p. 403.

10. *Ibid.*, p. 452.

11. *McKay's Guide to Bermuda, the Bahamas and the Caribbean*, New York, 1958, p. 48.

12. *The Guardian*, London, 30 October 1993.

13. Henry Fraser, Sean Carrington, Addington Forde and John Gilmore, *A–Z of Barbadian Heritage*, Jamaica, 1990.

14. Cited in Graham Dann and Robert Potter, 'Tourism and Post-Modernity in a Caribbean Setting', *Les Cahiers du Tourisme*, Aix-en-Provence, April 1994.

15. Caribbean News Agency, 13 May 1994.

16. Marcus Binney, John Harris and Kit Martin, *Jamaica's Heritage – An Untapped Resource*, Kingston, 1991.

17. *Caribbean Week*, 9–22 January 1993.

18. Alissandra Cummins, 'Exhibiting Culture: Museums and National Identity in the Caribbean', *Caribbean Quarterly*, vol. 38, no. 2, p. 33.

19. *Ibid.*

20. *Ibid.*

21. *Cuba Business*, London, June 1994.

22. William Chapman, 'A Little More Gingerbread: Tourism, Design and Preservation in the Caribbean', *Places*, London, vol. 8, no. 1, 1992.

23. Norma Rae, 'Contemporary Jamaican Art' in *Ian Fleming Introduces Jamaica*, London, 1965, p. 169.

24. *International Herald Tribune*, Washington DC, 2–3 July 1994.

25. Gerardo Mosquera, 'Hustling the Tourist in Cuba', *Poliester*, London, vol. 3, no. 10, 1994.

26. *Ibid.*

27. Karen Fog Olwig, 'Cultural Identity and Material Culture: Afro-Caribbean Pottery', *Folk*, vol. 32, Copenhagen, 1990.

28. Parris, *op. cit.*

CHAPTER 9

New Footprints in the Sand:

The Future

'To all the tourists, visitors, travellers or whatever other name you are called: I beg you, please don't come [here] .... Tourism is killing us. It is literally sucking the life out of us. We are running out of sweet water. Our lands have been sucked dry. Where once there were taro fields and fishponds today there are golf courses, hotels and urban sprawl.'[1]

This message came from Hawaii in 1994; it might equally have come from Goa. Both countries have groups who appeal to visitors to stay at home. Not so in the Caribbean. In the 20 years since young Caribbean radicals trumpeted 'Tourism is Whorism' and a Prime Minister told an international conference 'To Hell With Paradise', the radicals have become professors and the Prime Minister, James Mitchell of St Vincent and the Grenadines, has himself become caught up in resorts, condos and marinas.

There are now no organized voices raised in protest against tourism. It has been accepted; it is assumed that it is here to stay. It has brought modern airports and roads, and for some, the amenities of modern, urban living. It provides jobs and foreign exchange and with that money schools and hospitals can be built. The centre-right political orthodoxy that has prevailed in most of the Caribbean for the last decade or so preaches its virtues. Foreign experts from international bodies say that there is no alternative, that tourism is the last resort. Even a left-of-centre regime like Grenada encouraged it, and now Cuba has embraced it. Politicians boast that more tourists are better than fewer tourists. If there is popular protest it is expressed more covertly, in cool welcomes and indifferent service rather than in political argument and protest.

Of course, there are people in the Caribbean who criticize aspects of the tourist industry, its structures and its adverse impact on people, places and cultures. They are actively campaigning to make tourism work constructively. Many of these people feature in this book, adding their experiences and perceptions to the body of understanding about the curious and often dislocating relationship between hosts and guests.

One of the more critical positions is held by Professor Hilary Beckles at the University of the West Indies in Barbados. For him, tourism is a kind of new plantocracy reinventing the economic and social relations of slavery. Even so, does he believe tourism could be a tool for sustainable development? Not in the way that it is organized at present. According to Beckles, tourism has been adopted as an easier option than any other path to economic development. 'Society doesn't have to be so disciplined; it can grow by itself.' The region, he says, has failed to become creative and has failed to develop a philosophy of individual initiative and discipline in the workplace. 'Our minds have not been fashioned to create, so instead of creative services, information services, publishing, printing, we have become a dumping ground for low-grade data processing.' This is why the region 'fell back on tourism as the principal agency for growth', says Beckles. 'Local people are put on the back burners and the taxpayers' money is used so that the élite benefit.'

The 'new plantocracy' school is not alone in its critique. There are other groups and individuals who take issue with particular aspects of the industry. There are, for example, church groups who are concerned about the impact of tourism on morals, sexual and otherwise; they also comment on the way tourism is socially debilitating to vulnerable communities. Then there are environmentalists who try to stop the degradation, measure the damage and put together protectionist policies and guidelines to make tourism work for the environment and not against it (see Chapter 5). And there are the intellectuals and artists, who present the best of Caribbean culture as it is to the tourists rather than offering them phoney versions of it. Calypsonians, too, have made their contributions, with songs such as 'Alien' in St Lucia (see Chapter 4) and 'Jack' in Barbados (see Chapter 3).

Within the industry itself there are concerns. There are, for example, the hoteliers, who feel they are overtaxed, especially compared with the cruise lines (see Chapter 7). At the same time, their staff, who think the owners reap all the benefits, complain about a limited career structure with the best jobs still going to foreigners (see Chapter 3). At a more profound level, there are those, whether hoteliers or workers, taxi-drivers or tour guides, who feel that the industry does not belong to them at all.

As Antigua's Opposition Leader Baldwin Spencer explains: 'Most of the progress has come from tourism, but it is not in our hands. We can't lay a foundation on which we benefit.' Spencer is perhaps suggesting that although tourism has brought Antiguans a recognizably modern, consumer society Antiguans are not pinned into it. It is an elusive sort of benefit because Antiguans have not made their own investment in tourism and do not control it.

Academics put it another way. They argue that the problem, especially in the case of the 'microstates' of the Eastern Caribbean, is that the economic model of export-led agriculture and light industry, and a tourism based on foreign investment does not provide for so-called 'basic needs provision' for the people.[2] The public sector's *laissez-faire* approach, its inability to plan for the future and its failure to implement any plans that do exist are further key constraints to sustainable development. This is particularly critical in islands such as Aruba, Antigua, Barbados, the Bahamas and St Maarten which have adopted a mass-tourism profile. Such scenarios have prompted some unfavourable verdicts. For instance, Professor Robert Potter quotes the Canadian academic Paul Wilkinson's conclusions on Barbados, 'an example of the non-sustainability of a fragile island microstate embracing large-scale mass tourism in what is nearly a policy and planning vacuum.'[3]

The conclusion reached by many specialists is that high-density mass tourism and the open economies and closed ecosystems of small islands are not compatible with sustainable development. If this is so, the policy of the Caribbean's tourist industry to keep on bringing more and more visitors to its shores is seriously flawed.

There is, however, an alternative path to the mass-market, leaking-vessel approach. The alternative is an integrated tourism in which the industry is managed for the common good, focusing on ecological and human needs as well as business considerations. This concept, the 'new' tourism, was possibly coined as long ago as 1972 by the former Prime Minister of Jamaica, Michael Manley, at the start of his first term of office. At any rate, that administration attempted to change the top-down, white-on-black culture of the industry. Holidays for Jamaican workers were organized in the tourist resorts to break what Manley called the old élitist patterns in which hotels were 'shut away from the local population by psychology as much as by price'.[4]

'New' tourism later became associated with the late Prime Minister of Grenada, Maurice Bishop, just eight months after a bloodless coup had brought his People's Revolutionary Government (PRG) to power. Bishop's administration was to end in his murder in October 1983. However, during the short-lived regime, a new tourism began to take shape.

In December 1979, Bishop gave the opening address to a regional conference on the sociocultural and environmental impact of tourism on Caribbean societies. It was held at the Holiday Inn, on Grande Anse Beach, Grenada, and was an important opportunity for Bishop to explain his government's policies on tourism in front of what must have been a somewhat suspicious regional audience. Delegates included ministers of tourism, the Cuban ambassador to Grenada and the executive directors of the Caribbean Tourism Research and Development Centre and the Caribbean Tourism Association, the precursors of the Caribbean Tourism Organization.

It is worth paying some attention to Bishop's speech because Grenada under the PRG and, to some extent, Jamaica are probably the only Caribbean states to have created a political framework for the 'new' tourism and to have had the political will to develop it.

Bishop began his speech by emphasizing the PRG's commitment to tourism and to its expansion (he mentioned the forthcoming construction of the international airport at Point Salines, 'in the centre of our main tourist area'). He said that Grenada's tourism would reflect 'the nature of our revolution' and that the 'old tourism' would be replaced by a 'new tourism'[5]. He associated the old tourism with an imperialist age, when tourism was 'intended as a means of increasing dependence on the metropole and of providing development for the few and under-development for the vast majority of the people of our islands'.[6]

He summarized this 'old tourism' as:

a problem largely because of its colonial and imperialist connotations. It was foreign-owned and controlled, it was unrelated to the needs and development of the Caribbean people, it had no linkages with other sectors in the economy and it brought with it a number of distinct socio-cultural and environmental hazards such as the race question and undesirable social and economic patterns such as drug abuse, prostitution and consumerism.[7]

(As this book has attempted to explain, Bishop would still recognize 'old tourism' today in all of the Caribbean, including Grenada.)

Bishop then examined what shape he thought the new tourism should take. 'We start from the principle ... that Grenadians as all Caribbean people must be recognised as controllers of their own destiny and developers of their own process.' He went on to explore the tenets of the new tourism both from an internal perspective and from a regional and international one.

Tourism was a tool for development, he said, emphasizing its potential for creating linkages with the rest of the economy at many levels, including food and handicrafts. The government was also working towards what he called a proper 'internal climate' for tourism: this included a strong agro-industrial sector, the international airport, improved water supply and training and cultural programmes. He also anticipated that ordinary people could participate 'in the process of defining the type of tourist activity' that Grenada wanted.

Looking outwards, Bishop first identified tourism as being an 'instrument of world peace'. If this now appears a dated concept, it should be remembered that such vocabulary was an essential ingredient of international left-wing discourse during the Cold War. He then talked about diversifying the tourist market into Latin America, the Caribbean itself and Europe, beyond the United Kingdom. 'To break the relationship between tourism, class and colour', Bishop wanted to encourage non-white visitors and particularly other Caribbeans to become tourists. This was linked to another aim of the new tourism which was to support 'regional solutions to problems in tourism as in other sectors'. He urged 'hassle-free' travel among Caribbean nationals. The PRG did not, however, neglect the traditional market; on the marketing side, it formed a separate Ministry of Tourism, allocated it EC$2 million in funds (far more than ever before) and opened tourism offices in Toronto and New York.[8]

Bishop's hopes for a new tourism, however, were thwarted. Firstly, and crucially, they failed because the external market was against the regime. Hostile propaganda by the USA ensured that visitor arrivals slackened (see Chapter 2), while Bishop's ideas about encouraging Caribbean, Third-World and 'study' tourists never really took off. There were not enough of them and they did not spend as much money as the traditional tourist sector.[9]

Internally, the PRG made more progress towards its new tourism goals. Linkages began to be established. Between 1981 and 1982, both the private sector and the public sector grew, in particular the public sector which recorded a 34 per cent growth in gross production. The island's food import bills had also begun to decrease. Entrepreneurs were involved in tourist-linked operations such as furniture-making, brewing, soft drinks and basic food products, while the state set up Grenada Agro-Industries (making jams and jellies and so on) and Grencraft, which encouraged craft cottage industries. Such mixed economy initiatives even won the approval of the conservative World Bank which praised the PRG in 1982 for 'laying better foundations for growth within the framework of a mixed economy'.[10]

There were, however, difficulties with this strategy. One constraint on Grenada's brave new world was the financial burden of infrastructural development. The cost of the new airport, although subsidized by the Cubans to a great degree, became a drain on the PRG's finances, as did other public-sector initiatives, especially agricultural reform. Revenue had to be found somewhere and it was the hotel sector which was saddled with new taxes. In turn, this pushed up prices and made Grenada less competitive.

The new tourism experiment never really had time to settle down. Bishop's ideas became clouded by political rhetoric and the PRG finally collapsed on the steps of St George's, Fort Rupert when, along with three of his ministers, Bishop was murdered in the implosion of Grenadian radical politics in October 1983.

The end of the PRG saw the end of Grenada's 'new' tourism experiment. And no other government picked up the torch.

Closest to Bishop's 'new' tourism, however, in both theory and practice, is perhaps community tourism. This was pioneered in Jamaica by a former Jamaican Minister of Tourism, Desmond Henry (who also spoke at that Holiday Inn conference in Grenada in 1979). Henry defined community tourism as a 'from-the-bottom-up concept designed to stimulate community cooperation, pride and a sense of value; to utilise local resources, provide local income and encourage the training of new hospitality skills'.[11] Designed for areas of Jamaica outside the mass-tourism enclaves, it is also locally planned, locally controlled and maintained, and small-scale.

The centre of community tourism is Mandeville, the capital of the parish of Manchester. Diana McIntyre-Pike, chairwoman of the pioneering Central and South Jamaica Tourism Committee, describes community tourism as a process in which 'everyone is involved from the beginning in the planning and development – from the "big guys" to the man on the street'. Her Committee has encouraged locals to back it and the result is something quite new for the Caribbean. Among a whole range of activities, it offers visitors a chance to visit a private orchid garden, a bammy factory, a pickapepper factory, a therapeutic spa, Mandeville schools, a crocodile farm research station and to have a 'Jamaica chit-chat session' while staying in local homes. Village tourism in Belize and some approaches in ecotourism throughout the region (see Chapter 5) are similar initiatives which shift the focus away from both the beach and the expensive resort hotel.

Another option which rejects the equation that more tourists is good news, is retirement, second-home tourism. This has become popular on the small, rather chic islands of Montserrat, St Barthélémy and Nevis. In Montserrat, for example, former agricultural land has become a suburban landscape of well-tended expatriate homes with American-style letter-boxes at the end of drives. According to one study, 'only 287 expatriate resident retirees accounted for one-fifth of all visitor expenditures of the other much more numerous stayover segments: hotel, villa and private home guest'.[12] This is a high-spend alternative to conventional tourism. Anguilla with its up-market hotels also fits this profile. Both are small-scale, environmentally friendly, low-impact and high-spend. However, they fail the 'new' tourism test, being both élitist and controlled by outsiders.

What is significant about all these initiatives is that not only are they alternatives to what Auliana Poon, a Caribbean tourism consultant, has called the MSRP (mass, standardized and rigidly packaged) tourism but they are also attractive to the marketing gurus who are anxious to see the Caribbean develop 'niche' marketing. This means that the Caribbean must be able to offer holidays that appeal to a variety of special interests and needs; the tourist, for example, who wants to switch from canoeing to casinos, from camping to condos all in one holiday.

Without such a flexible approach, the Caribbean will be in trouble, warns Poon fiercely: 'Innovation must not only be total. It must be continuous .... Caribbean tourism will have to fall in line with the new tourism best practice – of flexibility, segmentation and diagonal integration – or fade out!'[13] Discussions are now centred on the potential for exploiting, for example, cricket (this means more than just selling the best seats to tourists) and dominoes in the same way as Reggae Sunsplash or scuba diving is offered as an alternative to beach tourism. An important part of such a strategy would also be to increase net visitor expenditure (by way of a more varied tourist environment and longer stays) rather than to increase visitor arrivals.

Countless workshops have been held to examine the new approaches and the need for the reform and realignment of the tourist industry. Indeed, as this book has tried to show, plenty of people have also pointed out that strategies such as rational long-term planning, environmental protection, diversification, improved linkages and so on needed to be addressed with some urgency. What seems to be missing, however, is a coherent philosophy and the willingness to turn talk into action. Instead, there is patchwork development, with some scattered examples of good practice.

At a regional level, the new tourism also needs to practise co-operation rather than competition. Many have cautioned against a narrow nationalism, yet Caribbean economic and political integration has been painfully slow, with regional agreements made but not implemented. The failure to adopt a common cruise-ship passenger head tax is a case in point (see Chapter 7). As Jean Holder, Secretary-General of the Caribbean Tourism Organization (CTO), told a Caribbean audience in 1993, so long as Caribbean states practised the creed, 'If at first you don't secede, try, try and try again', there would be no reason for major metropolitan countries or foreign corporations to respect the region.[14]

The CTO, with its membership of 34 states of the Caribbean Basin along with powerful private-sector organizations such as American Express and the Florida Caribbean Cruise Association, is, in fact, one body which operates at a regional level. It works to promote the

Caribbean 'as one destination', and also as a research resource, providing the region with its major source of information for the industry. Its research wing was started in 1974 as the Caribbean Tourism Research (and Development) Centre, instigated by the Caribbean Conference of Churches which questioned the kind of tourism suitable for the region. It was later run by Peter Morgan, the former Minister of Tourism for Barbados. It was launched, says Morgan, 'in order to find out if our grandchildren would curse us'. In 1989, it merged with the Caribbean Tourism Association to become the CTO. It holds together the strands of both public- and private-sector interests as well as having close links with the Caribbean Hotel Association, the Caribbean Hospitality Training Institute (see Chapter 3), the University of the West Indies and so on.

The CTO co-ordinates regional activity, but it has no mandate to enforce its ideas. This is a major weakness, and only occasionally does the CTO's Council of Ministers flex its muscles. When it does it can even stand up to external pressure as it did when it accepted Cuba's application for membership despite opposition from the United States.

The consensus on tourism in the Caribbean shows no signs of breaking down. Indeed, in many ways the industry's increasing profession-alism has made it feel more buoyant. However, grass-roots disillusion and ambivalence exist (see Chapters 3 and 4). And if governments cling on to the old-fashioned tourism concepts, the pressures on the people of the Caribbean will increase. Major political decisions are needed to reshape tourism so that it becomes more democratic. Local people need to participate in the decision-making process and share in the benefits and responsibilities. The new emphasis on training and a more confident workforce could help this process.

If tourism in the Caribbean continues to grow as predicted, more and more corners of the region will be touched by the industry. Those many communities on distant hillsides now undisturbed by tourism will inevitably be drawn into its orbit in the hope that it will ease their hardship.

The people of Vielle Case in Dominica, for example, have no experience of tourism, either old or new, although some of them will know all about mass tourism from their own holidays, perhaps in St Maarten, or from working in Antigua or Guadeloupe. But for the moment they are not waiters or receptionists, hair-braiders or taxi-drivers; they do not sell duty-free Colombian emeralds or T-shirts with 'Vielle Case Jammin' printed on them. For despite its beauty, few tourists go to the village of Vielle Case, which sits on cliffs high above the Atlantic on the north coast of Dominica, along a twisting, potholed road that leads only to one other, even more remote, settlement.

Yet even Vielle Case is gearing itself up for tourists. In April 1994, the Tourist Board's public awareness programme officer, Sobers Esprit, held a meeting about tourism with eight members of the village council. He told them that the Tourist Board was visiting communities all over the island to 'dialogue with the people' and to explain the potential for tourism. 'We want to build a partnership,' Esprit explained. 'We see tourism has a growing role to play in Dominica. Bananas are under strain, and we want to sustain the economy and raise foreign exchange. Tourism is going to be a major industry for increased growth.' After all, it may indeed be a last resort.

The village council was enthusiastic. One man said that they noticed the tourists in their buses on the way to the Carib Territory: 'We feel left out because the buses pass us by.' The council said that it recognized that tourism was 'our business' as much as the government's. It had drawn up a list of potential attractions in and around the village: a waterfall, a pond 'like a bath tub', an underwater cave and the fishermen's cove, old trails, tremendous views across the sea to Marie Galante and Les Saintes, a church where the first mass on the island was held, Carib artefacts and so on. 'We have the people who would make the tourists' time enjoyable so we can take advantage of tourism,' said another village council member, who also pointed out that it was important to sensitize the public about tourism.

The next stage, according to Esprit was to draw up a plan of action. This would include a beautifying project, improving access to sites and facilities and training villagers as guides. There was, he said, a small development fund to help finance the programme. 'Nothing like this has happened in the Caribbean,' he said. 'It's unique. Dominica is going out to the communities to get people to appreciate the potential.'

It may be a long time before Vielle Case sees, let alone benefits from, tourism. Until then it will remain a village of farmers and fishermen, its people largely self-sufficient and autonomous as they have been since even before emancipation.

It is impossible to imagine Vielle Case as an international resort; it is even hard to envisage something such as St Lucia's Jalousie Plantation Resort arising from that Gauginesque landscape. Yet the transformation of much of the Caribbean, including parts of St Lucia, has been fast and would have been unimaginable 20 years ago. For some already tourist-stifled destinations, the thought of more and more tourists appears untenable. Those larger states with room to spare such as Jamaica, Cuba and the Dominican Republic have more opportunities to manoeuvre as do those which have kept their tourism up-market and low-density.

Those who have hardly started down the tourism path say that they have learned from the mistakes of others and will not repeat them. If that is true (and Dominica identifies itself in that group), it is not impossible to imagine that a 'new tourism' could bring an improved quality of life to the people of Vielle Case. If that happens – and Dominica will need a clear-thinking and radical government to make it possible – then perhaps the people of Vielle Case will look back without regret to the day the man from the Tourist Board brought tourism, the engine of growth for the modern Caribbean, a little closer to their village. Others will not have been so lucky.

Notes

1. Cited in *Tourism in Focus*, London, Summer 1994.

2. Robert Potter, 'Basic Needs and Development in the Small Island States of the Eastern Caribbean' in D.G. Lockhart, D. Drakakis-Smith and J. Schembri (eds), *The Development Process in Small Island States*, London, 1993.

3. Quoted in Graham Dann and Robert Potter, 'Tourism in Barbados: Rejuvenation or Decline?' in D.G. Lockhart and D. Drakakis-Smith (eds), *Island Tourism*, London, 1995.

4. Michael Manley, *Jamaica: Struggle in the Periphery*, London, n.d., p. 94.

5. Maurice Bishop, address to Regional Conference on the Socio-Cultural and Environmental Impact of Tourism on Caribbean Societies, Grenada, December 1979.

6. *Ibid*.

7. *Ibid*.

8. Marcus Stephenson, 'Tourism is Everyone's Business', MA dissertation, Manchester Metropolitan University, 1990.

9. Tony Thorndike, *Grenada: Politics, Economics and Society*, London, 1985, p. 100.

10. James Ferguson, *Grenada: Revolution in Reverse*, London, 1990, p. 94.

11. Desmond Henry, untitled paper given at Regional Conference, Grenada, *op. cit.*.

12. Jerome McElroy and Klaus de Albuquerque, 'The Economic Impact of Retirement Tourism in Montserrat: Some Provisional Evidence', *Social and Economic Studies*, vol. 41, 1992, pp. 127–52.

13. Auliana Poon, 'Competitive Strategies for Caribbean Tourism: The New versus the Old', *Caribbean Affairs*, Trinidad, vol. 2, no. 2, 1989.

14. Jean Holder, 'Regional integration, Tourism and Caribbean Sovereignty', mimeo, 1993.

Select Bibliography

For a general coverage of the issues around Third-World tourism, two of the best (if now somewhat out of date) books are: Emanuel de Kadt (ed.), *Tourism: Passport to Development? Perspectives on the Social and Cultural Effects of Tourism in Developing Countries*, Oxford, 1978; and L. Turner and J. Ash, *The Golden Hordes: International Tourism and the Pleasure Periphery*, London, 1975. A more recent set of essays is David Harrison (ed.), *Tourism and the Less Developed Countries*, London, 1992.

A recent book specifically about Caribbean tourism, Dennis Gayle and Jonathan Goodrich (eds), *Tourism, Marketing and Management in the Caribbean*, London, 1993, is a mixed bag of essays, some country-specific, others looking at issues. The quality varies. Reports on Caribbean tourism include: Victor Curtin and Auliana Poon, *Tourist Accommodation in the Caribbean*, Barbados, 1988; Lesley France, *An Overview of Tourism in the Caribbean*, Newcastle-upon-Tyne, undated; Economist Intelligence Unit, *Tourism in the Caribbean: Special Report,* London, 1993; US Department of Commerce, *Tourism in the Caribbean Basin*, Washington DC, 1993; West Indian Commission, *Time For Action: Overview of the Report of the West Indian Commission*, Barbados, 1992.

There are few country-specific books. An exception is Frank Fonda Taylor, *To Hell with Paradise: A History of the Jamaican Tourist Industry*, Pittsburgh, 1993. However, there are books which have sections on aspects of the tourist industry or include views on tourism in particular countries. These include: Jamaica Kincaid, *A Small Place*, London, 1988 (Antigua); Philip Cash, Shirley Gordon and Gail Saunders, *Sources of Bahamian History*, London, 1991 (Bahamas); Neil Price, *Behind the Planter's Back: Lower-Class Responses to Marginality in Bequia Island, St Vincent*, London, 1988 (Bequia); David Harrison (ed.), *Tourism and the Less Developed Countries*, London, 1992 (Cuba); Simon Calder and Emily Hatchwell, *Cuba In Focus*, London, 1995; and Marcel Bayer, *Jamaica in Focus*, London, 1993.

For books on the Caribbean in general, with passing references to tourism, see: Tom Barry, Beth Wood and Deb Preusch, *The Other Side of Paradise: Foreign Control in the Caribbean*, New York, 1984; Jean Besson and Janet Momsen, *Land and Development in the Caribbean*, London, 1987; Gordon Lewis, *The Growth of the Modern West Indies*, New York, 1968; David Lowenthal, *West Indian Societies*, Oxford, 1972; Kathy McAfee, *Storm Signals: Structural Adjustment and Development Alternatives in the Caribbean*, London, 1991; R. Millet *et al.* (eds), *The Restless Caribbean*, New York, 1979; and Janet Momsen (ed.), *Women and Change in the Caribbean*, London, 1993.

Some Caribbean travelogues include observations on tourism; for a patrician view from the 1950s, Patrick Leigh Fermor, *The Traveller's Tree: A Journey Through the Caribbean Islands*, London, 1984, is the classic. A more recent batch includes Quentin Crewe, *Touch the Happy Isles: A Journey Through the Caribbean*, London, 1987; Zenga Longmore, *Tap-Taps to Trinidad: A Caribbean Journey*, London, 1989; and Lucretia Stewart, *The Weather Prophet*, London, 1995. Henry Shukman, *Travels with my Trombone*, London, 1992, contains interesting accounts of the islands' musical scene. Martha Gellhorn, *Travels with Myself and Another*, London, 1983, has a wonderful chapter on her Caribbean experiences during World War II.

Travel guides sometimes include useful background information on tourism: the *Caribbean Islands Handbook* has a considered approach to tourism. Also the Insight Guides provide good background information. Old travel guides tell it how it was.

Statistical information: *Caribbean Tourism Organisation Yearbook* is published annually. National tourist boards and/or ministries of tourism will also supply statistics and, of course, brochures. The Economist Intelligence Unit Country Profiles, London, are published quarterly and include some information on tourism; the *Caribbean Basin Commercial Profile*, Miami, is published annually.

Journals: *Caribbean Studies*, Trinidad, and *Caribbean Quarterly*, Jamaica, both have occasional papers on tourism in the region; *Annals of Tourism Research* publishes academic papers on all aspects of tourism and features the Caribbean from time to time; Malcolm Crick, 'Representations of International Tourism in the Social Sciences: Sun, Sex, Sights, Savings and Servility', *Annual Review of Anthropology*, vol. 18, 1989, sets out an overview of the academic material.

Periodicals: the monthly magazine *Caribbean Insight*, London, provides some coverage and occasional statistics; *Caribbean Contact*, Barbados, stopped publishing in 1994, but back issues occasionally have useful pieces; *Caribbean Week*, Barbados, fortnightly, available throughout the region, gives regular and helpful coverage to tourism issues.

Local Caribbean papers often carry stories about the tourist industry, in particular in those countries with a developed tourist industry. In particular, look out for *Outlet* (Antigua); the *Gleaner* (Jamaica); *Barbados Advocate* and *Barbados Sun*; and the *Nassau Tribune* (Bahamas).

Organizations involved in raising awareness about tourism include: Tourism Concern, Southlands College, Roehampton Institute, Wimbledon Parkside, London SW19 5NN, UK; Center for Responsible Tourism, PO Box 827, San Anselmo, CA 94979 USA; and Ecumenical Coalition on Third World Tourism, PO Box 35, Senanikom PO, Bangkok, Thailand. Caribbean Conference of Churches, PO Box 616, Bridgetown, Barbados. All produce newsletters and other information.

Many of the views and quotations which appear in this book were supplied by people in the Caribbean and elsewhere whom I interviewed in the course of my research. Their quotations appear without notes.

Books from the Latin America Bureau

The Latin America Bureau (LAB) publishes books on contemporary issues in Latin America and the Caribbean.

Current titles include:

- Introductions to Latin American and Caribbean society, culture, economics and politics
- Country guides – Jamaica, Bolivia, Venezuela, Cuba and Colombia are the first in the series
- A series on Latin American women's lives and experiences
- Latin American authors in translation: from street children to salsa, from rubber tappers to guerrilla radio stations

Highlights from LAB's Caribbean list include:

Guyana: Fragile Frontier – Marcus Colchester
Guyana's environment is in danger of wholesale destruction from logging, mining and other forms of extraction. *Fragile Frontier* describes the threat, and the forces – economic and political – behind it. Looking at the role of the IMF, World Bank and InterAmerican Development Bank, author Marcus Colchester shows how structural adjustment has paved the way for extraction-based development.

February 1996 90 pages ISBN 1 899365 02 8 (pb) £7.99

Afrocuba: *An Anthology of Cuban Writing on Race, Politics and Culture* – Pedro Pérez Sarduy and Jean Stubbs (eds)
Looks at the black experience in Cuba through the eyes of the island's writers, scholars and artists. Writings – poetry, fiction, political analysis and anthropology – from over thirty, mainly black, contributors give a multi-faceted insight into Cuba's rich ethnic and cultural reality.

1993 310 pages index ISBN 0 906156 75 0 (pb) £12.99 Distributed in the USA by The Talman Company

Dominican Republic: Beyond the Lighthouse – James Ferguson
An introduction to a country where extreme poverty exists alongside a booming tourist industry. Where workers from neighbouring Haiti are literally enslaved in a bankrupt sugar industry. Where political leaders date back to a dictatorship which ended more than thirty years ago.

1992 128 pages index ISBN 0 906156 64 5 (pb) £5.99

The Poor and The Powerless: Economic Policy and Change in the Caribbean – Clive Y. Thomas
A major survey of economic development tracing the history of colonialism and neo-colonialism from the perspective of the region's poor majority. Draws lessons from Jamaica, Grenada, Guyana, Barbados and Trinidad & Tobago.

1988 396 pages index ISBN 0 906156 35 1 (pbk) £9.99 Published in North America by Monthly Review Press

For a free 20-page LAB Books catalogue, write to LAB, Dept LR, 1 Amwell Street, London EC1R 1UL or call 0171 278 2829

LAB Books are distributed in North America by Monthly Review Press, 122 West 27 Street, New York, NY 10001 (Tel: 212-691-2555) and are available through Ian Randle Publishers, 206 Old Hope Road, Kingston 6, Jamaica (Tel 809-927-2084).

Index